51 IMPERFECT SOLUTIONS

51 IMPERFECT SOLUTIONS

*STATES AND THE
MAKING OF AMERICAN
CONSTITUTIONAL LAW*

JEFFREY S. SUTTON

OXFORD
UNIVERSITY PRESS

OXFORD

UNIVERSITY PRESS

Oxford University Press is a department of the University of Oxford. It furthers
the University's objective of excellence in research, scholarship, and education
by publishing worldwide. Oxford is a registered trade mark of Oxford University
Press in the UK and certain other countries.

Published in the United States of America by Oxford University Press
198 Madison Avenue, New York, NY 10016, United States of America.

Library of Congress Cataloging-in-Publication Data
Names: Sutton, Jeffrey S. (Jeffrey Stuart), 1960–, author.
Title: 51 imperfect solutions : states and the making of American constitutional law / Jeffrey Sutton.
Other titles: Fifty-one imperfect solutions
Description: New York : Oxford University Press, 2018.
Identifiers: LCCN 2017050044 (print) | LCCN 2017051410 (ebook) |
ISBN 9780190866051 (updf) | ISBN 9780190866068 (epub) |
ISBN 9780190866044 (hardback) | ISBN 9780190088811 (paperback)
Subjects: LCSH: Constitutional law—United States—States.
Classification: LCC KF4530 (ebook) | LCC KF4530 .S88 2018 (print) | DDC 342.73—dc23
LC record available at https://lccn.loc.gov/2017050044

1 3 5 7 9 8 6 4 2

Printed by Sheridan Books, Inc., in the United States of America

CONTENTS

———⟫◦⟪———

ACKNOWLEDGMENTS

—————◈—————

This book has had a long gestation period. When Ohio Attorney General Betty Montgomery hired me to be the Ohio State Solicitor in 1995, I knew little about our state constitutions and had even less experience with them. Three and a half years later, I could teach a semester-long course on the subject, focused solely (had I wished) on cases I had lost at the Ohio Supreme Court under the Ohio Constitution. My first encounters with state constitutional law thus largely came on the short end of disputes about school funding, vouchers, searches and seizures, tort reform, free exercise of religion, and criminal procedure. That was not a promising beginning. I did not enjoy losing those cases and to this day would be thrilled to file a petition for rehearing in some of them.

Over time, two thoughts dawned on me about my experiences as the Ohio Solicitor. One was that it could have been worse. If I was disappointed by a 4–3 ruling of the Ohio Supreme Court to invalidate the State's system for funding the public schools under the Ohio Constitution, to use one of too many examples, I would have been positively morose about a 5–4 ruling of the U.S. Supreme Court doing the same under the National Constitution. It's one thing for a state court to constitutionalize an issue for one State; it's quite another for the National Court to do the same for all fifty States.

My other thought was less small minded, less focused on one advocate's wins and losses. Ever since *Brown v. Board of Education*, a recurring theme in federal constitutional law has been that the States and their constituent parts—legislatures, governors, courts, local governments—have been the policy villains in this or that area of law and this or that era of history. The States, to their discredit, often supplied ample evidence to support these stories, Jim Crow being the most conspicuous example but hardly the only example. By the mid-1990s, however, I saw nothing of the sort in Ohio. Whether in the Governor's Office, the General Assembly, the Attorney General's Office, or the Ohio courts, I saw elected officials and judges who were sensitive to civil rights, who were doing their best to resolve difficult policy problems with finite resources, and who offered no hints of the kinds of state officials that dominate many constitutional law narratives of the past. Granted, I did see some political dysfunction when it came to criminal law policies. But that was a reality not just in Ohio and not just in the States, and it is a reality that has ebbed in the last ten years in state and federal legislative and judicial spheres.

During my stint in state government, I also worked with solicitors, solicitors general, and appellate chiefs from other states. Here too I saw nothing remotely suggestive of the stories that dominate federal constitutional law. Some issues united the States. Some issues divided them. But it was rare to see unreasonable grounds for disagreement. Quite the opposite: The occasional divisions reflected differences in regional priorities or close calls on close issues. After I left state government, I represented many States in federalism cases in the U.S. Supreme Court, including Alabama, Florida, Georgia, and Nevada, among others. In brief after brief in federalism cases about issues ranging from disability discrimination to age discrimination, we always featured the same point: The States had all enacted their own laws designed to stop these forms of discrimination, many of the laws had been passed long before the national government entered the picture, and these States remained just as committed to prohibiting such discrimination as any other government. If there were disagreements between my clients and the federal government in those cases, they were reasonable ones, as confirmed by the close votes in each case.

These were eye-opening experiences. They recalibrated my views about the role of the States in our federalist system of government and prompted me to wonder whether we were maximizing the benefits of our nearly unique form of government, one initiated after all by The United States of America.

Two other experiences supplemented and reinforced these thoughts. As an advocate at the U.S. Supreme Court, I witnessed increasing pressure placed on the federal courts to resolve national rights debates. And as a federal court of appeals judge for the last fifteen years, I have seen the same thing and had my share of experiences with it. I came to wonder: Why place such pressure on one Court and one Constitution to referee winner-take-all disputes when the country has fifty-one high courts and fifty-one constitutions?

So began the first inklings for some articles about state constitutional law, speeches, a textbook, and eventually this book. If federalism was an enemy of progress for one chapter in American history, perhaps federalism could be a solution, or at least a partial answer, to some of the deep divides that persist in today's chapter of American history. In a country that has come to believe deeply in judicially protected rights but has come to disagree fiercely about which rights to recognize, a renewed focus on state constitutions as a meaningful source of rights protection, but not a one-size-fits-all source of rights protection, might offer a useful way to handle our country's differences of opinion and a useful process for ameliorating and eventually resolving them.

Along the way, I have received considerable support in thinking about these issues. Start with my luckless law clerks. For fifteen years, they have suffered through countless lunchtime discussions about these issues and done their best to humor me about the topic, sometimes even contributing helpful insights along the way. Through more than twenty years of teaching state constitutional law at Ohio State and more than five years at Harvard, my law school students have energized me about the topic and contributed valuable insights of their own.

As with the writing of many books, my first work in this area started with speeches at law schools and articles published by law reviews. I am grateful for those invitations and the thoughts they provoked and forced me to organize. Here are the main speeches and articles in rough sequence: (1) *San Antonio Independent School District v. Rodriguez and Its Aftermath*, 94 Va. L. Rev. 1963 (2008), which grew out of a 2007 lecture at the University of Virginia Law School; (2) *Why Teach—And*

Why Study—State Constitutional Law, 34 Okla. City Univ. L. Rev. 165 (2009), which grew out of the 2008 Brennan Lecture at Oklahoma City University's Law School; (3) *What Does—And Does Not—Ail State Constitutional Law*, 59 Kan. L. Rev. 687 (2011), which grew out of a 2010 symposium on state constitutional law at the University of Kansas Law School; (4) *Hallows Lecture: Barnette, Frankfurter, and Judicial Review*, 96 Marq. L. Rev. 133 (2012), which grew out of the 2012 Hallows Lecture at Marquette University Law School; (5) the 2013 Sullivan Lecture at Capital University Law School; (6) *Courts as Change Agents: Do We Want More—Or Less?*, 127 Harv. L. Rev. 1419 (2014); (7) *Symposium Introduction: State Constitutions in the United States Federal System*, 77 Ohio St. L.J. 195 (2016), which grew out of a symposium on state constitutional law at the Moritz College of Law at The Ohio State University; and (8) *Our Fifty-One Constitutions*, the 2015 Henry Lecture at the University of Oklahoma Law School. Some of these speeches and articles were used in places in *State Constitutional Law: The Modern Experience*, a West textbook that I coauthored with the Honorable Randy Holland, Steve McAllister, and Jeffrey Shaman and that now is in its second edition. These speeches and articles form the foundation and some of the words for parts of several chapters of the book. I am grateful for the invitations to deliver these talks and to the law reviews and West for permission to use some of these materials here.

I am also grateful to several friends and family members who reviewed parts or all of the book: the Honorable James Bassett, Larry Baum, Joseph Blocher, Neil Devins, Jim Garland, the Honorable David Gilberston, Larry Herman, the Honorable Randy Holland, Dick Howard, Orin Kerr, the Honorable Erin Lagesen, Jeff Minear, Sandy Levinson, Michael McConnell, the Honorable Richard Pollack, Dan Schweitzer, Nathaniel Sutton, and Peggy Sutton.

The Sixth Circuit librarians have done wonderful work in tracking down resources. In addition to the head librarian, Owen Smith, they include Tom Vanderloo, Stephanie Woebkenberg, Neil Reed, and Ellen Smith. They also have provided helpful edits. Thank you.

Over the years, many interns in my office have helped with research that has been used in the book or related articles. Several of them deserve mention: Noah Schottenstein, Stefan Hayek, Brett Colbert, Marjorie Yano, Ali Haque, Russell Balikian, Jordan Pratt, Yariv Pierce,

Courter Shimeall, Andrew Fraser, David Twombly, Christina Karam, Jason Gerken, Corey Leggett, Natalie Holzaepfel, Lindsay Dunn, Danielle Scoliere, Danelle Gagliardi, Michael Disotell, Lisa Herman, Cailtyn Martin, Trent Thacker, Cheyenne Chambers, Alex Korecky, Alex Holtzman, Collin Flake, Danielle Wheeler, Andrew Jordan, William Seidleck, Matthew Diaz, Robert Smith, Chase McReynolds, Sara Schiavone, James Payne, Guiseppe Pappalardo, Adam Midkiff, Ben Hemmelgarn, Sean Lehman, James Kim, Danny Colston, Jack Burnside, and Larae Shraeder.

Dave McBride, Emily Mackenzie, Damian Penfold and Mary Rosewood at Oxford University Press have provided helpful editing suggestions throughout and have made the book better than it was when I delivered the manuscript to them.

People who write books on top of the day-to-day responsibilities of their job face one of two situations at home: a family whose love and care inspires them to do more or a family from whom they are escaping. I am deeply blessed to fall into the first category. My wife, Peggy, sons Nathaniel and John, and daughter Margaret are all anyone could ask for.

51 IMPERFECT SOLUTIONS

I

Introduction

ONE COULD FILL A bookshelf with compilations of landmark constitutional decisions. Valuable as these writings may be, they uniformly tell just part of the story. In describing opinions on equal protection, criminal procedure, due process, free speech, freedom of religion, and other bedrock constitutional guarantees, they all omit two essentials.

One omission is that they begin and end with discussions of rulings by the U.S. Supreme Court, rarely discussing, rarely indeed even mentioning, related rulings of the state supreme courts that construe similar state constitutional guarantees. Yet virtually all of the foundational liberties that protect Americans originated in the state constitutions and to this day remain independently protected by them. Those interested in the right to speak freely without risk of government suppression or the right to practice one's religion without restriction, to give two examples, ought to understand the role that the courts of all sovereigns in the country—national and state—play in construing these guarantees. In our federal system, nearly every state and local law must comply with two sets of constraints, those imposed by the Federal Constitution and those imposed by their state counterparts, as it is the rare guarantee of any significance that appears just in the National Constitution as opposed to most (if not all) of the state constitutions. And some liberty guarantees appear only in state constitutions. When individuals seek protection from their state or local governments, they generally will not care whether the state or federal constitution, the state or federal court, does the protecting.

The other omission is that the full story of landmark decisions of the U.S. Supreme Court cannot be understood in isolation. When the National Court enforces a federal right, prior state court decisions in the area often influence the decision, whether on the ground that interpretations of the original state constitutional guarantees illuminate the meaning of the later federal provision or on the ground that the States' experiences in recognizing the right warrant nationalizing it. The States' experiences are just as relevant, indeed more relevant, in the other direction. When the National Court *declines* to enforce a right, the state courts become the *only* forum (fora, if you prefer) for enforcing the right under their own constitutions, making it imperative to see whether and, if so, how the States fill gaps left by the U.S. Supreme Court. Both accounts must be aired to understand the true sources of American liberty and their availability today.

This book aims to fill these gaps. It tells the story not of cases but of rights, not of one court but of many courts, not of federal and state judges but of American judges.

The book does something else. It talks about the role of the States in developing American constitutional law from a different vantage point. At many times in American history, the States have set a *negative* example that has affected the development of constitutional law. This book builds on those accounts by offering stories in which the States set *positive* examples that hold the potential to be just as influential in the development of American constitutional law.

Chapter 2 lays the foundation for the book by offering some basics about American federalism. It explains how most state and local laws in this country remain subject to two sets of constitutional constraints—those under the federal and state constitutions. It shows how that was not always so when it comes to the liberty and property protections associated with the Bill of Rights and indeed was not the case for most of the first 150 years of American history. Not until the U.S. Supreme Court's extension of most of the Bill of Rights to the States, completed for the most part by the early 1960s, did any of these federal individual rights guarantees apply to the States. Our system of dual sovereigns now comes with dual protections against overreaching state and local laws. In the aftermath of that development, the chapter explains why American lawyers and judges would do well to pay attention to the liberty and property protections in the federal *and* state constitutions and the reasons why the state guarantees often offer a promising source of protection.

All of this is a windup to the heart of the book, four stories about four individual rights, each revealing the complex interaction between the state and federal courts in construing similar state and federal constitutional guarantees.

The first story, featured in Chapter 3, concerns school funding. State law developments are particularly salient when the U.S. Supreme Court declines to recognize a right. In *San Antonio Independent School District v. Rodriguez*, the U.S. Supreme Court in 1973 (less than two months after *Roe v. Wade*) refused to create a constitutional right to equal funding between and among public school districts in Texas. In the decades since, one state supreme court after another (and many state legislatures to boot) have required their own States to create greater equal-funding remedies than the ones the *Rodriguez* plaintiffs had sought—but failed to obtain. Since *Rodriguez*, the States have adopted so many school-funding innovations that it's fair to ask whether the plaintiffs won by losing. The answer is more complicated than one might expect.

State law developments are just as relevant in the years *before* the U.S. Supreme Court recognizes a new constitutional right and in the years *after* it implements the right. Chapter 4 describes the development of the exclusionary rule—a criminal defendant's right to exclude evidence obtained through an unreasonable search and seizure—an account that cannot be understood without considering the state-federal dialogue that led to it and that continues to shape it to this day. Construing their own constitutions more than a century ago, the U.S. Supreme Court and several state courts raised the idea, often haltingly and often just in passing, of excluding evidence obtained in violation of protections against unreasonable searches and seizures as a way of vindicating the guarantee. The suggestions gradually led to holdings, as several state courts adopted an exclusionary rule, abandoning the common law rule that the illegality of a seizure did not affect the independent evidentiary question whether the items discovered during it could be admitted in a later criminal trial. In 1914, the U.S. Supreme Court appeared to adopt an exclusionary rule for *federal* law enforcement, making its own break from the common law rule. By 1949, when the Court was asked to nationalize the exclusionary rule through the Fourteenth Amendment but declined the invitation, sixteen States had adopted their own exclusionary rules. And by 1961, when *Mapp v. Ohio* extended the rule to the States, roughly half of the States had adopted the rule for themselves under their state constitutions, a point that the U.S. Supreme Court emphasized in justifying its decision.

The apparent end of this chapter of the story opened another. In 1984, the U.S. Supreme Court created an exception to the exclusionary rule for federal and state police officers who rely in good faith on the existence of a warrant. Since then, close to twenty States (and counting) have refused to embrace the good faith exception under their own constitutions, confirming that a dialogue begun in the nineteenth century is apt to continue well into the twenty-first century. A pragmatic question posed by Chapter 4 is this: How much did criminal defendants as a group win *and* lose by prevailing in *Mapp*? And which venues, the state or federal courts, were most responsible for the winning? The answer, again, is more complicated than one might think.

The plight of Carrie Buck offers a variation on these themes in Chapter 5. Most lawyers and many Americans know about the U.S. Supreme Court's ignominious rejection of her claim that the Fourteenth Amendment prohibited the State of Virginia from sterilizing her against her will. What few people know is that many state courts grappled with the same issue long before the Supreme Court decided *Buck v. Bell*. Before 1927, many state courts had granted relief under federal and state law to men and women seeking relief from compelled sterilizations on a variety of state and federal constitutional grounds. Yet after 1927, after Justice Holmes' unrestrained praise for eugenics in *Buck v. Bell*, an 8–1 decision joined by Chief Justice Taft and Justice Brandeis, few state courts showed any willingness to enforce their own state constitutional guarantees in similar cases. The compelled-sterilization story offers several warnings. Be careful about assuming that state court judges, even majoritarian-elected state court judges, cannot be trusted to enforce countermajoritarian guarantees. And never place too much faith in any one set of judges or any one court or, for that matter, any one branch of government as the sole protector of our liberties. The aftermath of *Buck* demonstrates what happens if Americans rely too heavily on just one of those courts, the U.S. Supreme Court, as the exclusive guardian of our rights: We run the risk of creating state courts that lack the necessary fortitude to fill the gap when we need it most.

We meet the plight of a religious minority, the Jehovah's Witnesses, in Chapter 6. Before and during World War II, Witness families faced a startling wave of discrimination in this country, all stemming from actions required by their faith. They sought to assert their free exercise and free speech rights by seeking an exemption from public school requirements that they participate in flag-salute and pledge-of-allegiance ceremonies at the beginning of each school day. Here too we have landmark rulings by the U.S. Supreme Court: one rejecting the Witnesses' claim (*Minersville School District v. Gobitis*), and the other, just three years later, granting relief to the families and overruling *Gobitis* in the process (*West Virginia State Board of Education v. Barnette*). And here too we have a set of underappreciated rulings by the state courts during the same era, several of which anticipated *Barnette* and set the stage in word and deed for it. But this story differs in one respect from the others. The state court judges, truth be told, were largely just as slow to recognize the risks to liberty in these disputes as their federal counterparts. All in all, this is a story about across-the-board judicial failure—perhaps explained by the unfolding world war—with the state and federal judges together sleeping through the initial efforts to enforce these individual rights and waking up at roughly the same time.

Why these four rights, the reader might ask? Each set of cases presents a distinct tale of caution or hope and illustrates the types of complications that sometimes arise in prematurely nationalizing constitutional rights and the occasional benefits that flow from measured restraint in refusing to do so. Why not cover other prominent rights disputes: segregated schools, same-sex marriage, an individual right to possess a weapon, property rights, and so on? The short answer is that many of these stories have been covered in considerable detail elsewhere. The long answer is that I will discuss some of these other disputes in abridged fashion in the epilogue and try to put them in the context of these other chapters.

Last of all, Chapters 7 and 8 raise the idea of reform. I offer several ways in which lawyers, state and federal judges, and law schools might take both sides of American constitutional law more seriously—and in the process strengthen each indispensable half.

In offering federal *and* state accounts of the development of these constitutional rights, the book strives to shelve one account of American constitutional law and to replace it with another. The book tries, usually successfully, not to take sides on what the state and federal courts *should* have done in construing these guarantees. Its focus instead is on describing what they did in order to see if there is anything to learn along the way. That's why I pay little attention to whether the state and federal court decisions were right. And that's why I pay little attention to whether the state and federal courts should have applied originalism or living constitutionalism or pragmatism to the issues. That's also why I frequently take for granted that vigorous individual rights protection by some court is beneficial even if that may not always be the case—even if legislative and executive branch protections of individual rights, as I sometimes point out, often offer equally promising, if not more promising, ways to resolve these problems. With these qualifications in mind, I try to put each of these rights disputes in the context of a remarkably complex, nuanced, ever-changing constitutional system—that of American federalism—one that ought to make lawyers and litigants pause before reflexively assuming that the U.S. Supreme Court should nationalize answers to vexing constitutional questions. If there is a central conviction of the book, it's that an underappreciation of state constitutional law has hurt state *and* federal law and has undermined the appropriate balance between state *and* federal courts in protecting individual liberty.

2

American Constitutionalism: A Second Source of Power Comes with Dual Constraints on That Power

BEFORE EXPLAINING THE ROLE of federal *and* state constitutions in protecting individual rights, let me offer a basic—and surprisingly accurate—analogy for thinking about them. Imagine the final game of the Final Four of the NCAA Men's College Basketball Tournament. Let's say that the University of Kansas faces the University of Kentucky, a storied matchup that leads to an epic game. Toward the end of regulation, with the game tied, a Kentucky player drives the lane, and a Kansas player fouls him in the act of shooting, just as time expires. The shot rims out, but the Kentucky player has two free throws. That's not a bad situation for the Bluegrass State, as the team gets two chances to win the game. But how would Kentucky fans react if the coach ordered his player to take just one of those free throws, giving him just one chance, not two, to win? The referee couldn't force the player to take the second shot any more than he could force the player to make it. If Kentucky ended up losing the game (because the player missed the one shot and the team lost in overtime), the Kentucky coach's eyebrow-raising choice would be unforgivable.

If you think this scenario is implausible, so do I. But that leaves us with some explaining to do. Why is it that when we switch from American basketball to American law, we see American lawyers regularly taking just one shot rather than two to invalidate state or local laws (or state or local executive branch action) on behalf of their clients?

A few features of American constitutional law confirm the similarities between the two situations. In this country, state and local laws face two sets of constitutional constraints: those under the U.S. Constitution and those under the relevant state constitution. The Framers of the U.S. Constitution modeled all individual rights guarantees after guarantees that originated in a state constitution—usually one of the state constitutions ratified between 1776 (after, in most cases, the colonies declared independence from England) and 1789 (when the people ratified the U.S. Constitution). Take some of our most celebrated rights: free speech; free exercise of religion; separation of church and state; jury trial; right to bear arms; prohibitions on unreasonable searches and seizures; due process; prohibition on governmental taking of property; no cruel and unusual punishment; equal protection. *All* of them, and all of the other individual rights guarantees as well, originated in the state constitutions[1] and were authored by a set of not inconsequential political leaders in the States, such as John Adams, Benjamin Franklin, Robert Livingston, James Madison, and George Mason.[2]

The upshot is that American constitutional law creates two potential opportunities, not one, to invalidate a state or local law. Individuals who wish to challenge the validity of a state or local law thus usually have two opportunities to strike the law—one premised on the first-in-time state constitutional guarantee and one premised on a counterpart found in the U.S. Constitution.

Yet most lawyers take one shot rather than two, and usually raise the federal claim rather than the state one. In the course of serving on the U.S. Court of Appeals for the Sixth Circuit for fifteen years, I have seen many constitutional challenges to state or local laws within the States of my circuit: Kentucky, Michigan, Ohio, and Tennessee. Yet I recall just one instance in which the claimant meaningfully challenged the validity of a law on federal *and* state constitutional grounds.[3] One might be tempted to think that federal judges hear lawsuits only under federal law. Don't be. We hear many state common law and state statutory claims. That's because our power to hear federal statutory and constitutional claims comes with authority to hear related claims that arise under state law. And our power to hear disputes between citizens of one State against citizens of another permits claims under state or federal law—or both.

As the State Solicitor of Ohio from 1995 to 1998, I oversaw appellate litigation for the Attorney General, which included defending challenges to state and local laws in the state and federal appellate courts. While I saw more claimants who raised federal and state constitutional challenges to the laws (that's how I first became acquainted with state constitutional law), that remained the once-in-a-while exception. Even then, even when the claimants filed claims under both constitutions, their lawyers tended to focus their briefing and oral arguments on the federal claims and the federal precedents undergirding them.[4]

If you doubt the conclusion I draw from my own experience, do two things. Ask a state court judge about the frequency with which claimants raise federal and state constitutional challenges to state or local laws and the seriousness with which they raise the state claims (if they raise them at all). Then read the literature. One article after another talks about the second-tier status of state constitutional claims and the infrequency with which they are raised.[5]

One article deserves special note. In 1977, a highly influential U.S. Supreme Court Justice, William Brennan, devoted a law review article to the topic. One of the most widely read law review articles in American legal history, the Brennan piece asks the same question I am asking: Why is it that lawyers, required by the ethical canons to put their clients' best foot forward and often incentivized by a fee to do the same, usually focus just on the U.S. Constitution in challenging the validity of state or local laws? The article laments the infrequency with which litigants and state court judges have respected and honored both sides of our federalist system: Dual governing powers come with dual limits on those powers. A loss in the U.S. Supreme Court under the U.S. Constitution need not foreshadow a loss in a State High Court under a comparable guarantee found in the state constitution. What was true in 1977 appears to be just as true in 2018. Lawyers still raise claims under their States' constitutions as quintessential arguments of last resort, if they raise them at all.

All of this is difficult to understand. Just as each free throw gives the basketball player an equal chance to score a point, each free speech challenge gives the lawyer an equal chance to invalidate a speech-infringing law on behalf of the client. Most clients do not care why or how they win. Whether the court invalidates a speech-infringing law under the state or federal constitution rarely makes a difference to the future enforceability of the law. If the law violates the Federal

Constitution, the Supremacy Clause prohibits a state or local government from enforcing the law. If the law violates the State's constitution, that constitution bars state or local governments from enforcing it. Either way, the law is null and void. That usually makes clients, a results-driven group if ever there were one, happy. Yet most lawyers often don't take the second shot.

Maybe the two scenarios are not as parallel as I suppose. While a second free throw costs nothing, a second argument costs time and money to develop. True. But the analogy still holds. American law offers many second (and third) shots, and American lawyers, as I can attest, are not known for their reticence in taking them. Consider a case in which the police conduct an illegal search of a suspect's home *and* an illegal interrogation of a suspect. No lawyer worth his salt would raise only a Fourth Amendment challenge, as opposed to Fourth *and* Fifth Amendment challenges, to the police misconduct. Just so with another type of second shot. If the police conduct an illegal search, it is difficult to justify taking just one opportunity (the Fourth Amendment) rather than two (the Fourth Amendment *and* the state counterpart) to invalidate it.

What's going on? Are American basketball players smarter than American lawyers? Have American law schools trained their graduates to be half-equipped to obtain relief for their clients? Have American lawyers, even after taking an oath to uphold the federal *and* state constitutions, even after practicing for many years and learning that their State has a constitution, become so specialized that they are half-prepared to win?

The point of this chapter is twofold: (1) to explain how we got here—how the bench and bar became so one-sided in their understanding of American constitutional law and diminished the States' constitutions in the process, and (2) to consider reasons for changing course—why American lawyers and judges (and citizens) would benefit from taking our state constitutions more seriously than they currently do.

How We Got Here

The States created the first thirteen constitutions in this country,[6] indeed many of the first constitutions in the world.[7] The era between the Declaration of Independence in 1776 and the U.S. Constitutional Convention in 1787 was *the* seminal era of constitution writing. The most inspired constitution writing in this country, perhaps at any time, perhaps anywhere, occurred before 1787, and it occurred in the States. In the words of Gordon Wood: "The office of our governors, the bicameral legislatures, tripartite separation of powers, bills of rights, and the unique use of constitutional conventions were all born during the state constitution-making period between 1775 and the early 1780s, well before the federal constitution of 1787 was created."[8] More innovations in the drafting of constitutions occurred before the fabled meeting in the summer of 1787 to draft the U.S. Constitution than after it.

That's not to belittle the Framers of the U.S. Constitution. In "split[ting] the atom of sovereignty,"[9] the Framers created American federalism, a unique way of dividing governmental power and a unique way of aggregating it. That innovation and the many compromises that came with it make the U.S. Constitution a rightly celebrated framework of government. The horizontal separations of power among the three branches of the national government, together with the vertical separation of powers between the national government and the States, provide the soundest protection of liberty any people has known.

But to the extent we celebrate the U.S. Constitution for the express individual rights guarantees added to it later, credit for these innovations goes elsewhere. Whether it's the individual liberty guarantees added in 1791 (the Bill of Rights), in 1865 (the Thirteenth Amendment), in 1868 (the Fourteenth Amendment), in 1870 (the Fifteenth Amendment), or in 1920 (the Nineteenth Amendment), all of the language underlying these guarantees originated in the States.[10]

When it came time to draft the first eight amendments in the Bill of Rights, for example, Madison and others drew from the existing state constitutions.[11] By 1791, four States already protected the right to bear arms.[12] Nearly every State guaranteed the free exercise of religion.[13] And so on.[14]

Against this backdrop, the idea of dual constitutional challenges to state or local laws, or for that matter federal laws, would have seemed strange to the authors of the state and federal constitutions. Lawyers of the founding generation would have thought that one layer of constitutional protection was enough. If a state or local government infringed an individual's liberty, property, or other rights, that individual's state constitution would supply the answer. And if the federal government did the same, the Bill of Rights would supply the answer. Yes, a few exceptions existed at the founding. Section 10 of Article I of the U.S. Constitution placed some limits on the States by prohibiting them from "pass[ing] any Bill of Attainder, ex post Facto law, or Law impairing the Obligation of Contracts." And yes, most state constitutions prohibited their governments then, and prohibit them now, from impairing contracts or adopting ex post facto laws.[15] But these minor variations prove the major premise, that at the founding the U.S. Constitution imposed limits mainly on the federal government.

Any doubt about the major premise was laid to rest in 1833 in an opinion by Chief Justice Marshall in *Barron v. City of Baltimore*.[16] At stake was whether the Takings Clause of the Fifth Amendment limited the actions of the City of Baltimore. The Court clarified that this provision, and all of the individual rights provisions of the Bill of Rights, applied only to the federal government, not to the States or, as in that case, to a city.[17] As *Barron* confirms, the key individual rights guarantees in the U.S. Constitution originally restricted only the federal government.

What of the possibility that the state constitutions could restrict not just state and local governments but the federal government as well? Shouldn't a citizen of Maryland be able to invoke the U.S. Constitution *and* her own constitution in challenging the validity of a federal law or, say, the actions of a federal law enforcement officer? The Supremacy Clause of the U.S. Constitution—making federal law supreme over contrary state law[18]—suggests an answer. The Supreme Court's decision in a second case from Maryland, *McCulloch v. Maryland*, removes all doubt about the answer.[19] In another opinion by Chief Justice Marshall, *McCulloch* prohibited the State of Maryland from imposing its own taxes on the Second National Bank of the United States on top of those imposed by the federal government.[20]

Because the original national government truly was one of limited and enumerated powers and because the States had general and assumed powers, most individual rights litigation for roughly the first

150 years of American history was premised on the state constitutions and arose in the state courts. Even the origin of judicial review—the power of a court to invalidate a law under the constitution and a prerequisite to *any* such individual rights litigation—began in the States. The first use of the power occurred in the state courts and arose under the state constitutions.[21] State courts in at least seven states invalidated state or local laws under their State constitutions before 1787.[22] The state courts not only laid the foundation for judicial review under the U.S. Constitution, as recognized in *Marbury v. Madison*,[23] but they also were the key courts to exercise the power for more than a century after independence.[24]

An examination of constitutional law treatises from this era confirms the point. Most of each treatise was devoted to state constitutional law. Thomas Cooley's treatise, "The General Principles of Constitutional Law in the United States of America," is representative.[25] The chapters devoted to individual rights mainly concerned state constitutional law. And most of the individual rights decisions in the book came from the state courts. So too of other treatises of the era.[26] Odd though it may sound to modern ears, most of the constitutional-rights litigation of the first 150 years after 1776 took place in the States.

Passage of the Fourteenth Amendment in 1868 began to change things even though state constitutions by then were teeming with individual rights.[27] The due process and equal protection guarantees of the Fourteenth Amendment, unlike the Bill of Rights, applied by their terms to the States. Of particular significance to the future of individual rights litigation, the U.S. Supreme Court gradually incorporated most of the Bill of Rights into the Due Process Clause of the Fourteenth Amendment—an early form of substantive due process. By the time the age of incorporation had (largely) come to rest in the early 1960s, most of the core federal protections of property and liberty applied equally to the federal government and the States. That's when it became possible for litigants to raise two claims of constitutional invalidity against most state and local laws.

What we have today is not an inevitable feature of the Framers' vision. It is in reality quite remote from anything the Framers could have imagined. The original constitutional plan created largely exclusive federal and state spheres of power as opposed to largely overlapping spheres of power.[28] Which makes sense: Why would a libertarian group of Framers, skeptical of governmental power and intent on dividing it in all manner of ways, have *doubled* the governmental bodies that could regulate the lives of Americans? And tripled and quadrupled them if one accounts for cities and counties? A system of largely separate dual sovereignty (federal *or* state power in most areas) has become a system of largely overlapping dual sovereignty (federal *and* state power in most areas). Good or bad, textually justified or not, this feature of American government is not going away. American constitutional law today thus permits at least two sets of regulations in every corner of the country and what comes with it: the potential for dual challenges to the validity of most state or local laws. That has been true since the end of the Warren Court for most liberty guarantees, and it is difficult to envision a scenario in which that reality disappears.

This history, much abridged for sure, suggests two explanations for the seeming reluctance of lawyers and courts to take one part of American constitutional law seriously. The first is a function of time. Because it took until the 1960s for the U.S. Supreme Court to complete the individual rights revolution by incorporating most of the Bill of Rights into the Fourteenth Amendment, it was not until then that American lawyers, law schools, and state courts had any reason to think about using state and federal court systems, and state and federal constitutions, to vindicate civil rights. We thus are not talking about a set of litigation opportunities, a litigation strategy, that existed for most of American history. It's been roughly fifty years since the U.S. Supreme Court completed much of this transformation. That's not a long time, less than a fourth of American legal history. And that's even less time if we consider the most recently incorporated right: the Second Amendment in 2010.[29]

The second reason emerges from a central explanation for the success of the federal rights revolution: the States' relative underprotection of individual rights. Who could blame lawyers and their clients for being reluctant to develop a strategy built in part on state constitutional rights? The U.S. Supreme Court recognized many of the rights it did between the 1940s and the 1960s *because* many state courts (and state legislatures and state governors) resisted protecting individual rights, most notably in the South but hardly there alone. One can forgive lawyers from this era for hesitating to add state constitutional claims to their newly minted federal claims. Why seek relief from institutions that created the individual rights vacuum in the first place?

It's no small matter that the federal claims kept succeeding. Even the most progressive state courts in this era would have had trouble keeping up with the rights innovations of the U.S. Supreme Court in the midst of this constitutional reordering. Take the perspective of a criminal defense lawyer at the time. Who needed the liberty protections in the state constitutions when the National Constitution produced the likes of *Gideon, Mapp, Miranda*, and other transformative decisions? Surely the goal was to *continue* raising federal claims, whether in federal or state court.

There has to be more to it than that, though. Chief Justice Burger replaced Chief Justice Warren in 1968, and the kinds of advantages that once prompted resort to federal law and federal courts have been more fluid than fixed. Just as the Burger Court was less willing to innovate new constitutional rights, the same has been true, perhaps more true, for the Rehnquist and Roberts Courts. It was during the transition from the Warren Court to the Burger Court that Justice Brennan authored his (potentially) pathmaking article—a call to arms for individual rights litigants to seek relief under the States' constitutions in the wake of a loss in the U.S. Supreme Court. Some litigants, it is true, listened. Some went to state court. And some won. But for present purposes, the question is why just some, as opposed to most, lawyers took Justice Brennan's advice—why American lawyers did not follow the example of American basketball players by taking two shots rather than one *whenever* the opportunity presented itself. I will return to this topic in Chapters 7 and 8.

Let me turn to the other theme of this chapter and the second piece of groundwork for the American constitutional law stories that follow. We now know the potential benefits of seeking relief under a State's constitution: Lawyers are paid to help clients win, and lawyers will have some explaining to do if they opt to take just one chance, rather than two, at knocking out a state or local law.[30] But why would a State's high court grant relief under its constitution after the national high court has rejected a similar claim under its constitution?

Reasons to Think Anew About State Courts as Guardians of Individual Rights and State Constitutions as Sources of Those Rights

State courts have authority to construe their own constitutional provisions however they wish. Nothing compels the state courts to imitate federal interpretations of the liberty and property guarantees in the U.S. Constitution when it comes to the rights guarantees found in their own constitutions, even guarantees that match the federal ones letter for letter. As long as a state court's interpretation of its own constitution does not violate a federal requirement, it will stand, and, better than that, it will be impervious to challenge in the U.S. Supreme Court.[31]

So why might a state court grant relief under its state constitution when the federal court rejected a request for relief in construing similar or even identical language in the U.S. Constitution? The first answer is that it can. Our federal system gives state courts the final say over the meaning of their own constitutions. As a matter of power, the fifty-one highest courts in the system may *each* come to different conclusions about the meaning of, say, due process in their own jurisdictions.

The second answer is better. As a matter of reason, there often are sound grounds for interpreting the two sets of guarantees differently. State constitutional law not only gives the client two chances to win, but in many cases it also will give the client a better chance to win. Imagine two judges who are identical twins. They are the same in every relevant respect, save one: The first sibling sits on the U.S. Supreme Court, while the other one sits on the New Jersey Supreme Court. My submission is that, all else being equal, a lawyer for an individual-liberties claimant should have an easier time convincing the twin who sits on a state supreme court to rule the client's way than convincing the twin who sits on the U.S. Supreme Court to do the same.

The U.S. Supreme Court faces several disadvantages relative to the state courts when it comes to defining constitutional rights and crafting constitutional remedies. Because the Supreme Court must announce rights and remedies for fifty States, one national government, and over 320 million people, it is more constrained than a state supreme court faced with an issue affecting one State and, say, twelve million people. Legal commentators talk about liberal and conservative judges, but all

U.S. Supreme Court Justices generally appreciate the risks associated with rulings that prevent the democratic processes from working in fifty-one different jurisdictions. The more innovative a constitutional claim, the more hesitant the U.S. Supreme Court may be about entering the thicket. That dynamic disappears in the state courts. Innovation by one state court necessarily comes with no risks for other States and fewer risks for that State.

New constitutional rights not only require the articulation of a new constitutional theory. They also require the management of a new constitutional right. Most judges worry about the next case when they think about identifying a new constitutional right. But U.S. Supreme Court Justices have more to worry about than state court judges in view of the scope of their jurisdiction, the enormous breadth of which ensures that it is "always raining somewhere"[32] and that any new right will face a bundle of varied circumstances. In some settings, the challenge of imposing a constitutional solution on the whole country at once will increase the likelihood that federal constitutional law will be underenforced, that a "federalism discount" will be applied to the right.[33] State courts face no such problem in construing their own constitutions.

State courts also have a freer hand in doing something the Supreme Court cannot: allowing local conditions and traditions to affect their interpretation of a constitutional guarantee and the remedies imposed to implement that guarantee.[34] Does anyone doubt that the Wyoming Supreme Court might look at property rights—and takings claims— differently than the New York Court of Appeals? Or that the Alaska and Hawaii Supreme Courts might look at privacy issues differently than other States or, for that matter, the U.S. Supreme Court? Might the regulation of weapons generate a different reading in a supreme court of a state with a large rural population from one with a large suburban and urban population? Might the state courts of Utah and Rhode Island and Maryland construe a free exercise clause differently than other state courts given their histories? State constitutional law respects and honors these differences between and among the States by allowing interpretations of the fifty state constitutions to account for these differences in culture, geography, and history.

The U.S. Supreme Court has no such option. It cannot, or at least it should not, premise an interpretation of the National Constitution on the local traditions, cultures, or history of one State, one region of the country, or one group of citizens.[35]

A mistaken or an ill-conceived constitutional decision is also easier to correct at the state level than it is at the federal level.[36] Not only do state court decisions cover a narrower jurisdiction and affect fewer individuals, but the people at the state level also have other remedies at their disposal: an easier constitutional amendment process and, for richer or poorer, judicial elections. State courts, like state legislatures, thus have far more freedom to "try novel social and economic experiments without risk to the rest of the country"[37] than the U.S. Supreme Court.

Be mindful when considering the comparative advantages of the state and federal courts in rights innovation that many American constitutional issues do not lend themselves to winner-take-all solutions.[38] Many of the most frequently litigated guarantees are open-ended and generate intensely difficult interpretive debates. So difficult are some of these questions that lawyers and law professors alike insist that there are no right answers to some of the questions or, worse, that policy preferences underlie the judges' answers to them. Some judges even say so.[39]

As to these vexing areas of the law, what better time to permit the state courts to adopt their own interpretations of similarly worded constitutional guarantees found in their constitutions? When difficult areas of constitutional construction arise—equal protection, free speech, free exercise, or property rights—why should we assume that the U.S. Supreme Court is somehow an Oracle of Truth? And why should we impose on the members of that Court the remarkable (and what must be exhausting) burden of treating it as the only supreme court in the country capable of offering an insightful solution to a difficult problem? That's a recipe for decreasing, not increasing, respect for the U.S. Supreme Court. Three or so levels of scrutiny—rational basis, intermediate, or strict—may be the best way to assess equal protection claims under the National Constitution, but they are hardly the ordained way and hardly the way *required* by original meaning, living constitutionalism, pragmatism, or any other school of interpretation.[40]

Rational-basis review works for free exercise challenges to neutral, generally applicable laws as a matter of national constitutional law, says the National Court,[41] but the same may not be true for each state constitution.[42] A modest standard for enforcing the Takings Clause[43] works for national taking-of-property claims, says the Court,[44] but it is by no means clear that every State should embrace the same approach in addressing similar challenges under its own constitution.[45] Or think of the many lawsuits filed in the federal and state courts over the constitutionality of state systems for funding public schools in the aftermath of the U.S. Supreme Court's rejection of a similar claim under the Equal Protection Clause.[46] The more difficult the constitutional question, as these cases show, the more indeterminate the answer may be. In these settings, it may be more appropriate to tolerate fifty-one imperfect solutions rather than to impose one imperfect solution on the country as a whole, particularly when imperfection may be something we have to live with in a given area.[47]

Two sidenotes deserve mention at this point. In some settings, the only way a lawyer can win is through the state constitution because it is the only constitution with a provision on point. State constitutions have a variety of clauses found nowhere in the U.S. Constitution: single-subject clauses, uniform-law clauses, right-to-remedy clauses, to name a conspicuous few of many.[48] And some state constitutions have idiosyncratic clauses found in few of their state counterparts.[49]

The other sidenote is that 20 percent of the States' high courts have mandatory appellate jurisdiction.[50] In these States, the claimant is guaranteed to receive review in its state supreme court. By contrast, almost all of the docket of the U.S. Supreme Court is discretionary, and the Court grants review in a small percentage of cases, well under 5 percent of them in a given year.

So far, I have given two reasons why state constitutional law matters: (1) every lawyer should prefer to have two arrows in his quiver rather than one; and (2) it often will be easier to vindicate a state constitutional right in a State's high court than a federal constitutional right in the U.S. Supreme Court.

There is a third reason: It may facilitate the development of *federal constitutional law*. Respect for state constitutional law as an independent source of rights, and its revitalization as a litigation tool, may be the best thing that could happen for federal constitutional law. For too long, we have lived in a top-down constitutional world, in which the U.S. Supreme Court announces a ruling, and the state supreme courts move in lockstep in construing the counterpart guarantees of their own constitutions.

Why not do the reverse? That is the way other areas of the law traditionally develop, be it tort, property, or contract law. In these settings, the state courts are the vanguard, the first ones to decide whether to embrace or reject innovative legal claims. Over time, the market of judicial reasoning identifies winners and losers. An opinion by a Cardozo or a Traynor (or one of the many superb justices sitting on the state courts today) might become the benchmark, after which other state courts opt to follow that view or variations on it. Or the state courts might go their separate ways. In either occasion, the federal courts (and national legislature) profit from the contest of ideas, as they can choose whether to federalize the issue *after* learning the strengths and weaknesses of the competing ways of addressing the problem.

If this approach works so well for American tort, property, and contracts law, why not do the same for American constitutional law? Not all federal constitutional issues, I realize, give us the luxury of time to allow competing approaches to emerge. But if time allows and if the federal courts place a premium on creating sound federal constitutional law rather than quickly decided law, there is little upside to ending the federal constitutional debate first. Better, it would seem, to allow the state courts to work their way through the constitutional issues under their own similarly worded constitutions—developing their own tests and doctrines along the way—after which the National Court can assess the States' experiences and develop its own federal constitutional rules. Let the state courts be the initial innovators of constitutional doctrines if and when they wish, and allow the U.S. Supreme Court to pick and choose from the emerging options.[51] Recall that the individual rights guarantees of the Bill of Rights were based on preexisting state constitutional guarantees, not the other way around. That was a good model for writing the Bill of Rights, and it is a good model for interpreting them.

If ever there were a propitious time for thinking twice about how we develop constitutional law, now may be it. The current U.S. Supreme

Court is not the Warren Court. It still recognizes new constitutional rights, sure enough. In recent years, the Court recognized an individual right to possess a gun in *District of Columbia v. Heller*[52] and a right to same-sex marriage in *Obergefell v. Hodges*,[53] and placed new limits on imposing the death penalty in *Kennedy v. Louisiana*,[54] to name a few examples that come quickly to mind. But most observers, I suspect, would agree that the Burger, Rehnquist, and Roberts Courts have been less likely to innovate new constitutional rights than their forebears.

The same has not been true of the state supreme courts over the last three decades. Whether it is school funding,[55] property rights,[56] the definition of marriage,[57] or other modern rights disputes,[58] the state courts in recent years have gone from being civil rights followers to leaders in many areas. There is a rights-innovating side to federalism: A loss in the U.S. Supreme Court no longer inevitably foreshadows a loss in the state courts when the claim is premised on a state constitutional counterpart. State constitutional litigation can proceed without waiting for, or worrying about, the shadow of federal constitutional law.

What follows are four chapters that try to put these features of American constitutional law in the context of landmark rights disputes and the unexplored story of how state constitutional law played a role in handling them or could have played a greater role in doing so.

3

Equality and Adequacy of School Funding

IN *Brown v. Board of Education*, the Supreme Court observed that "education is perhaps the most important function of state and local governments" and held that it was a public service that "must be made available to all on equal terms."[1] *Brown* removed one barrier to equal educational opportunities in 1954 by prohibiting the segregation of public schools. But it left in place another: the obstacle faced by poor school districts that wished to provide an education to their students "on equal terms" relative to the education offered by wealthier school districts within a State. That left this critical question: Would the federal or state courts (or, for that matter, state legislatures) solve this problem—by equalizing funding between rich and poor public school districts within the States and thus increase the likelihood that *all* American children would have an equal start in life? The answer comes in surprising forms and surprising ways.

The Federal Story

The U.S. Supreme Court had an early opportunity to face this question and to try to correct these funding disparities and resulting inequities. Nineteen years after *Brown*, the Court decided another equal protection case, *San Antonio Independent School District v. Rodriguez*,[2] which gave the Court an opportunity to remove, or at least ameliorate, wealth-based barriers to equal educational opportunities. The lawsuit challenged the constitutionality of Texas's system for funding public schools under the Equal Protection Clause and featured two theories of unconstitutionality. One was premised on the notion that education is a fundamental right; the other was premised on the notion that wealth is a "suspect class." Both theories came to the same end. If accepted, each would require the Court to gauge the constitutionality of Texas's system for funding public schools based on the unforgiving demands of strict scrutiny, a test that would force the State to justify marked disparities between the quality of a public education offered to children living in property-rich and property-poor school districts.[3]

The disparities were stark. To illustrate them, the *Rodriguez* plaintiffs compared the fortunes of two San Antonio school districts: Edgewood and Alamo Heights. Located in the inner city, Edgewood educated 22,000 students in twenty-five elementary and secondary schools and had the lowest real-property values and family income in the metropolitan area. Even though Edgewood imposed the highest property tax rate in the metropolitan area in 1967–68, it generated the lowest amount of revenue: a total of $356 per pupil, which consisted of $222 guaranteed by the State (made up of state and local property taxes), $108 in federal funds, and $26 of discretionary local property-tax revenue.[4] Alamo Heights, the most affluent school district in the San Antonio metropolitan area, had an easier time of it. In 1967–68, it generated $594 per pupil, which consisted of $225 provided by the state guarantee, $36 in federal funds, and $333 of discretionary local-property-tax revenue.[5] When the *Rodriguez* plaintiffs filed their complaint, these disparities were not atypical in Texas, and they meant that the Texas students with the greatest educational needs received the worst (or at least the lowest-funded) education. These disparities often had a racial correlation. Edgewood was 90 percent Hispanic and 6 percent African American, while Alamo Heights was mainly Caucasian, with 18 percent of its student body made up of Hispanic students and with less than 1 percent of it made up of African American students.[6]

Texas's heavy reliance on local property taxes, the plaintiffs also alleged, affected the quality of education a property-poor district could offer, at least as measured by conventional statistics such as class size and the credentials and experience of a district's teachers. Consider these comparisons in the 1968–69 school year: 100 percent of the Alamo Heights teachers had college degrees, while 80 percent of the Edgewood teachers had them; 37.17 percent of the Alamo Heights teachers had advanced degrees, while 14.98 percent of the Edgewood teachers had them; 11 percent of the Alamo Heights teachers depended on emergency teaching permits, while 47 percent of the Edgewood teachers depended on them; Alamo Heights' maximum teaching salary was 25 percent greater than Edgewood's maximum salary; Alamo Heights' teacher-student ratio was 1 to 20.5, while Edgewood's was 1 to 26.5; and Alamo Heights provided one counselor for every 645 students, while Edgewood provided one counselor for every 3,098 students.[7]

In the absence of additional state (or federal) revenue, nothing short of alchemy would permit Edgewood to remove this disparity. At $5,960 per student, the average assessed property value of the district was the lowest in the metropolitan area, and Edgewood already imposed the area's highest property-tax rate ($1.05 per every $100 of value). Alamo Heights, by contrast, had an average assessed property value in excess of $49,000 per student, and a tax rate of $0.85 per every $100.

The debate in the Supreme Court was not about the accuracy of these fiscal comparisons. Or about the challenges poor school districts face in closing this funding gap. It was about the standard of review.

American constitutional law has all manner of tests for assessing the validity of legislation. But in most constitutional cases, courts essentially choose between two standards of review: lax or rigorous. Under a lax form of review, often called rational basis review, a court will uphold a law so long as it can envision an explanation, any plausible explanation at all, for the law and the classifications it draws. Under the rigorous form of review, often called strict scrutiny, a court will invalidate a law unless the government establishes a powerful reason for it and can show that there was no other way to advance that interest. To illustrate, the U.S. Supreme Court often applies rigorous review to laws that turn on suspect classifications based on race or religion but lax review to laws that turn on distinctions between, say, individuals and businesses.

The outcome in *Rodriguez* largely turned on which type of review the Court picked. If strict scrutiny applied, the State faced the daunting task of establishing a compelling interest to justify these disparities and of establishing that it had done everything within its power to eliminate them. But if rational basis review applied, the State could point out that these disparities were the unfortunate, but unavoidable and unsurprising, consequence of *any* public school system premised on local, rather than statewide, control, and that local control of public schools had many competing advantages. The success of the parties' arguments had national implications, as a widespread reliance on local property taxes to fund public schools had created similar disparities throughout the country.[8]

The timing of the Supreme Court's decision in *Rodriguez* did not help the plaintiffs.[9] Not long after they filed the lawsuit in 1968, the district court placed the case on hold while the State attempted to pass legislative reforms designed to correct or at least lessen the disparities identified in the lawsuit. After two years, the reform efforts fell short, and the spotlight returned to the courts. In 1971, a three-judge federal district court (required at the time to assess the constitutionality of a state law) held the system unconstitutional. The U.S. Supreme Court reversed that decision on March 21, 1973.

One need not be a scholar of Supreme Court history to appreciate that there were some differences between the late Warren Court of 1968 and the early Burger Court of 1973. President Richard Nixon made four appointments to the Court during the first four years of his presidency: Chief Justice Burger replaced Chief Justice Warren; Justice Blackmun replaced Justice Fortas; Justice Powell replaced Justice Black; and Justice Rehnquist replaced Justice Harlan. By 1973, the Court had become a different forum in which to advance the argument that education was a fundamental right or that wealth-based classifications were presumptively invalid. The five-member majority that rejected the plaintiffs' claims in *Rodriguez*, as it happened, consisted of the four Nixon appointees plus Justice Stewart.

The author of the majority opinion, Justice Powell, understood the challenges of running a public school system firsthand. From 1952 to 1961, he had chaired the Richmond School Board, where he helped to oversee the desegregation of the school district in the aftermath of *Brown v. Board of Education*.[10] In explaining why education was not a fundamental right subject to strict scrutiny, Justice Powell noted that education is not mentioned in the U.S. Constitution, precluding the possibility of granting fundamental-right status on that basis alone.[11] Nor, he added, does an individual have a fundamental right to a governmental benefit simply because it is important, even indispensable.

Otherwise, access to health care, housing, and food all would be fundamental rights, and all governmental decisions in these areas would be subject to the most rigorous form of review.[12]

In explaining why wealth was not a suspect classification, Justice Powell observed that Texas did not deny its residents a public education on the basis of wealth. Quite the other way: The State guaranteed all residents a free public education regardless of wealth. At stake was not the denial of a government benefit on the basis of wealth but the provision of a relatively worse public benefit on the basis of wealth.[13]

The four dissenters saw things differently. Writing only for himself, Justice Brennan maintained that strict scrutiny should apply because the Texas public-financing system implicated a fundamental right expressly mentioned in the Constitution—free speech—one that has little value if States may deny their citizens the kind of education necessary to exercise that right in a meaningful way.[14] Justice White, joined by Justices Douglas and Brennan, thought that the Texas system flunked even rational basis review.[15] By giving poor districts no opportunity to improve their lot, by insisting that the property tax be the only method for raising additional funds beyond the State's contribution, Texas did not realistically permit a property-poor district like Edgewood to raise the same (or even close to the same) amount of funds as a district like Alamo Heights.[16]

Justice Marshall authored the lead dissent, which Justice Douglas joined. As one of the winning lawyers in *Brown*, Justice Marshall surely appreciated the significance of the case. How could the promises of *Brown* be fulfilled, he must have wondered, unless the courts not only eliminated de jure segregation by race but also curbed the effects of de facto segregation by wealth? These stakes, Justice Marshall wrote, made it imperative that education be deemed a fundamental right and property wealth a suspect classification.[17] Fundamental-right status, he added, should not turn solely on whether the Constitution mentions the right. The uncontestable connection between education and other constitutional guarantees sufficed to subject discrimination against a "powerless class" to strict scrutiny.[18]

The dissenters had fallen one vote short. For Texas and the rest of the states, that meant they could continue to fund their public school systems based on local property taxes and run them based on local control.

For the plaintiffs, that meant significant funding disparities would continue between rich and poor school districts. Or so it seemed.

The State Stories

While the U.S. Supreme Court permitted continuity, the States demanded change. *Rodriguez* tolerated the continuation of a funding system that allowed serious disparities in the quality of the education children received based solely on the wealth of the community in which their parents happened to live or could afford to live. But the States nonetheless eventually demanded change, in some instances because the political processes prompted it and in other instances because the state courts required it.

Before explaining how the States responded to, and helped to alleviate, this problem, it is worth remembering how they created it. As a matter of history, a condensed history to be sure, what had happened in Texas before 1968 had happened to one degree or another in most States. At the founding, there were no statewide systems of public schools, and if there were schools at all, they were privately run or haphazardly organized at the local level.[19] Sparked by the leadership of Horace Mann and the "Common Schools" movement he launched in Massachusetts,[20] States in the mid-nineteenth century began to authorize their cities and counties to organize schools that would offer a free public education. In the words of Mann: "Education then, beyond all other devices of human origin, is a great equalizer of the conditions of men—the balance wheel of the social machinery."[21] To that end, many States amended their constitutions, requiring the legislature (in the words of many a state constitution) to create a "thorough and efficient" system of public schools.[22]

Although the States authorized the creation and funding of these public schools, and the States retained responsibility for them, local funding and local control remained the hallmarks of the early public schools.[23] Societal change spurred by the Industrial Revolution placed the first stresses on the system.[24] As the country moved from a largely agrarian society to one divided into rural, suburban, and urban communities, wealth disparities increased, prompting States in the early twentieth century to begin awarding "flat grants" to all school districts that turned on the number of students or teachers in a district.[25] While these grants provided considerable support to protect poorer communities, they did nothing to decrease property-wealth disparities because they did not vary in amount depending on a school district's relative wealth.[26] In an effort to address this problem, States in the mid-twentieth century began adopting "foundation programs."[27] So long as a district imposed a state-established property-tax rate on the assessed value of all property in the district, the State guaranteed each district a comparable amount of state and local funding per child. By 1965, many States funded their schools through a foundation program, with only eleven States still providing "flat grants."[28] Texas, to use the *Rodriguez* example, proceeded through each of these stages of reform, and by 1968 it too had adopted a state-run foundation program along these lines.[29]

While each of these reforms sought to correct funding inequities, they had not cured them by 1968 in Texas or elsewhere. Under the foundation program, Texas authorized school districts to fund their operations in just two ways: through local property taxes and supplemental state funding.[30] Because state funding provided less than a majority of overall primary and secondary school funding, the local property tax remained a cornerstone of every school district's budget. In 1970–71, for example, only 48 percent of an average school district's budget funding came from the State, while local property taxes provided 41.1 percent and the federal government contributed 10.9 percent.[31] And because local property taxes were the only means by which a community could *increase* funding, a district's property-tax base went a long way to determining the size of its budget.[32]

Having made "education . . . perhaps the most important function of state and local governments"[33] in the nineteenth century, what did the States do to correct these disparities in the late twentieth century? Two footnotes (of all things) from the *Rodriguez* opinions foreshadowed some of what the States would do after 1973 and one explanation for why they would do it. In footnote 85 of Justice Powell's majority opinion, he observed that the plaintiffs, in urging the invalidation of the current funding system, "offer little guidance as to what type of school financing should replace it."[34] One possibility, they suggested, was the creation of a "statewide financing" system, which would eliminate school districts as fund-raising bodies and presumably would require all revenue to be raised by the State and to be allocated evenly by it. The other alternative was "district power equalizing," by which a State would "guarantee" that at a "particular rate of property taxation the district would receive a stated number of dollars," no matter how little or how much its local property taxes generated, thereby neutralizing property-wealth disparities among districts up to that rate of taxation.[35]

In footnote 100 of Justice Marshall's dissent, he wrote that nothing in the majority's opinion prevented the state courts from requiring their legislatures to redress these problems under their own state constitutions as opposed to the U.S. Constitution. "[N]othing in the Court's decision today," he explained, "should inhibit further review of state educational funding schemes under state constitutional provisions."[36]

In the years before *Rodriguez*, and in the two score and more years since, most state legislatures embraced wealth-equalization formulas for funding their public schools. Most States, whether before *Rodriguez* or after, adopted a foundation program, which represented a first step toward addressing property-wealth variations by guaranteeing a minimum amount of combined state and local funding regardless of how little money a school district contributed. By the mid-1970s, eighteen States had gone further, embracing variations on the "district power equalizing" approach advocated in *Rodriguez*.[37]

As of today, every State has enacted a school-financing equalization scheme of one form or another.[38] And as of today, just one State— Hawaii, perhaps due to its unique history and geography—has adopted the other remedial option mentioned in *Rodriguez*, the elimination of school districts in favor of a statewide funding system, though even Hawaii allows local communities to supplement the State's funding allocations.[39]

While these state legislative initiatives addressed many of the problems identified in the *Rodriguez* litigation, they did not address all of them. By guaranteeing a minimum level of spending for all school districts and by offering uniform incentives to increase spending, the States made progress, at least as measured by dollars spent, in improving the educational lot of those living in the poorest areas of the country.

But they did little to solve the equity problem—the lingering funding gap between the richest and poorest school districts—because none of these reforms meaningfully limited the amount of revenue wealthy school districts could raise.

This continued disparity generated a fleet of state court lawsuits from 1971 to 1989.[40] As in *Rodriguez*, the claimants targeted the gap in funding between rich and poor school districts and the difficulties that property-poor districts faced in closing the gap. But instead of relying on the U.S. Constitution, the claimants premised their lawsuits on equal protection clauses and other guarantees found in their States' constitutions.[41] While some of these claims succeeded, most did not.[42] And even when the plaintiffs won, they and the courts struggled to identify realistic remedies for eliminating or meaningfully closing the equity gap. Consider the difficulty of each remedial option: either require a statewide school-funding system that precludes local school districts from supplementing state aid or impose a floor *and* a ceiling on local spending.[43]

These obstacles led to a second wave of state court lawsuits. From 1989 to the present, claimants targeted another problem that the earlier reforms had not resolved: a method for determining a State's guaranteed level of funding and the amount of that funding. At the center of these claims was the critique that a statewide funding guarantee accomplished little if the guaranteed amount was too low. In contrast to the earlier lawsuits, these claims met with considerable success. Invoking the education clauses that appear in all state constitutions in one form or another—that the State guarantees residents access to a "thorough and efficient system of common schools,"[44] to use the Ohio example—the claimants argued that the States must provide a minimum level of funding to offer an adequate education for all students.[45] Since 1989, plaintiffs have won nearly two-thirds of these lawsuits.[46]

All told, roughly forty-four States by now have faced state-constitutional challenges to their systems of funding public schools.[47] Plaintiffs have won twenty-seven of these challenges at some point[48] and in the process compelled legislatures to adopt a host of additional reforms, many of which increased funding and closed equity gaps.[49] The experiences of two States—Texas and Ohio—illustrate the types of reforms prompted by these lawsuits.

Texas

The Supreme Court of Texas held that the State's school-financing system, the same system upheld in *Rodriguez*, violated the Texas Constitution in three cases in the 1980s and 1990s.[50] In *Edgewood I* and *Edgewood II*, the court struck down the State's school-financing system under the "efficient" clause of the Texas Constitution,[51] faulting the State for "concentrat[ing] . . . resources in property-rich school districts that are taxing low when property-poor districts that are taxing high cannot generate sufficient revenues to meet even minimum standards."[52] The court required the State to craft a system that yielded a "direct and close correlation between a district's tax effort and the educational resources available to it" and that afforded children in rich and poor districts a "substantially equal opportunity to have access to educational funds."[53]

In later cases dealing with a different component of the funding system, the same court found that the newly crafted system complied with the requirements of the efficiency clause.[54] And with ample reason: The legislature had "reduc[ed] the effects of the vast disparities among the more than 1,000 independent school districts [in the State of Texas],"[55] and it had reduced the ratio of taxable property wealth per student between the wealthiest and poorest districts from 700:1 in 1989 to 28:1 by 1995.[56] By 1995, the court could say that "[c]hildren who live in property-poor districts and children who live in property-rich districts now have substantially equal access to the funds necessary for a general diffusion of knowledge."[57] And by 2005, the court could say that "standardized test scores have steadily improved over time, even while tests and curriculum have been made more difficult."[58]

Today, while the Texas funding system doubtless has continuing defects (most school systems do), it would be difficult to premise a challenge to that system based on disparities between the funding experiences of the Edgewood and Alamo Heights school districts, the two districts featured in *Rodriguez*. In the 2003–04 school year, the Edgewood and Alamo Heights school districts both spent about $8,600 per child.[59] That year, in point of fact, the still poorer Edgewood school district spent slightly more per pupil than the still wealthier Alamo Heights.[60]

Ohio

The Ohio experience is of a piece. In 1997, and again in 2000, the Ohio Supreme Court held that the State's school-financing system violated the "thorough and efficient" clause of the Ohio Constitution.[61] Among other failings, the court faulted the system for its over-reliance on local property taxes and for failing to provide sufficient funding for the operational and building needs of the public schools.[62]

In response to these decisions, the Ohio General Assembly substantially increased public school funding,[63] injecting "billions of additional dollars" into the system.[64] It developed a new formula for calculating the amount of money needed to provide an adequate education, increasing the guaranteed amount of per-pupil spending from $4,177 in 2000[65] to $4,814 in 2002.[66] It established a "parity aid" program, dispersing additional funds to low-wealth districts to enable them "to spend funds on discretionary items in the same manner as wealthier districts."[67] It reduced reliance on local property taxes.[68] And it "dedicated a large amount of its budget to constructing and repairing school facilities,"[69] allocating nearly $2.7 billion to the effort during the 1998–2002 fiscal years,[70] and over $5.8 billion during the 2003–09 fiscal years,[71] and committing to allocate at least $1.7 billion during the 2010–11 fiscal years.[72] By contrast, during the 1992–96 fiscal years, the State had contributed just over $173 million to helping local school districts repair facilities and build new ones.[73] While the *DeRolph I* record in 1997 showed a public education system that was "starved for funds, lack[ed] teachers, buildings, and equipment, and [that] had inferior educational programs,"[74] the record was "very different" by 2001.[75] The plaintiffs in *DeRolph III* complained less about the absence of basic educational services and more about things like the failure of some schools to offer college-level courses in certain subjects and the lack of space for science labs in some elementary schools.[76]

The Ohio litigation, however, did not end with the kind of soft judicial landing that occurred in Texas. In 2003, the Ohio Supreme Court issued what looked like a compromise ruling that brought all wings of the Court together based on some agreed-upon requirements to remedy lingering inequities and other deficiencies in the system.[77] But the State moved for reconsideration, after which the Court ordered both parties to try to settle the case through a special commissioner.[78] The settlement efforts came up short, prompting the Court to vacate *DeRolph III* and to order (through *DeRolph IV*) "a complete systematic overhaul" of the funding system.[79] Matters did not end there either. On remand, the trial court tried to enforce the most recent order. The State wouldn't budge. It filed an original writ of prohibition back in the Ohio Supreme Court, seeking to bar the trial court from doing anything with the case. That worked . . . in a way. In what became the last decision, *DeRolph V*, the Ohio Supreme Court issued a Janus-faced decision. Looking backward, the Court said that enough was enough with the litigation: It granted the writ of prohibition, it prevented the trial court from exercising power over the case, and it required the lower court to dismiss the action. Looking forward, the Court said that the legislature's work was not done: "The duty now lies with the General Assembly to remedy an educational system that has been found by the majority in *DeRolph IV* to still be unconstitutional."[80] Since 2003, the legislature has continued to make improvements to the school-funding system. Not everyone is satisfied with the changes, but no one has challenged the system in state court since then.

Rodriguez and its aftermath prompt a few observations and at least one question. First, any serious effort at civil rights litigation should account for the possibility that the state guarantees may be the most promising source of rights, the state courts the most promising venue for vindicating them. The goal is to win at least once. The Rodriguez, DeRolph, and Kirby families likely did not care who ordered relief or why. They just wanted a better system of public schools for their children and other children. No matter the name of the court that granted relief or the source of the right, any such system would be just as helpful. One consequence of a system of dual sovereignty is that it permits dual claims of unconstitutionality against state and local laws. While federal judges generally are not known for offering legal advice, I have some company in pointing out that a citizen troubled by state action may look to the federal and state constitutions for recourse.[81]

Not just living constitutionalists, such as Justices Brennan, Marshall, and Ginsburg, have made the point, as the just cited authorities confirm. So too has Justice Scalia. In his last majority opinion for the Court, an 8–1 decision, Justice Scalia explained that "[t]he state courts may experiment all they want with their own constitutions, and often do in the wake of this Court's decisions." As support for that proposition, he cited an article about *Rodriguez* and the many state court experiments launched in its aftermath.[82] Judges of all stripes appreciate the point, and all civil liberties advocates as a result would do well to keep a diverse portfolio of state and federal constitutions at the ready.

Second, *Rodriguez* demonstrates that there is a gentler side to federalism. Whether one agrees with *Rodriguez* or thinks it a missed opportunity, the reality is that, "[w]hile the Supreme Court has tolerated continuity in this area, the democratic processes have demanded change."[83] Like it or leave it, *Rodriguez* unleashed school-funding innovation throughout the country that continues to this day. And whether one welcomes the state court lawsuits that followed *Rodriguez* or thinks them a blight on state separation of powers, the *Rodriguez* coda puts the lie to the notion that the federal courts have a monopoly on progressive decision-making.

Rodriguez and *Brown v. Board of Education* in truth are bookends of one story, not two. For the last several decades, a prominent narrative of American constitutional law has been that only the federal courts and only the federal constitution can be trusted to protect individual liberty. No era in American history offered more proof to support this narrative than Jim Crow. And no case offered more support for it than *Brown*. But as Justice Marshall appreciated in his anguished dissent in *Rodriquez*, the elimination of race-based barriers to a quality education would mean little if replaced by wealth-based barriers to a quality education. What could have ended there did not. In truth, only an appreciation of *Brown* and *Rodriguez* captures a fair understanding of American constitutional law, of federalism, and of the roles of the federal *and* state courts (and legislatures) in protecting liberty. If it's fair to say that the States set an unfortunate example when it comes to the making of American constitutional law before *Brown*, it's fair to ask whether they set a promising example for the making of American constitutional law after *Rodriguez*.

Third, the school-funding story highlights an essential distinction between the state and federal constitutions. When it comes to individual liberties, the U.S. Constitution is largely negative. It imposes *limits* on what governments may do. Hence "Congress shall make no law," begins the First Amendment. "No State shall," adds the Fourteenth Amendment. But as Emily Zackin points out in her fascinating book *Looking for Rights in All the Wrong Places*, the state constitutions contain negative *and* positive rights.[84]

The state constitutions not only identify limits on government; they also impose obligations on government. So it is that nearly all State constitutions impose an obligation to create a system of free public schools along these lines: "The General Assembly *shall make* such provisions, by taxation or otherwise, . . . [to] secure a thorough and efficient system of common schools throughout the State."[85] The fortunes of school-funding advocates markedly improved when they shifted their theories of the case from the negative equal-protection-like clauses of the state constitutions to the positive school-funding clauses of the state constitutions.[86] State constitutions contain other affirmative guarantees as well, such as environmental protection and labor and employment rights, to name a few.[87] They, too, represent an underappreciated component of American constitutional law.

Fourth, all of this prompts a provocative question: Is it possible that the *Rodriguez* plaintiffs ultimately won by losing? In one sense, the answer is surely no. Although states like Texas and Ohio eventually made considerable progress in improving the adequacy and equity of their school funding systems after *Rodriguez*, these advances did little for the plaintiffs who filed the case in 1968. It took time for these innovations to take root, and as a result, at least a half generation, if not a full generation, of students failed to reap the benefits of the reforms.

In another sense, however, the answer may be yes, or at least it's worth considering whether the answer is yes. In the context of institutional litigation, the question is not just what the claimants can do for themselves in the here and now; it's also what they can do for other children and for other States in the future. Viewed from this vantage point, the *Rodriguez* story suggests some of the ways in which the claimants potentially gained by losing.

The *Rodriguez* plaintiffs faced two daunting tasks in urging the U.S. Supreme Court to establish that education is a fundamental right or that wealth is a suspect class. They had to convince the Court to break new ground in embracing untested theories of constitutional law, and they had to convince the Court to define a right and create a remedy that it could apply uniformly to fifty sets of state laws, 248 million people in 1990 (over 320 million today), and nearly 16,000 school districts in 1979 (over 14,000 today).[88] In addressing the plaintiffs' arguments, the Court did not lose sight of the risks of imposing one solution to such a difficult policy problem on the entire country. Justice Powell noted that the creation of a school-funding system required "expertise and . . . familiarity with local problems,"[89] that "[t]he very complexity of the problems of financing and managing a statewide public school system suggests that 'there will be more than one constitutionally permissible method of solving them,'"[90] and that the Court under these circumstances needed to be wary of imposing "inflexible constitutional restraints that could circumscribe or handicap the continued research and experimentation so vital to finding even partial solutions" to difficult policy problems.[91]

Many of these constraints do not apply to the state courts or at least not to the same degree. Compare the situation of a state supreme court faced with a similar claim under state law. The justices would face one funding system, not fifty. As residents of the State, the justices would be familiar with the funding system at issue and its strengths and weaknesses. As elected officials (in most cases), many justices would have skill sets that might help them craft workable remedies or explain more persuasively why court involvement would be a mistake. If the justices chose to identify an enforceable right and remedy, they would do so for just one jurisdiction and a small fraction of the number of people. And any unforeseen consequences of their ruling could be modified far more easily.

In a case like *Rodriguez*, the U.S. Supreme Court faced institutional-capacity challenges that the state courts simply do not. If these challenges influenced the *Rodriguez* Court in rejecting all claims for relief, they surely would have influenced the *Rodriguez* Court in *granting* some relief. Think about it from the plaintiffs' perspective. A victory in the U.S. Supreme Court, true enough, would have had the virtue of being uniformly enforceable nationwide. But it would have come with the vice that the Court almost certainly would have applied a federalism discount to its articulation of the constitutional right and remedy. The more a litigant asks of a court in a complex setting like this one, the less it may be able to expect if the court has nationwide jurisdiction.

A victory for the *Rodriguez* plaintiffs not only might have been diluted by the U.S. Supreme Court's institutional constraints, but it also would have prevented accountability over educational funding from shifting to the States. If there is one thing that the last four and one-half decades have shown in the area, it is this: When *Rodriguez* indicated that solutions to the country's public-school funding problems would have to come from state courts (or state legislatures), the political pressures at the state level increased—to considerable effect. One can fairly wonder whether the reforms developed by fifty state legislatures and required by twenty-eight state supreme courts over the last forty-five years would have been as far-reaching if the *Rodriguez* Court had not shifted the spotlight on this issue to the States.

Had *Rodriguez* applied strict scrutiny to educational spending, taxing, and policy choices, as the plaintiffs requested, the decision almost certainly would have spawned a host of unintended consequences. The most acute risk is that strict scrutiny would have been too blunt an instrument to manage the calibrated policy choices that States and school districts must make in running a public school system. Imagine the next generation of constitutional challenges if education were a fundamental right entitled to skeptical review: Strict scrutiny over curriculum choices? Class size? Class schedules? Advanced Placement classes? Membership on a sports team? The possibilities are limitless. The questions unanswerable.

The Court, it's true, might have drawn lines between categories of educational policy that warrant strict scrutiny and those that do not, or it might have diluted strict scrutiny. But that would have generated a tangled web of line-drawing and difficult-to-apply hybrid levels of review. Strict scrutiny and education policy in the end often will be hard to reconcile, which may be why the lion's share of successful state constitutional challenges in this area have turned not on state-law equal-protection theories but on the state courts' interpretations of their constitutions' education clauses.

A shortage of money drives many of these education disputes. Yet even the most aggressive decisions of the U.S. Supreme Court have stopped short of compelling States to raise taxes.[92] State courts face similar challenges in encouraging, or even trying to compel, legislatures to raise money.[93] Witness the on-again, off-again denouement of the *DeRolph* litigation in Ohio. But it is far easier for a court to work with, or at worst play cat and mouse with, one state legislature than it is to do so with fifty of them. If the problem at the heart of many of these cases is a revenue-driven one, a state court is more likely to have success in prodding dollars out of one legislature than the U.S. Supreme Court would have with fifty legislatures.

Perhaps the biggest constraint on the U.S. Supreme Court, had it been willing to grant relief for the *Rodriguez* plaintiffs, would have been the utter indeterminacy of the policy issues underlying these disputes. Education policy does not naturally lend itself to one-and-only-one-way solutions. How would the Court have determined an adequate amount of money for a State to spend on a child's education? Even a State committed to funding an adequate education still must develop a method for determining what that costs. All kinds of approaches have been tried—from different methods for defining the costs of the various inputs for a good education to output-based approaches that identify high-performing school districts and average out the cost of the education they provide.[94] Once a State has decided what an adequate or even a good education costs, it also must decide how to pay for it and how to neutralize the advantages of wealth while preserving long-held customs of local control over a community's schools. If there is an incontrovertible answer to all of these questions, it remains hidden. And if the Supreme Court had taken on the task of answering these questions, it almost certainly would have been forced to demand less rather than more. Some imperfection, I fear, is something we have to live with in this area. But fifty imperfect solutions—each grounded in constitutional guarantees the States have chosen for themselves, crafted to meet the peculiar needs of each State, and implemented by accountable state officials—are almost certainly superior to one imperfect solution.

The equity problem is no less vexing. Unless a State takes the path of becoming one school district for funding purposes, as only Hawaii has done,[95] and unless that State prevents cities and counties from supplementing state aid, as Hawaii no longer does,[96] any policymaker or court that wants true equity must establish not just a floor of adequate school-district spending but a ceiling as well. True equity requires the floor and the ceiling to be the same, or at least close to the same after accounting for cost-of-living differences within a State. But a ceiling requires capping of some sort, and the States that tried it have gotten nowhere. Whether it was California, Washington, Colorado, or Vermont, all either lacked the political will to enforce the ceiling or slipped too many holes into the capping laws to establish meaningful equity.[97]

Nor is it self-evident that capping is a policy that the citizens of this country, or even of any one State, ought to be forced to accept. What court or legislature wants to tell a family that it is free to buy another expensive car or a second home, but if it spends an extra dime on its child's public education, it has violated state law? That is a heavy lift. Even if floor-and-ceiling equity is a policy worth trying, it surely is a policy worth trying State by State over time, not by the United States all at once.

A State worried about monetary inputs into a public school system also is apt to care about educational outputs.[98] Accountability tends to follow money, at least in a democratic system of government. The more a State spends on education, the more its citizens will care about ensuring that these resources produce results. But how do you measure output? Proficiency tests? Graduation rates? Attendance? Or some other measure? I know of no comprehensive answer, and if you ask three teachers you will get at least three answers. Efforts to measure the success of additional expenditures, like so many other facets of the education-policy puzzle, turn on difficult questions on which reasonable minds can disagree.

So far, everything I have said assumes that there is a positive correlation between the quality of an education and the level of education funding. But is that true? While there is undoubtedly some connection between the two, no one seriously maintains that money is the only indicator of a quality education.[99] One suspects that most students would learn more in the long run if they were the product of a supportive, two-parent, educated family than if they graduated from a high-spending school district. The literature at any rate is all over the map, and a national Supreme Court willing to announce a ruling based on one side of this complex debate would be brave indeed.[100]

Many reform proposals in this area push for centralization of educational school policy—most at the state level, some at the national level.[101] While centralization, as opposed to local control, may make considerable sense as a way of resolving equity issues, it is far from clear that it amounts to good educational policy. The key question is this: Will centralization of educational policy breed better schools or just similar schools?

The point of identifying these policy issues is not to take sides on them. It is to demonstrate that they defy easy solution and to suggest the difficulties the U.S. Supreme Court would have faced had it decided to define what the state legislatures could and could not do in this area. Nor do I mean to say that state court litigation is the best way, or even necessarily an appropriate way, to meet these challenges. All else being equal, the States, I suspect, are more likely to address these problems effectively through sustained and engaged legislative and executive branch initiatives that balance the benefits of centralization with the benefits of local control. Just as federal courts face institutional limitations in defining rights and creating remedies in an area like this one, so do state courts, and most of those limitations do not restrict conventional policymakers.

Neither is the value of a nationwide solution to a nationwide problem lost on me. Yet the question is whether the problem in a given case is uniform in nature and, if it is, whether it is susceptible to a uniform solution, particularly if a nationwide solution runs the risk of curbing effective local innovation. That is one telling way in which *Rodriguez* differed from *Brown*. There is nothing complicated in principle about a Supreme Court ruling that says the Equal Protection Clause prohibits a State from denying students entrance to a school based on their race. Not so with school funding. In the final analysis, the policy issues underlying *Rodriguez* seem more amenable to fifty imperfect solutions than one imperfect solution, particularly if (as I suggest) a one-solution approach would have faced so many remedy-limiting constraints.

As with any effort to play with history, it's unknowable whether the *Rodriguez* plaintiffs gained more in the long run by losing their case than they stood to gain by winning it. Enough has happened since the decision, however, to make the question worth asking. Whatever the answer, one thing remains clear: In *Rodriguez*, the U.S. Supreme Court said the States could stick with the status quo, yet they did not. And in some cases, the States may have done more than the U.S. Supreme Court ever could have done for the claimants' cause.

4

Search and Seizure: The Exclusionary Rule

THE PROTECTION AGAINST UNREASONABLE searches and seizures is not new. It is rooted in the English common law, whose courts long ago developed a "[r]esistance to the government's power to search and seize."[1] Pre-Revolution English courts did not hold back in describing the significance of the guarantee: "To enter a man's house by virtue of a nameless warrant, in order to procure evidence, is worse than the Spanish Inquisition; a law under which no Englishman would wish to live an hour; it [is] a most daring public attack made upon the liberty of the subject."[2] By 1776, the right was sufficiently embedded in the common law that seven of the first eleven state constitutions protected their citizens from illegal searches and seizures: Virginia (1776), Delaware (1776), Pennsylvania (1776), Maryland (1776), North Carolina (1776), Massachusetts (1780), and New Hampshire (1784).[3] All six of the other States would eventually ratify guarantees against improper searches and seizures.[4]

The National Constitution borrowed from the state constitutions, particularly the Pennsylvania and Massachusetts Constitutions. In words unaltered since its ratification in 1791, the Fourth Amendment says:

> The right of the people to be secure in their persons, houses, papers, and effects, against unreasonable searches and seizures, shall not be violated, and no Warrants shall issue, but upon probable cause, supported by Oath or affirmation, and particularly describing the place to be searched, and the persons or things to be seized.

Missing from the federal guarantee and all of the state guarantees is any language about the consequences of a violation. They do not tell courts what to do with items obtained from an illegal search or seizure that the government later attempts to introduce into evidence in a criminal trial against the victim of the police misconduct. The guarantees thus do not command exclusion, and, as is often true of silence, they do not bar suppression as a remedy either. The question was, and the question remains, how to construe that silence: Does a prohibition on unreasonable searches and seizures (or like guarantees) command the exclusion of evidence in a later criminal prosecution?

Early English, State, and Federal Courts Did Not Require the Exclusion of Evidence at a Subsequent Criminal Trial

As a matter of history, neither the English nor the early American common law required exclusion of illegally obtained evidence. "It matters not how you get it," an English court said; "if you steal it even it would be admissible in evidence."[5] The same was true in this country. The government could offer papers and books into evidence "no matter how they were obtained."[6] Even evidence "procured in modes and by means . . . not justified by the rules of fair dealing, by good morals, [] or by law" was admissible.[7]

In the words of Professor Akhil Amar, "history emphatically rejects any idea of exclusion. The English common law cases underlying the Fourth Amendment never recognized exclusion. England still does not recognize exclusion. Canada resisted exclusion as a remedy until the 1980s. None of the Founders ever linked the Fourth Amendment to exclusion. In the first century after Independence, no federal court ever recognized exclusion" and "[n]o state court . . . ever excluded evidence in this first century" under its own constitution.[8]

All of this did not leave the victims of an illegal search without a remedy. Large full-time police forces did not exist in pre-Revolution England, yet law enforcement proceeded nonetheless. An agent of the crown, often a private individual temporarily deputized to investigate a crime, could obtain a warrant to search a home.[9] But if a search was conducted in the absence of a warrant, the remedy was to file a trespass lawsuit for damages or a lawsuit to return the property to its owner, known as a replevin action.[10] A valid warrant provided a defense to the lawsuit. But the absence of a warrant removed the cloak of legitimacy from the search, making the individual who conducted the search a private trespasser. Through a trespass suit, the individual could obtain money damages and eventually return of the property.[11] So too in this country. An officer's illegal search was treated as a trespass, and the remedies were tort actions for damages and a replevin action to obtain the return of the property, not the exclusion of the evidence at a criminal trial.[12]

Even after the state and federal charters elevated the right to be free from unreasonable searches and seizures to a constitutional guarantee, the courts continued to separate the constitutional and evidentiary inquiries over the next century. The remedy for the victim of an illegal search remained the right to sue in trespass for money damages and in replevin for return of the property, not to exclude the evidence from a later criminal trial against the victim.[13]

The leading evidence treatises of the day confirmed the rule. "[T]hough papers and other subjects of evidence may have been illegally taken from the possession of the party against whom they are offered, or otherwise unlawfully obtained," Professor Greenleaf explained, that "is no valid objection to their admissibility if they are pertinent to the issue."[14] For roughly the first one hundred years after the founding, Professor Wigmore observed that "the admissibility of evidence is not affected by the illegality of the means through which the party has been enabled to obtain the evidence."[15]

Although the state and federal courts held the line between the illegality of a search and the admissibility of evidence discovered during it over this period, that was not for lack of effort by defendants to adopt a contrary rule. An early federal case arose from the illegal seizure of a ship suspected of transporting slaves, after which the vessel's owners argued that the trespass precluded a court from "us[ing] any evidence acquired in virtue of such abuse."[16] Sitting as a circuit judge, Justice Story rejected the claim:

> In the ordinary administration of municipal law the right of using evidence does not depend, nor, as far as I have any recollection, has ever been supposed to depend upon the lawfulness or unlawfulness

of the mode, by which it is obtained. If it is competent or pertinent evidence, and not in its own nature objectionable, as having been created by constraint, or oppression, such as confessions extorted by threats or fraud, the evidence is admissible on charges for the highest crimes, even though it may have been obtained by a trespass upon the person, or by any other forcible and illegal means.[17]

An often-cited state court decision came to the same conclusion: "If the search warrant were illegal, or if the officer serving the warrant exceeded his authority, the party on whose complaint the warrant issued, or the officer, would be responsible for the wrong done; but this is no good reason for excluding the papers seized as evidence, if they were pertinent to the issue."[18] Consistent with the common law rule that preceded them, these cases typified the prevailing view in the federal and state courts through the eighteenth century and most of the nineteenth.[19]

Gindrat v. People, 138 Ill. 103 (1891), illustrates the common law rule. Two thieves entered a Chicago jewelry store and asked to see some rings.[20] When the jeweler brought out a tray of his finest, the duo surreptitiously substituted a 25-cent imitation for a $125 diamond ring.[21] Later that night, an officer searched the thieves' residences without a warrant and found cheap imitation jewelry, and the two were convicted of larceny on the basis of that evidence.[22] The Supreme Court of Illinois upheld the convictions, rejecting the claim that the trial court should have excluded the inculpatory evidence under the Illinois Constitution's analogue to the Fourth Amendment.[23] "If the jewelry which [the detective] produced and identified at the trial was otherwise competent evidence," the Court asked, "should it be excluded from the jury merely because he gained possession of it by the commission of a trespass?"[24] A long line of cases said no, admitting the evidence "without stopping to inquire whether possession of it had been obtained lawfully or unlawfully."[25] The thieves, the court held, could sue the detective only for damages, a thought that may (or may not) have sweetened the bitter taste of their four-year stay in prison.[26] Otherwise, there was no need to be "over-sensitive in regard to the sources from which evidence comes."[27]

State v. Flynn came to a like-minded conclusion, upholding the admission of testimony by an officer who uncovered evidence of illegal liquor sales during a search of Flynn's home. After concluding that the search was valid, Samuel Dana Bell, Chief Justice of the New Hampshire Supreme Court, noted that "evidence . . . will not be rejected because it has been either illegally or improperly obtained."[28] A suspect with evidentiary artifacts in his home, the court colorfully explained, holds hostage "mute witnesses" to his crime, and the official who enters the home in pursuit of these artifacts seeks only to liberate them.[29]

A final example from the period merits mention not for the result it reached but for the result it advocated. In *Williams v. State*, 100 Ga. 511 (1897), a police officer and a detective, acting on a tip, forcibly entered Sarah Williams's home, searched the home and Williams herself, and seized several pieces of evidence—proceeds from alleged liquor sales—from her apron pocket.[30] The Supreme Court of Georgia upheld the conviction for violating Sunday liquor laws after acknowledging that the evidence against her had been obtained in an "unlawful, unreasonable, and outrageous" search.[31] Reasoning that the right to be free from unreasonable searches and seizures protected only against government abuse, the Court said: "If an official . . . exceeds or abuses the authority with which he is clothed, he is to be deemed as acting, not for the state, but for himself only; and therefore he alone, and not the state, should be held accountable for his acts."[32] The remedy lay against the individuals for trespass, not against the State (and public) for suppression of the evidence and relief from a conviction.

But the Georgia High Court did not leave it at that. The exclusion of the evidence, the court added, would elevate the state constitutional guarantee against unreasonable searches and seizures into "a real, and not an empty, blessing."[33] Yet the Court did not think it appropriate to fashion such a remedy itself. "Whether or not prohibiting the courts from receiving [illegally obtained] evidence . . . would have any practical and salutary effect in discouraging unreasonable searches and seizures, and thus tend towards the preservation of the citizen's constitutional right to immunity therefrom," the Court explained, "is a matter for legislative determination."[34] While the Georgia legislature took up the suggestion, it did so later rather than sooner, adopting the remedy sixty-nine years later through the Search and Seizure Act of 1966. Today, Georgia Code § 17-5-30 allows criminal defendants to file pretrial motions to suppress illegally obtained evidence.

The U.S. Supreme Court recently confirmed this eighteenth- and nineteenth-century history. "Because officers who violated the Fourth Amendment were traditionally considered trespassers," it explained, "individuals subject to unconstitutional searches or seizures historically enforced their rights through tort suits or self-help."[35] It then acknowledged what came next: "In the 20th century, however, the exclusionary rule—the rule that often requires trial courts to exclude unlawfully seized evidence in a criminal trial—became the principal remedy to deter Fourth Amendment violations. *See, e.g., Mapp v. Ohio*, 367 U.S. 643, 655 (1961)."[36]

The Development of the Exclusionary Rule

In 1886, in *Boyd v. United States*,[37] the U.S. Supreme Court became the first American court to adopt an exclusionary rule for illegal searches—kind of. The development of an exclusionary rule is surprisingly complicated, filled with starts and halts, sprinkled with varying justifications until a deterrence-based approach to the issue emerged as the justification for the rule and the limit of its reach. The story is a classically American one, turning on interaction between the federal and state courts, between the federal and state constitutions, even between the state legislatures and state courts. And the story continues to evolve, remaining more itinerant than stationary and just as susceptible to change as when the first permutations of the rule came into existence.

In *Boyd*, the federal government charged two individuals with illegally importing thirty-five cases of plate glass and asked a court to order that they be forfeited. At the request of the government, the district court ordered the Boyds to produce an invoice concerning the earlier importation of plate glass, relying on a federal tax law that required taxpayers to produce such invoices or accept the allegations in the government's complaint as true. The Boyds produced the invoices, and a jury ruled that the goods must be forfeited.

The Boyds convinced the Supreme Court to reverse the forfeiture ruling, which, "though technically a civil proceeding, is in substance and effect a criminal one."[38] The Court ruled that the trial court's order to produce the invoice, the federal law that required the production of the invoice, and the introduction of the invoice into evidence all violated the Federal Constitution. One theory of the Court, and the only one on which all members joined, was that the government violated the Fifth Amendment's self-incrimination clause. That the Fifth Amendment required the exclusion of evidence violating its prohibitions made some sense, particularly in the context of a federal law that put the individual to the push-me-pull-me "choice" of producing a document or conceding the government's allegations. The clause provides its own rule of exclusion, prohibiting the government from compelling an individual "in a criminal case to be a witness against himself."[39] What the Fifth Amendment prohibits, the Fifth Amendment excludes from a criminal trial, and so the Court held.[40]

The same could not be said of the Court's Fourth Amendment explanation for its ruling. Writing for the Court and over the disagreement of two colleagues, Justice Bradley reasoned that the required production of the invoice amounted to a search,[41] that the Fourth Amendment applied to this quasi-criminal forfeiture,[42] and that the search was unreasonable.[43] In deciding that the Fourth Amendment required suppression of the invoice, or at least together with the Fifth Amendment required its exclusion, the Court observed that the two amendments "throw great light on each other."[44] One of the prohibited activities—"unreasonable searches and seizures"—is "almost always made for the purpose of compelling a man to give evidence against himself, which in criminal cases is condemned in the [F]ifth [A]mendment."[45] The other prohibited activity—requiring an individual "in a criminal case to be a witness against himself"—"throws light on the question as to what is an 'unreasonable search and seizure' within the meaning of the [F]ourth [A]mendment."[46] The Court concluded "that the seizure of a man's private books and papers to be used in evidence against him" is "substantially" the same as "compelling him to be a witness against himself."[47]

Justice Miller, joined by Chief Justice Waite, concurred, accepting the one ground for decision (the Fifth Amendment) but not the other (the Fourth Amendment). They rejected the idea that a court order requiring the production of an invoice at trial amounted to a search of the residence or a seizure of the item.[48] All the order required was that the papers "are to be produced in court, and, when produced, the

United States attorney is permitted, under the direction of the court, to make examination in presence of the claimant, and may offer in evidence such entries in the books, invoices, or papers as relate to the issue."[49] How such a procedure rose to a search or seizure escaped the concurring Justices.

The majority's Fourth Amendment analysis, it's worth adding, did not come out of nowhere. The Boyds raised the Fourth Amendment in their brief and invoked a well-known English case, *Entick v. Carrington,* in doing so.[50]

In the years soon after *Boyd,* a few state courts adopted its reasoning in addressing similar subpoenas for private documents and papers. One account claims that "[n]o departure" from the common law rule "occurred in American state courts until 1901" in *State v. Slamon.*[51] So far as I can tell, *Slamon* is indeed the first state court to depart from the common law rule, and it did so in the following setting.[52] A state officer obtained a search warrant for stolen goods held by Frank Slamon.[53] During the search, the officer found a letter written to Slamon, the substance of which supported the State's theory that he had committed grand larceny.[54] Slamon challenged the admission of the letter on two state grounds—that it violated the Vermont Constitution's prohibition against a "search or seizure" unsupported by a particularized warrant and its prohibition against "compell[ing] a person 'to give evidence against himself.' "[55] In assessing the first argument, the Vermont Supreme Court explained that the seizure was illegal because the warrant did "not particularly describe" the letter.[56] It then acknowledged the common law rule—that "it is generally considered immaterial how a paper passes into the possession of the one offering it in evidence."[57] "But this rule," it continued, "is subject to another rule which is applicable—that, when a party invokes the constitutional right of freedom from unlawful search and seizure, the court will take notice of the question and determine it."[58] Relying on *Boyd,* the court "h[e]ld that the letter was inadmissible" under the guarantee against self-incrimination.[59] "The seizure of a person's private papers, to be used in evidence against him, is equivalent to compelling him to be a witness against himself."[60]

Three other cases from the era seem to follow a similar approach, all invoking *Boyd* and all relying on their state constitutions to suppress the evidence. Two of the cases come from Iowa, the constitution of which (at least at the time) contained a prohibition on unreasonable searches and seizures but not a self-incrimination clause. The first arose from a statutory rape charge. The incriminating evidence came from an involuntary examination of the defendant "of those parts of the person not usually exposed" to determine whether he suffered from the same kind of venereal disease with which the victim had been infected.[61] In suppressing the evidence, the court deemed the examination an illegal "search," and suppressed it on that ground (among others).[62] The search after all had the "purpose of securing evidence by an invasion of the private person of the defendant."[63]

A more typical exclusionary-rule dispute arose from an atypical method of competition. Adopting a business plan that would have made Ayn Rand blush, an ice dealer tried to destroy a rival's product by placing loads of salt on it.[64] A justice of the peace obtained a warrant to look for the remnants of the salt in the accused's residence, and all agreed that the later seizure of a salt barrel violated the Iowa Constitution's prohibition on unreasonable searches and seizures, apparently because the warrant was issued without proper authority and was sought "for the sole 'purpose of obtaining testimony' against the [defendant]."[65] As in *Slamon*, the Court acknowledged the common law rule—"that the mere fact that evidence has been developed by the wrongful act or trespass of an officer or any other person will not necessarily render it inadmissible."[66] Still, the Court continued, "we are confronted by the further fact that the evidence objected to was obtained by a palpable abuse of judicial process."[67] Unwilling to allow "a fraudulent or unlawful use of process [to] be sanctioned by the courts," it held that in such cases the "parties will be restored to the rights and positions they possessed before they were deprived thereof by the fraud, violence, or abuse of legal process."[68] "It is true," the Court acknowledged, that some cases provide "seeming support" for the illegality/suppression dichotomy, "but most of them, when examined, will be found to be instances in which the incriminating evidence has been discovered by persons acting without color of authority, or by officers as the incidental result of the service of a warrant of arrest or other writ of process legally issued. None can be found, we think, where the state has been permitted to obtain a search warrant in confessed violation of law, and thereby take papers or

SEARCH AND SEIZURE   51

property from the home of the man suspected of the crime, and use the matter thus procured in securing his conviction."[69]

The other state cases from this same period, by contrast, distinguished *Boyd* as a compelled-speech Fifth Amendment case.[70]

One account claims that these early cases "stand[] as a valuable monument to the confusion engendered by Justice Bradley in *Boyd*."[71] Confirming that theory is the fact that the Iowa Supreme Court overruled *Sheridan* and *Height* twenty years later.[72] Silas Weaver, who had written *Sheridan*, was still a sitting justice when the Iowa Supreme Court overruled his decision (in *Tonn*), and he was none too happy. He dissented from that outcome—and from a key theme of this book: that the States have a duty to construe their constitutions independently. "We have long since chosen to follow the [line of precedent] established and adhered to by the Supreme Court of the United States," said Weaver, "and I have yet to see or hear any sound argument for introducing confusion into our cases by reversing ourselves and repudiating the lead of the one court which above all others is in position to speak upon the subject with controlling effect."[73] *Boyd* and the *Sheridan* line of state court cases represent the first instances of American courts invoking a constitutional prohibition against unreasonable searches or seizures as a basis for suppressing evidence. But their relevance to the development of an exclusionary rule remains more historical than doctrinal. A testimonial-based rule of exclusion not only is redundant (if linked to Fifth Amendment violations), but it also would cover only the seizure of private papers that convey the thoughts and views of the individuals who wrote them and that the individual has an exclusive right to possess, as opposed to, say, contraband or stolen property.

Eighteen years after *Boyd*, the U.S. Supreme Court seemed to confirm that the decision did not alter the common law rule in traditional search-and-seizure cases. At the outset of its opinion in *Adams v. New York*, 192 U.S. 585 (1904), the Court disclaimed any intent "to detract from" *Boyd*.[74] If the Court meant what it said, it did not succeed. The appeal arose from a state court trial and concerned the action of state law enforcement, leaving available the ready option of denying relief on the ground that the yet-to-be-incorporated Fourth Amendment did not apply to the search or criminal trial. In rejecting Adams' appeal, the New York Court of Appeals relied only on the state constitution's counterpart guarantee and rejected the defendant's effort to use the Fourth Amendment to challenge a state search and prosecution.[75] Had the Court wished to leave *Boyd* as is, surely the cleanest way of doing so would have been to explain that the Fourth Amendment did not apply—and leave it at that.[76] It did not take this path.

What the Court authorized in *Adams* is difficult to square with what it banned in *Boyd*. The conviction arose from the defendant's possession of gambling paraphernalia, discovered when officers seized gambling slips and incriminating private papers (some of them not mentioned in the warrant) found in the course of a search.[77] In rejecting the constitutional claim, the New York Court of Appeals (applying state law) explained that the "underlying principle" is "not [to] take notice of the manner in which witnesses have possessed themselves of papers or other articles of personal property."[78] Any "remedy" for an illegal search and seizure, the Court added, was "an independent proceeding" against the individual who conducted the search.[79]

In affirming, the U.S. Supreme Court returned to the common law rule. There is no doubt, it said, that a search warrant may be used "to discover stolen property or the means of committing crimes,"[80] and the items discovered may be used in the criminal proceeding. None of this changes, the Court added, "if, in the search for the instruments of crime, other papers are taken."[81] Nonetheless, the defendant had contended, "if a search warrant is issued for stolen property and burglars' tools be discovered and seized, they are to be excluded from testimony by force of [the Fourth and Fifth] [A]mendments."[82] But the two amendments, the Court responded, "were never intended to have that effect."[83]

Adams instead appeared to reaffirm the common law rule, leaving little of the Fourth Amendment portion of *Boyd* intact, whether it was *Boyd*'s penumbral leveraging of the Fifth Amendment into a Fourth Amendment rule of exclusion or its view that illegally seized private papers or private property may not be admitted in a criminal trial if obtained in the course of an illegal search. "Evidence which is pertinent to the issue is admissible, although it may have been procured in an irregular, or even in an illegal, manner."[84] "[T]he weight of authority as well as reason," the Court explained, favored the common law rule, which permitted the introduction of "competent" evidence "tending to establish the guilt of the accused" and did not require the courts to "stop to inquire as to the means by which the evidence was obtained."[85]

During the decade after *Adams*, the state courts, whether construing the federal constitution or their own, tended to return to or to continue to stand by the common law rule. In the four instances when the state courts suppressed evidence, that was generally because the government effectively had compelled the individual to be a witness against himself, not because the government had conducted an illegal search. The four cases, from Georgia, Missouri, Indiana, and New York, are all *Boyd*-type cases focused on the forced production of evidence against the individual in a way that implicated self-incrimination concerns. In the Indiana case, for example, a state law required pharmacists to produce "prescriptions and applications for intoxicating liquor sold by him."[86] The Court prohibited this "compelled" production "for use as evidence before a court or grand jury."[87]

So matters lay until 1914. Just as it appeared that the state and federal courts would hold to the common law division between the illegality of a search and the admissibility of evidence seized through it, the U.S. Supreme Court breached the line in a stand-alone Fourth Amendment case. In *Weeks v. United States*, 232 U.S. 383 (1914), the Court adopted an exclusionary rule applicable to federal prosecutions using illegally seized evidence—for the "first" time, so later cases would say.[88]

As with *Boyd* and *Adams*, *Weeks* involved private papers—the defendant's "letters and correspondence"—that a federal official had taken from his house without a warrant and without his permission.[89] Relying on the seized papers, the federal government charged Weeks with using the mail to transport lottery tickets.[90] Unlike *Boyd* and unlike *Adams* (and unlike any other criminal cases until then of which I am aware), Weeks tried to get the papers back *before* his trial in the course of the same criminal proceeding, not a separate civil action in replevin.[91] The trial court twice denied the request, once before trial and once during it.[92]

This last reality casts doubt on whether *Weeks* should be treated as the seminal exclusionary rule case or whether this repeated character-ization has contributed to a legend that time has distanced from the true setting of the case and ought to be corrected. Several features of

Weeks suggest it stood by the common law rule, not the innovation of exclusion.

Exhibit A is the reality that Justice Day authored *Adams* and *Weeks* and that both opinions were unanimous.[93]

Exhibit B is the reality that *Weeks* never purports to abandon the common law rule.

Exhibit C is the reality that everything *Weeks* did squares with the common law rule. Keep in mind that, in separating the illegality and evidentiary issues, the common law did not deny a judicial remedy for illegal searches and seizures and did not deny judicial responsibility for assessing whether a search had infringed an individual's Fourth Amendment rights. To the contrary, it required courts to assess the legality of a search, and it provided a remedy. Two indeed: a right to ensure that property wrongfully taken could be rightfully returned and a right to obtain damages for the trespass. Some of what Weeks sought through the courts was just what the common law allowed: the return of his property. That explains why the Court framed the question as "the duty of the court" to require "the return of certain letters" that the federal marshal had seized "without authority of process."[94] The Court reaffirmed *Adams*'s characterization of and adherence to the common law rule—that courts, "when engaged in trying a criminal case, will not take notice of the manner in which witnesses have possessed themselves of papers or other articles of personal property, which are material and properly offered in evidence."[95] To do otherwise, the Court explained, would permit "collateral issue[s]" to enter into "the source of competent testimony," an approach condemned by such a number of "state cases that it would be impracticable to cite or refer to them in detail."[96] Notice, by the way, the Court's reference to, and belief in the relevance of, the state court decisions. The constitutional problem, the Court explained, was not the use of the papers in evidence but the failure of the trial court to return them when they were timely—in "due season"—requested.[97] As the Court put it: When Weeks made "a seasonable application for" the letters, "heard and passed upon by the court, there was involved in the order refusing the application a denial of the constitutional rights of the accused, and that the court should have restored these letters to the accused. In holding them and permitting their use upon the trial, we think prejudicial error was committed."[98]

If *Weeks* innovated anything, it was the Court's response to the happenstance of the timing and setting of the defendant's request. Unlike prior cases, Weeks did not file a separate *civil* action for replevin or for that matter a civil trespass action for damages. He sought repossession relief in the criminal case, indeed before the criminal case, which was not how the remedy traditionally had been deployed.[99] In this way, a court presiding over a criminal trial could use a long-accepted civil remedy for illegal searches—a trial-level request for return of the property and, if denied, a ground for appeal from the criminal conviction, which (and here is the key innovation) would require that the conviction be vacated as a remedy for the prejudicial failure to return the property when timely asked.[100] All of this may explain why *Wolf* and *Mapp* treat *Weeks* as the first exclusionary rule case. And perhaps the first use of this civil remedy in a criminal case deserves the appellation and acclaim.

Even then, the two cases overstate what happened. *Wolf: Weeks* "held that in a federal prosecution the Fourth Amendment barred the use of evidence secured through an illegal search and seizure. This ruling was made for the first time in 1914."[101] *Mapp: Weeks* established "that use of the seized evidence involved 'a denial of the constitutional rights of the accused.'"[102] Contrary to these characterizations, *Weeks* establishes an individual's constitutional right to the return of illegally seized property, not necessarily a constitutional right to exclude it at a subsequent criminal trial, and that is all the Court condemned in the case. By its terms and by its linkage to the right to possess one's own property, *Weeks* involves only a right with respect to private property, as opposed to contraband or stolen property, that the accused lawfully has a right to possess.[103]

In view of the facts of *Weeks* and its reasoning, one could imagine a world in which the *Weeks* rule helped Fremont Weeks but few others charged with crimes. Once the Court established that defendants could obtain the return of illegally seized property, trial courts, it is true, could compel the return of property (improperly taken). Yet that would not preclude the government from later issuing a subpoena to obtain the property, from testifying about what they saw, or, for that matter, from holding onto contraband (which need not be returned).[104]

Silverthorne Lumber v. United States, 251 U.S. 385 (1920), put these possibilities to the test. And it prompted the Court to reboot the rule. Federal law enforcement officers raided a company's offices and seized several documents, all in violation of the Fourth Amendment. Consistent with the common law return-of-property rule and with *Weeks*, the company asked the trial court to compel the government to return the documents. The trial court agreed. Before returning the papers, however, the officers copied them and used the copies to figure out what laws the company had violated. They then issued subpoenas to obtain the original papers. On its own terms, *Weeks* would seem to have allowed the officers to do just what they did, including using the evidence in a criminal trial. Yet the Court suppressed the evidence and for the first time adopted a deterrence rationale for doing so. In a 7–2 decision authored by Justice Holmes, the Court explained that, if the government could circumvent the exclusionary rule so easily, that would "reduce[] the Fourth Amendment to a form of words."[105] Instead, the Court reasoned (and truly innovated), the guarantee "covers [both] physical possession [and] any advantages that the Government can gain over the object of its pursuit by doing the forbidden act."[106] The government could no more make its case against the company with the illegally seized papers themselves than it could with "the knowledge[,] gained by [its] own wrong," of their existence and contents.[107]

Back to the state courts. They soon faced the question about how to construe *Weeks* and *Silverthorne* and whether to adopt a *Weeks*-like exclusionary rule or something broader under state law. Despite *Weeks*'s description as a repossession case and despite its insistence that it was not altering the common law illegality/admission-of-evidence distinction, the state courts generally treated *Weeks* as a suppression case in deciding *whether* to adopt a suppression rule under their own constitutions.[108]

Nonetheless, in the immediate decades after *Weeks*, most state courts refused to adopt an exclusionary rule under their own constitutions. Foremost among them was the New York Court of Appeals, the same court from which *Adams* arose. In *People v. Defore*, a police officer arrested John Defore in the hall of his boarding house on a charge that he had stolen an overcoat.[109] After making the arrest, the officer entered Defore's room and searched it.[110] The search produced a bag, and the bag produced a blackjack, a hand weapon.[111] Defore moved to suppress the blackjack, possession of which amounted to a crime under

New York law, and the trial court refused.[112] Writing for New York's
high court was Benjamin Cardozo, then a judge, soon to be a U.S.
Supreme Court Justice, but most remembered for his influence on the
development of American law through his work as a New York Court of
Appeals judge. The Court declined to suppress the evidence under state
or federal law. Acknowledging that *Weeks* "merit[s] our attentive scrutiny," Judge Cardozo explained that "[t]hose judgments do not bind
us, for they construe provisions of the federal Constitution, the Fourth
and Fifth Amendments, not applicable [just yet] to the States."[113] As
to the merits, he acknowledged that the search was illegal, "an act of
trespass" for which the officer could be sued for damages, removed,
or prosecuted.[114] Standing by the common law rule, he insisted that a
trespasser's evidence does not become incompetent merely because it
is the product of a trespass.[115] To hold evidence gathered by the state
through a trespass inadmissible but to permit the introduction of evidence obtained by a trespass from a private citizen "without a badge
of office" would "exalt form above substance."[116] Importation of the
federal exclusionary rule into the New York Constitution, Cardozo
warned, would allow "[t]he criminal to go free because the constable
has blundered," effectively permitting "[t]he pettiest peace officer [to]
have in his power[,] through overzeal or indiscretion[,] to confer immunity upon an offender for crimes the most flagitious."[117] "The Federal
rule," he observed, "is either too strict or too lax": It suppresses evidence
of the most outrageous crimes based on the negligence of an officer yet
does not apply to evidence discovered by all trespasses, whether private
or public.[118] Notice the battle of the titans over form and substance—
with Cardozo claiming that the exclusionary rule "exalt[s] form above
substance"[119] and Holmes claiming that the absence of an exclusionary
rule would "reduce the Fourth Amendment to a form of words."[120]

Between 1914 and 1949, thirty States rejected the *Weeks* modifica-
tion of the common law rule in construing their own law, and seventeen embraced *Weeks* (or at least the widening interpretation of *Weeks*).
One explanation why States during this period first embraced an exclusionary rule, by the way, had nothing to do with *Weeks*. It had to
do with another national development: Prohibition. After many state
laws placed limits on alcohol sales and consumption and eventually the
Eighteenth Amendment did the same, all manner of Americans became

lawbreakers, which sensitized state court judges to the consequences of illegal searches in ways that might not have affected them if the law enforcement investigations had led to other criminal charges.[121]

Up to now, the story of the exclusionary rule proceeded on independent federal and state tracks, with each charter and each forum affecting the other but remaining independent through it all. *Wolf v. Colorado*, 338 U.S. 25 (1949), raised the question whether that should change, whether the Fourth Amendment and the exclusionary rule should apply to state prosecutions. Yes to the one, no to the other, the Court answered. In an opinion by Justice Frankfurter, the Court explained that "[t]he security of one's privacy against arbitrary intrusion by the police—which is at the core of the Fourth Amendment—is basic to a free society. It is therefore implicit in 'the concept of ordered liberty' and as such enforceable against the States through the Due Process Clause."[122] In holding that the Fourth Amendment would apply to the States, Frankfurter embraced a modest theory of incorporation, one in which the Court acted more as a follower than as a leader. By 1949, every State had a prohibition on unreasonable searches and seizures. That makes *Wolf* a lot like a modern case, *McDonald*, which embraced a similar theory of incorporation for a right to bear arms after nearly every State in the country had recognized such an enforceable individual right.[123]

Wolf reached a different conclusion when it came to extending the exclusionary rule to the States. Reasoning that the rule "was not derived from the explicit requirements of the Fourth Amendment," that it was instead "a matter of judicial implication," that "most of the English-speaking world does not regard" the rule "as vital" to the protection of privacy, and that thirty States had rejected the rule (and just seventeen had adopted it), the Court declined to incorporate the rule into the liberty protections of the Due Process Clause of the Fourteenth Amendment.[124] This approach, the Court concluded, did not "depart from basic standards" and would permissibly allow the victims of improper searches to use the traditional "remedies of private action and such protection as the internal discipline of the police . . . may afford."[125]

Between 1949 and 1961, the number of state courts that embraced an exclusionary rule under state law grew from seventeen to roughly half of the States.[126] Two of the States were Alaska and Hawaii, which did not "pass anew on this question since attaining statehood" but had embraced an exclusionary rule as territories.[127] Five other States (Alabama, California, Delaware, North Carolina, and Rhode Island) took different paths. Alabama enacted a statute that excluded a narrow category of evidence; Rhode Island and North Carolina adopted a more typical exclusionary rule by statute; and California and Delaware construed their state constitutions to contain an exclusionary rule.[128] The state exclusionary rules thus did not emerge alike. Some came through the legislature, while others were embraced by the courts interpreting their state constitutions as a "judicially declared rule of evidence."[129] Some applied to all illegally seized evidence, while others applied only to egregiously seized evidence.[130]

Cue *Mapp v. Ohio*.[131] It nationalized the exclusionary rule in 1961, and transformed a multitude of common law approaches to the admission of evidence obtained from an illegal search into just one. A 1957 bombing of the Cleveland home of a young Don King, then a gambling promoter and eventually a ubiquitous boxing promoter, prompted a police investigation. The police eventually came to the home of Dollree Mapp. The search was not a picture of rectitude. Three Cleveland police officers knocked on her door and demanded to be let in, all in an effort to track down gambling kingpin (and Don King rival) Virgil Ogletree.[132] After calling her attorney, she refused, claiming they needed a warrant.[133] Three hours later, the officers returned, joined by four more officers, and, when Mapp did not answer the door, they "forcibly" opened it.[134] At that point, Mapp's attorney arrived, yet the officers refused to let him see her and, in a twist, the officers (now in possession of the property) refused to let *him* enter the residence. (The record does not reveal whether the officers insisted that the *attorney* get a warrant.) Dollree Mapp came down the stairs to meet the officers and asked to see the warrant.[135] One of the officers held up a piece of paper purporting to be a warrant, and Mapp grabbed it "and placed it in her bosom."[136] There was a skirmish, and the officers recovered the document, almost assuredly a mere piece of paper masquerading as a warrant,[137] the ultimate in a "form of words."[138] The officers found pornography, and the State charged Mapp with possessing obscene books and pictures.[139]

The police never produced a warrant at Mapp's trial, and the Ohio Supreme Court had "considerable doubt" whether the police ever obtained one.[140] In rejecting Fourth Amendment and state constitutional challenges to Mapp's conviction, the court declined to abandon the common law rule, observing in the process that the officers did not take the evidence "from [the] defendant's person by the use of brutal or offensive physical force" against Mapp.[141] Justice Herbert, joined by Justice Bell, dissented. They urged their colleagues to adopt an exclusionary rule under the Ohio Constitution in view of the "trend away" from the Ohio position, to avoid "steriliz[ing]" the state guarantee, and to ensure that "there will no longer be a judicial stamp of approval on the use of unlawful means to justify an end result."[142]

Much of Mapp's defense to her criminal conviction in the state courts turned on the free speech guarantees of the First Amendment. In her view, the State had no right to criminalize the private possession of pornography. The state courts rejected that claim too, though based on a supermajority requirement in the Ohio Constitution. At the time, it took five justices to invalidate a state law, and just four members of the seven-member court voted to invalidate the law on free speech grounds.

The U.S. Supreme Court granted review of the Ohio Supreme Court's free-speech and search-and-seizure decisions. Notably, however, Mapp did not ask the Court to overrule *Wolf* and indeed counsel at oral argument "disavowed that he was seeking to have the *Wolf* case overturned."[143] The search-and-seizure portion of Mapp's argument sought relief under *Rochin v. California* because the officers' conduct "shock[ed] the conscience" and thus required the suppression of the evidence.[144] The national and state civil liberties unions, as *amici curiae*, devoted one paragraph of their argument and twelve seconds of their portion of the divided oral argument to overruling *Wolf*.[145] One other feature of *Mapp* deserves mention: The advocate for the State was Gertrude Bauer Mahon, an assistant prosecutor for Cuyahoga Country, and to my knowledge one of the first women to argue a landmark case in the U.S. Supreme Court.

In overruling *Wolf*, the *Mapp* majority decision, written by Justice Clark, explained that the prior decision was "bottomed on factual considerations," at least five in all, that no longer applied.[146] One, nearly two-thirds of the States had opposed the use of an exclusionary rule under their own constitutions when the Court decided *Wolf*, but by the time of *Mapp* more than half of the States had adopted their own exclusionary rules in one way or another.[147]

Two, the experience of one of those States, California, turned on the realization by its supreme court that "'other remedies have completely failed to secure compliance with the constitutional provisions.'"[148] Other States, too, came to the conclusion that "other remedies have been worthless and futile."[149]

Three, "time has set its face against what *Wolf* called the 'weighty testimony' of *People v. Defore*," in which Judge Cardozo famously said the criminal should not "go free because the constable has blundered" and less famously said that the federal exclusionary rule is under- and over-inclusive—"either too strict or too lax."[150] The force of Judge Cardozo's reasoning, the Court explained, "has been largely vitiated by later decisions of" the Court.[151] Better, the Court reasoned, that the criminal should be set free than that the Court should fail to heed the wisdom that the government "teaches the whole people by its example. . . . If the government becomes a lawbreaker, it breeds contempt for law."[152] It took Justice Holmes (*Silverthorne*) and Justice Brandeis (*Olmstead*) to trump Judge Cardozo.[153]

Four, in explaining why "all evidence obtained by searches and seizures in violation of the Constitution" may not be admitted in state court,[154] the Court added that *Wolf* was internally inconsistent: "[T]he admission of the new constitutional right by *Wolf* could not consistently tolerate denial of its most important constitutional privilege, namely, the exclusion of the evidence which the accused had been forced to give by reason of the unlawful seizure. To hold otherwise is to grant the right but in reality to withhold its privilege and enjoyment. . . . [T]he purpose of the exclusionary rule 'is to deter—to compel respect for the constitutional guaranty in the only effectively available way—by removing the incentive to disregard it.'"[155]

Five, a national exclusionary rule made "very good sense" as a way to ensure uniform treatment between the state and federal courts rather than a "double standard" and as a way to prevent federal officers in nonexclusionary States from "step[ping] across the street to the State's attorney with their unconstitutionally seized evidence."[156] After nearly fifty years of experience with an exclusionary rule in the federal courts and after the "impressive" experiences of the States, where "[t]he movement towards the rule of exclusion has been halting but seemingly inexorable," *Mapp* reasoned that it could not fairly be said that the criminal justice system will be "disrupted" by a national exclusionary rule.[157]

The Development of a Good Faith Exception to the Exclusionary Rule—And Exceptions to the Exception

One might have expected the exclusionary rule story to end with the linking of the federal and state requirements and the creation of a national rule. But much of what led to the linking of the limitations on federal and state law enforcement—a deterrence-premised effort to promote a vigorous set of privacy protections—led to their delinking over the next fifty years when the U.S. Supreme Court lowered the federal protection in reviewing a *federal* prosecution.

Twenty-three years after *Mapp*, the Supreme Court in *United States v. Leon* considered whether to apply the exclusionary rule to evidence obtained by police officers "acting in reasonable reliance on a search warrant issued by a detached and neutral magistrate but ultimately found to be unsupported by probable cause."[158] Officers in Burbank, California investigated a potential drug-trafficking operation by conducting surveillance of three houses. Relying on observations during the investigation, the officers submitted an application for a warrant to search the houses and the suspects' cars for a long list of items. A state court issued the warrant. The search produced drugs and other evidence of drug trafficking, and the defendants were indicted for *federal* drug crimes. The defendants moved to suppress the evidence. The district court found that the affidavit attached to the warrant application did not establish probable cause because it failed to establish the reliability and credibility of the informant and some of the information relied upon in the affidavit appeared to be stale. Applying the *Mapp* exclusionary rule, the district court suppressed the relevant evidence, and the court of appeals affirmed.

Writing for six Justices, Justice White started by saying that the case required the Court to resolve "the tension between the sometimes competing goals of, on the one hand, deterring official misconduct and removing inducements to unreasonable invasions of privacy and, on the other, establishing procedures under which criminal defendants are 'acquitted or convicted on the basis of all the evidence which exposes the truth.'"[159] Some of the initial explanations for an exclusionary rule, he explained, no longer justified it. The rule is not "a necessary corollary of the Fourth Amendment," as the guarantee "contains no provision expressly precluding the use of evidence obtained in violation of its commands."[160] Nor has the theory that the rule "is required by the conjunction of the Fourth and Fifth Amendments . . . withstood critical analysis or the test of time."[161]

That left the principal justification for the rule—deterrence—a judicially created remedy designed to safeguard Fourth Amendment rights through its deterrent effect rather than through a personal constitutional right of the party.[162] Yet deterring police misconduct, he explained, is not furthered "when an officer acting with objective good faith has obtained a search warrant from a judge or magistrate and acted within its scope" because "[i]n most such cases, there is no police illegality and thus nothing to deter."[163] "Penalizing the officer for the magistrate's error, rather than his own, cannot logically contribute to the deterrence of Fourth Amendment violations."[164] In the last analysis, the balance of competing interests—deterring police misconduct versus considering all truthful evidence of what happened—favored the admission of the evidence, particularly since "it cannot be expected . . . to deter objectively reasonable law enforcement activity."[165] "[T]he marginal or nonexistent benefits produced by suppressing evidence obtained in objectively reasonable reliance on a subsequently invalidated search warrant cannot justify the substantial costs of exclusion."[166]

As a rule of *federal* constitutional law, *Mapp* gave the state courts no realistic opportunities to *dilute* the requirements of their state constitutions in state criminal prosecutions—unless, in a fit of malpractice, a defendant's attorney failed to raise a federal defense to a state prosecution. If a Fourth Amendment violation occurred, the state courts had to apply the (nearly) exception-less federal exclusionary rule given the Supremacy Clause's federal ratchet. The same was not true in the other direction. By lowering rather than raising the Fourth Amendment floor, *Leon* made relevant once more the meaning of the state constitutions' search-and-seizure guarantees, in particular whether they contained *Leon* exceptions of their own.

Leon launched three decades (and more) of state constitutional disputes over the point. One distinguished commentator says that the Supreme Court's "rationale" in *Leon* "has been overwhelmingly rejected by state courts asked to adopt an exception to the exclusionary rule for good faith reliance on a defective warrant under state constitutions and statutes."[167] That conclusion may overstate the point, but at least one-third of the States for one reason or another have opted to exclude evidence under state law even when the police officers acted in good faith reliance on the validity of a warrant issued by a neutral magistrate or judge.

Idaho v. Guzman[168] exemplifies this line of cases. An informant notified police that Guzman was storing more than one-hundred pounds of marijuana at his home, and the officer verified a thread of the story through surveillance showing that a man meeting Guzman's description lived at the address.[169] The officer's affidavit neglected to provide a basis for the informant's credibility, and the trial court ruled that the warrant-issuing judge did so without probable cause.[170] Under *Mapp*, that meant the evidence normally would be excluded—unless the *Leon* good faith exception applied.

In its 1992 decision in *Guzman*, the Idaho Supreme Court opted not to apply *Leon* under the Idaho Constitution's conventionally worded search-and-seizure provision.[171] The Court began by confirming that probable cause did not support the warrant in view of a conclusory affidavit.[172] Invoking a decision by Justice Herman Taylor, apparently a mountaineer, the Court observed: "he who sits in judgment at the halfway station as to the existence of 'probable cause' must be the magistrate, and not the affiant who must bear the burden of facts up the mountain to that station, rather than his conclusions. He cannot leave at the foot of the mountain his load of facts, and with lightened and easy steps recite at the halfway station his conclusions as to facts which he does not choose to carry so far."[173]

The Court invoked the same state court case to show that, soon after *Weeks* and *Silverthorne* and well before *Mapp*, "Idaho has had an independent exclusionary rule based upon the state constitution."[174] Had it wished to demonstrate the "independen[ce]" of the Idaho rule, the

Court would have done well to explain its rejection of a good faith exception to the exclusionary rule based on reasons specific to Idaho's Constitution rule or even to its sister States. The focus of its justification instead turned on a critique of *Leon* and an embrace of Justice Brennan's *Leon* dissent, a pattern that repeated itself in many of the other state cases, whether embracing *Leon* or rejecting it. A state court does not amplify the independent nature of a state constitutional guarantee merely by taking sides on a debate about the meaning of a *federal* guarantee—least of all a guarantee that originated in state constitutions.

Be that as it may, Justice Bistline, in writing for his Court, rejected *Leon*'s claim that deterrence was the key function of the exclusionary rule. The rule, he insisted, also protects the integrity of the warrant process by encouraging magistrates to take care when issuing warrants and by preventing a second constitutional violation through the admission of illegally obtained evidence.[175] The Court also disagreed with *Leon*'s cost-benefit analysis. In the first place, Justice Bistline found it strange to subject rules of evidence to such an analysis, as the analysis might call into question the validity of a host of other evidentiary rules: marital privileges, religious privileges, attorney-client privileges, for example.[176] In the second place, he thought *Leon* misjudged the costs and benefits of the rule. On the cost side, *Leon* overstated the frequency of suppression and failed to appreciate the source of the costs: "As the state is only deprived of what it was not entitled to possess in the first place, to say the fourth amendment exacts a cost to the state is like saying that a thief pays for committing a theft when he is required to return what he stole."[177] On the benefits side, *Leon* focused too heavily on police officer deterrence, overlooking the institutional benefits of exclusion, such as a spur to better police training and greater care by magistrates before issuing warrants.[178] While Justice Bistline spent most of his time embracing some U.S. Supreme Court decisions and opinions over others, he did note that "we are in agreement with" similar decisions by the New York, North Carolina, Vermont, and Connecticut Supreme Courts.[179] When Justice Bistline said "we," he overstated matters, as his opinion did not curry favor with several members of the five-justice supreme court. One justice had resigned by the time of his opinion, one justice dissented in full, one justice concurred in the result that *Leon* did not apply, and one justice concurred in some, but not much of, Justice Bistline's analysis.[180] Still, three justices rejected *Leon*, even if they managed to do so on federal-centric grounds in some instances and on unexplained grounds in others.

Just as a state court's authority to construe its own constitution allows the court to extend greater protections than the Federal Constitution, so too it allows a court to extend less protection under its own constitution, even none at all beyond the common law remedies. In a case from Utah, Justice Thomas Lee in a concurring opinion looked at the *Guzman* issues through the other end of the lens.[181] Unlike Idaho, Utah had no exclusionary rule before *Mapp*. It instead had adhered to the common law rule that the method by which police obtained evidence did not determine its admissibility.[182] After *Mapp*, Utah honored the federal rule, and the Supreme Court of Utah eventually decided— first by a plurality and later by a majority—that Utah's Constitution contained a similar protection.[183]

The point of Justice Lee's opinion was to question this seemingly reflexive adoption of a state exclusionary rule, one that did not analyze the terms or history of the Utah Constitution but simply cited other state supreme court decisions that followed *Mapp* in construing their own constitutions.[184] The Utah Constitution's search-and-seizure guarantee, Justice Lee reasoned, says nothing about excluding illegally obtained evidence.[185] In reviewing the relevant history from the 1895 convention, Justice Lee found that the general understanding at the time would have supported the common law rule—that illegally obtained evidence was admissible.[186] "[N]o appellate court *in any state*," he reasoned, "had excluded unlawfully obtained evidence under its constitution."[187] Having found "little ground for attributing to the framers of section 14 the view that evidence collected in violation of its terms would be deemed inadmissible in court," he concluded that the Utah guarantee did not contain an exclusionary remedy and that any debate over a good faith exception to it necessarily was beside the point.[188]

Where does that leave us? To date, forty-six States have adopted exclusionary rules under their state constitutions.[189] Two of the four remaining States, California and Florida, had adopted independent exclusionary rules through case law, but their state constitutions were amended to abrogate them.[190] The remaining two States, Maine and

Maryland, apparently still have no judicially announced exclusionary rules for evidence gathered in violation of their state constitutions.[191]

Of the forty-six States, twenty States (by most counts) have rejected *Leon* through court decisions construing their own constitutions.[192] Consistent with the Idaho Supreme Court's decision, some courts rejected the notion that the exclusionary rule serves only a deterrence function. "Its function," one court explained, "is not merely to deter police misconduct. The rule also serves as the indispensable mechanism for vindicating the constitutional right to be free from unreasonable searches."[193] Others balanced the competing interests differently. "We will not impose such a significant limitation upon our state exclusionary rule," the Vermont Supreme Court explained, "on the basis of the Court's cost-benefit analysis in *Leon*."[194] And many decisions concluded that *Leon* could not be reconciled with their state constitution's textual requirement that probable cause exist for a search.[195]

Five States have codified an exclusionary rule: Georgia, Massachusetts, North Carolina, South Carolina, and Texas. The Texas statute predates *Mapp v. Ohio*.[196] It also contains a good faith exception.[197] The North Carolina statute is similar. It codifies an exclusionary rule *and* a good faith exception.[198] Efforts were made in the other three States to add a good faith exception to their statutory rules of exclusion, but the courts rejected each effort.[199]

What insights does this federal-state story offer? First, constitutional law can be, and should be, interactive between the States and the national government. The development of the exclusionary rule followed (and continues to follow) a Hegelian path, as the state and federal courts respond to strengths and weaknesses of their own decisions *and* to those of other sovereigns. Since *Boyd*, change in each respect has been a constant. Little has remained static.

From this perspective, *Mapp* is a story with some potentially promising features, one in which the U.S. Supreme Court paid attention to the institutional strengths of the two sets of courts and learned from the experiences of each. The point is not that *Mapp* was correctly decided. The creation of a national exclusionary rule is difficult to justify on originalist grounds—on the ground that the public meaning of the

Fourth Amendment, whether in 1791 or 1868, created a rule of evidentiary exclusion, as opposed to a rule about permissible searches and seizures. The eighteenth- and nineteenth-century common law rule cuts the other way. At most, the history suggests that suspects had a right of replevin—a right to the return of all noncontraband property, as in *Weeks*. But a right to the return of seized property is not a right of exclusion, as the officers may testify about what they saw or subpoena what they returned. It thus is difficult to see how an originalist "exclusionary" rule would affect the outcome of many cases.

But *Mapp* does not purport to justify itself on originalist grounds. By its terms, it's a combination of evolving constitutionalism and common law pragmatism. The Court has done so before. It may do so again. The question is whether *Mapp* can be justified on its own terms and by the verdict of history.

On the plus side, if the U.S. Supreme Court wishes to innovate new constitutional rights in this way, there is something to be said for the *Mapp* process and the *Mapp* timeline as the way to do it. The first experimentation in this area came from the national laboratory, not the States, and came from a laboratory that was relatively small given the few areas of *federal* criminal law in the late nineteenth and early twentieth centuries.[200] The U.S. Supreme Court led by example in *Boyd, Weeks,* and *Silverthorne* in improvising in fits and starts a rule of exclusion, one applicable only to federal law enforcement. That allowed the States to decide for themselves how to weigh the costs and benefits of evidentiary exclusion. Guided in part by the federal example, some States followed the U.S. Supreme Court's path. Others, led by the New York Court of Appeals and Judge Cardozo's decision in *Defore*, did not.

In 1949, sixty-three years after *Boyd* and thirty-five years after *Weeks*, the U.S. Supreme Court considered whether to create a national exclusionary rule in *Wolf.* Discretion carried the day. At the same time that the Court made the Fourth Amendment applicable to the States, it declined to require the States to adopt an exclusionary rule. The Court gave the States more time to decide for themselves whether to create the rule under their own constitutions. What looked like delay to some (in view of the trend in favor of an exclusionary rule in the States), counted as informed patience to others (in view of the same trend). From either perspective, the Court by waiting and seeing gave the States more time to decide for themselves how to balance these costs and benefits and more time for the Court to assess their work product.

By 1961, the extra period of experimentation had proved useful to the U.S. Supreme Court. The twelve years provided more empirical information about the pros and cons of exclusion. Recall that one of the explanations for *Mapp* was the California experience, in which the California courts had found that other methods of deterrence—private rights of action against police officers and internal disciplinary proceedings—had done little to decrease illegal encounters between the police and citizens.[201] The additional time also diminished the extent of the assumption of power that invariably occurs when the Court nationalizes a right, as it allowed more States to develop exclusionary rules on their own under their own constitutions. Perceived respect for coequal sovereigns goes up when the High Court's decision affects fewer States.

Perhaps most importantly, the delay had the potential to increase the legitimacy of the eventual decision. Even accepted on its own terms, evolving constitutionalism amounts to a warrantless seizure of power—deserving its own rule of exclusion—if it turns only on changing norms subjectively held by a majority of Justices, as opposed to changing norms objectively provable beyond 1 First Street. Time allowed the *Mapp* majority to rely on the experiences of roughly half of the States to show that a new norm of exclusion was not one of their own making. Whether that number, that percentage, is the right one is open to debate. What matters is that the Court paid attention to the best evidence of shifting norms, the experiences in the States.

On the debit side, two features of the *Mapp* decision cannot be ignored. If the Court wishes to nationalize a right in an area of core state sovereignty—how and when to ferret out crime and under what restrictions—it's not a good idea to do so in a case in which the litigant failed to argue the point. It was a self-inflicted wound to resolve the point in that case in that way. The Court could have asked for additional briefing and argument on whether to overrule *Wolf*, as the Court has done before. Or it could have waited for another vehicle to resolve the point. It's fair to wonder whether some of the backlash to *Mapp* arose from this feature of the case.

Another problem, perhaps growing out of the first, is that the *Mapp* opinion is a methodological disaster. In its eagerness to overrule *Wolf*, the Court offered a grab bag of explanations, the diversity of which said more about the interpreters' desire to nationalize the exclusionary rule than the constitutional guarantee they were interpreting. In her engaging and thoughtful (pre–law school!) master's thesis at Oxford University, titled "The Development and Erosion of the American Exclusionary Rule: A Study in Judicial Method," Justice Kagan, a supporter of a national exclusionary rule, offered a similar critique.[202] The decision "flouted judicial convention," was "spectacularly confused," and "left the primary basis of the exclusionary rule in doubt." By "blend[ing] constitutional and nonconstitutional rationales" and by "combin[ing] arguments based on individual rights with those found on societal interests," the Court left unclear whether the rule turned on the Fourth Amendment, the Fifth Amendment, deterrence, or judicial integrity.[203] "Transformations in the law," she explained, "should not be accomplished by fiat. It is important that the Court not only rule but persuade—not only command but convince."[204] Agreed.

But these two flaws should not obscure a broader point. If we put the restless trigger finger of *Mapp* and its mishmash reasoning to the side, if we assume indeed that Justice Kagan (or an equally incisive Justice) had put her rigor to the task of justifying the decision, we can remember a feature of *Mapp* that should not be forgotten. And this is a compliment. By living and learning from the experiences of the States and national government over seventy-five years, *Mapp* potentially exemplified a promising route for nationalizing a right, at least on pragmatic, evolving-norm grounds.

Second, if the build-up to *Mapp* offers a useful model for innovating new rights on pragmatic and living-constitutionalism grounds, the aftermath of *Mapp* offers a cautionary account of the risks and complications of nationalizing a new constitutional right. With the announcement of *Mapp*, the advocates of a strong national rule seemed to carry the day with a winner-take-all decision. All law enforcement, whether state or federal, faced the strong medicine of suppression whenever a defendant could show that an officer or magistrate had botched the probable-cause prerequisite for a search or seizure. In the years immediately after *Mapp*, the Court eventually settled on a unified rationale for a national exclusionary rule—deterrence[205]—one seemingly appropriate for a uniform rule.

While that uniform rationale may have justified extending the remedy of exclusion to all fifty-one jurisdictions, it became its own across-the-board limiting principle. The post-*Mapp* story illustrates the promise *and* peril of raising the national floor of constitutional rights and of linking the meaning of federal and state constitutions—for criminal defendants in *both* jurisdictions. If deterrence of police misconduct was the point, why should the rule apply when the police acted in good faith? It should not, *Leon* held, dealing a blow to the practical impact of *Mapp* and *Weeks/Silverthorne,* and lowering the barrier to admission in state *and* federal cases. Once the Court diluted the exclusionary rule, it diluted the rule in all of its applications.

By 1984, when the Court decided *Leon*, it had abandoned the idea of giving Bill of Rights guarantees one interpretation when applied to the federal government and another interpretation when applied to the States via Fourteenth Amendment incorporation.[206] The extension of the exclusionary rule to the States thus may have come with a price. Few, if any, cases sought to add a good faith exception to the exclusionary rule in the forty-seven years between *Weeks* and *Mapp*. And it is fair to ask whether that would have happened, and if so whether it would have succeeded. Only after *Mapp*, only after its perceived intrusion on the States' long-held authority to investigate and prosecute crime without federal interference, did the Court think to apply a federalism discount to the exclusionary rule, one that limited its reach in state *and* federal prosecutions.

Any fair assessment of *Mapp* must ask whether it led to less protection, not more, for criminal suspects overall. As to *federal* criminal defendants, it's difficult to believe that, without *Mapp*, there would have been a *Leon*, and if that's right, that makes *Mapp* a net loss when it comes to protection from the federal government. That does not make *Mapp* wrong. A pragmatic, evolving-norm approach to constitutional interpretation is not a ratchet. By its nature, it can lead to increases and decreases in constitutional protections as times change. But it does raise the question whether criminal defendants lost by winning *Mapp*, at least with respect to suspects of crime investigated and prosecuted by the federal government.

What of state investigations? Wasn't *Mapp* a net victory for suspects of crime living in the States that had not adopted an exclusionary rule already? Not necessarily. If *Leon* responded in part to *Mapp*, so too may have *Stone v. Powell*, 482 U.S. 465 (1976). When *Stone* opted to prevent state criminal defendants from raising Fourth Amendment claims in habeas corpus petitions—and Fourth Amendment claims alone—is it possible that a backlash to *Mapp* was part of the explanation? And is it possible that, if the Court had waited longer for more States to create exclusionary rules of their own (say three-fourths of them), *Stone v. Powell* would have come out differently?

Stone, it's worth telling, has almost uniformly prevented *federal* prisoners from raising Fourth Amendment claims in collateral challenges to their convictions and sentences—what lawyers call a § 2255 petition.[207] Before *Stone*, the Court held in 1969 that federal inmates could bring a § 2255 petition for relief based on a Fourth Amendment violation.[208] Yet after *Stone*, the U.S. Supreme Court suggested that federal inmates were no more entitled to collateral relief under the Fourth Amendment than state inmates were.[209] Nearly every circuit has embraced the suggestion and rejected Fourth Amendment claims under § 2255 by federal prisoners.[210] The only holdout is the Eighth Circuit, and the inmate lost that case on the merits anyway.[211] Here, then, we have a second example of a lowering of state *and* federal protections after the adoption of a national standard.

More examples follow. In *United States v. Calandra*, the Court held that the exclusionary rule does not apply to *any* grand jury proceedings, whether federal or state.[212] No case to my knowledge had limited the exclusionary rule in this way before *Mapp*, and after 1974 (the year of *Calandra*) the limitation applied to all state and federal Fourth Amendment claims. Justice Kagan (in truth, graduate student Kagan) reached a similar conclusion.

> Prior to *Calandra*, Supreme Courts had regarded the exclusionary rule as an absolute prohibition: According to the rule, no part of the criminal justice system could use the fruits of an unconstitutional search against that search's victim. As early as 1920, in *Silverthorne Lumber Co. v. United States*, Justice Holmes had declared by way of dictum that the exclusionary rule stipulated not merely [that]

evidence so acquired [by means of an unconstitutional search] shall not be used before the court but that it shall not be used at all.[213]

Not so after *Calandra.*

United States v. Janis is of a piece. The Court held that the exclusionary rule did not apply to any civil proceedings, whether federal or state.[214] Here too we have an erosion of the exclusionary rule as it existed before *Mapp*. "Several lower federal courts . . . had held that unconstitutionally gained evidence was inadmissible in certain kinds of civil proceedings.[215] Not anymore after *Janis.*

Just as important as all of this, perhaps more important than all of this, may be a broader pushback question. If *Leon, Stone, Calandra*, and *Janis* cut back on the scope of *Mapp* for the federal and state courts, what of the possibility that the benchmark for Fourth Amendment violations in both courts decreased after *Mapp*? It's one thing to review a state court's interpretation of "unreasonable searches and seizures" in the abstract. It's quite another to review such a decision when a verdict of unconstitutionality leads to a verdict of state court evidentiary exclusion and often to a state court acquittal, dropped charges, or a new trial. If one thinks judges are influenced by the consequences of their decisions, a school of legal philosophy (legal realism) with a wide following, the linkage of exclusion to the definition of an unreasonable search presents a risk to the underlying Fourth Amendment standard, especially in cases involving technical violations of the standard or egregious crimes.

Consider some data points. In 1968, seven years after *Mapp*, the Court decided another case from Ohio: *Terry v. Ohio.*[216] In a decision written by Chief Justice Warren, the Court permitted stops and frisks whenever an officer had reasonable suspicion (as opposed to probable cause) that criminal activity was afoot. Only Justice Douglas dissented. If *Leon* and other cases reduced the number of Fourth Amendment violations that required evidentiary exclusion, *Terry* diminished the Fourth Amendment standard itself. Would *Terry* have come out differently before *Mapp*? Who can know? But the possibility deserves consideration.

Nor is *Terry* the only case that raises this question. From 1968 to 2016, the U.S. Supreme Court decided 231 cases about the meaning of the Fourth Amendment, and 152 have come out in favor of the government.[217] Courts and commentators alike have noted the toll that Fourth Amendment rights have taken since *Mapp*.[218]

What of the possibility that *Mapp* watered down broader liberty safeguards even beyond the Fourth Amendment? Four years after *Mapp*, the Court decided *Linkletter v. Walker*.[219] It addressed "a most troublesome question in the administration of justice": Does *Mapp* apply "retrospectively" to cases decided before it?[220] In an opinion by Justice Clark, the author of *Mapp*, the Court addressed whether the exclusionary rule applied to an illegal search in the State of Louisiana that had occurred one year *after* the illegal search of Dollree Mapp's apartment in the State of Ohio. At the time, the norm was to apply constitutional rulings retroactively to all affected individuals—a custom captured by the words emblazoned above the front pedestal of the U.S. Supreme Court ("Equal Justice Under Law") and captured by the Fourteenth Amendment ("nor deny to any person within its jurisdiction the equal protection of the laws"). "It is true," the Court acknowledged, that "we have applied new constitutional rules to cases finalized before the promulgation of the rule."[221] Even so, the Court decided that "the exigencies of the situation require" a prospective ruling[222] due to concerns about "the wholesale release of the guilty victims."[223]

In dissent, Justice Black, joined by Justice Douglas, criticized "the arbitrary and discriminatory nature of the judicial contrivance utilized here to break the promise of *Mapp* by keeping all people in jail who are unfortunate enough to have had their unconstitutional convictions affirmed before June 19, 1961."[224] The Court, Justice Black wrote, should not "perpetrate a grossly invidious and unfair discrimination against Linkletter simply because he happened to be prosecuted in a State that was evidently well up with its criminal court docket."[225]

The potential administrative complications prompted by the innovations of *Mapp*—the release of thousands of state convicted prisoners—thus prompted reassessments of the justifications for *Mapp* and changes to the custom of applying new constitutional rules retroactively at all. As for the retooling of *Mapp*, the Fifth Amendment explanation for an exclusionary rule, initially identified in *Boyd* and mentioned in *Weeks*, disappeared. The Court had previously applied new constitutional rules with respect to coerced confessions, a violation of the Fifth Amendment, retroactively, making it awkward to link *Mapp* with the Fifth Amendment any longer. The idea that the Fourth Amendment by its nature required exclusion disappeared as well. For that too would make Fourth Amendment violations just like other constitutional violations and other new constitutional rules. That left the deterrence rationale of *Mapp*, which supplied the key explanation for *Linkletter*. "[T]he purpose" of *Mapp*, *Linkletter* explained, was "to deter the lawless action of the police" and thus "to effectively enforce the Fourth Amendment," but "[t]hat purpose will not at this late date be served by the wholesale release of the guilty victims."[226]

As for the Court's new nonretroactivity rule, the Court acknowledged that it went against the grain. But it noted that prior decisions had applied new constitutional rules to all affected individuals "without discussion." And today's circumstances, mainly the number of affected individuals, justified a new rule, one that by its terms was not limited to Fourth Amendment violations and one that it would apply on a case-by-case basis going forward. Before long, the Court applied *Linkletter*'s nonretroactivity principle not just to final convictions but to convictions not yet final at the time of the new constitutional rule and in the midst of direct or collateral review.[227] And before long, the Court found other "exigencies" that limited the retroactive application of other constitutional rulings: adverse comments on a defendant's decision not to testify[228] and right to counsel violations,[229] to name a few. Notably, after the Court issued its *Miranda* decision, it did not apply the ruling retroactively.[230] The *broad* nonretroactivity regime, announced in *Linkletter* and prompted by *Mapp*, ended in 1987 with its decision in *Griffith v. Kentucky*.[231]

As all of this suggests, one potential price of a nationwide exclusionary rule—or a nationwide rule on any constitutional right—may be a nationwide ebbing of the underlying standard, if not cutbacks on other constitutional rights and principles. Is this price worth the cost? Would the availability of individual money-damages actions—largely available on the same terms as *Leon*, namely when the officers did not act in bad faith[232]—have provided just as much deterrence without this potential impact on the meaning of the standard? Or perhaps the timing of *Mapp* might have made a difference? Had the Court waited for roughly three-quarters (or even two-thirds) of the States to adopt exclusionary rules, would that delay or patience, pick your perspective, have limited these consequences?

Third, while the Court was in a position to assess these risks when it decided *Mapp*, difficult though that assessment may have been, it's doubtful the Court considered the possibility of another development after 1961. As noted in Chapter 2, federal-state lockstepping—the tendency of many state courts to link the meaning of their constitutional guarantees to the meaning given to counterpart federal guarantees by the U.S. Supreme Court—increased markedly after the Warren Court. That development, a development that remains with us today, raises the stakes of the nationalization question. The risk embedded in a backlash to a U.S. Supreme Court decision is not just that the federal standard could decline in the aftermath of the decision but that the state courts would follow suit in construing their own constitutions (and even reduce the guarantee below what it was before *Mapp*). Linkage between the federal standard and state exclusion ran the risk of a two-step blow. It created the risk that the U.S. Supreme Court would dilute the unreasonable-search-and-seizure test *and* the risk that the state courts would march in unison in construing their own constitutional guarantee.

The problem of lockstepping grows out of a perception, fair or not, that the federal standard is too generous as is. That might explain why some States refuse to construe their state constitutional criminal procedure guarantees more broadly than the federal guarantees. And it is assuredly why two States amended their constitutions in 1982 (Florida) and 1990 (California) to *prohibit* their state courts from extending search-and-seizure guarantees beyond the floor established by the U.S. Supreme Court.[233] How unfortunate. The first and third most populated States, blessed with two impressive state courts, have been sidelined when it comes to addressing the meaning of "unreasonable searches and seizures" independently.

Perhaps the reader wonders whether this backlash had less to do with *Mapp* and more to do with national political developments—which led to the Nixon administration and which led to four new appointments to the Supreme Court: Chief Justice Burger, Justice Blackmun, Justice Powell, and then-Justice Rehnquist. I had the same question. That may be true, and that may suggest that I have overstated the pushback to the Warren Court. But it's also possible that the Warren Court, the *Mapp* decision included, fed some of these national political developments. I would not be the first person to raise this possibility.[234]

None of this, to be clear, proves *Mapp* did more harm than good when it comes to safeguarding citizens from unreasonable searches and seizures. It proves only that the question is complicated. And it proves, I would submit, that the question is worth asking more frequently when parties or interest groups seek one-perfect-solution victories at the U.S. Supreme Court. Maximizing liberty does not invariably follow from a national rule. Keep in mind that, by 1961, roughly half of the States had an exclusionary rule of their own, prompting the complicated (but deeply important) question: How many of the States would have embraced one on their own within the next decade? Within the next two decades? By today?

Justice Souter, then serving on the New Hampshire Supreme Court, spoke for many state court judges when he gave this ambivalent take on the proper relationship between state and federal court interpretations of identical language: "If we place too much reliance on federal precedent we will render the State rules a mere row of shadows; if we place too little, we will render State practice incoherent."[235]

Fourth, *Mapp, Leon*, and these other cases show something else. It's dangerous for judges (but easy for judges) to think of the courts as the only protectors of liberty or to assume too quickly that they are the best protectors of liberty. Consider the questions raised by the exclusionary rule debate in all directions, whether for it or against it. What does the evidentiary tool of suppression, as opposed to a money-damages action, have to do with an unreasonable search or seizure? What assurance can we have that officers invested in the success of an investigation will respect limits on their own authority? How does exclusion serve deterrence when the constable has merely made a mistake? And why should the people (and their safety) suffer for that individual officer's mistake? Are there not other ways— money-damages lawsuits established by federal law against state law enforcement[236] and federal law enforcement[237]—to create a national floor that will deter the most shoddy or egregious police work? Does a good faith exception swallow the exclusionary rule?

Some of these questions may be susceptible to empirical answers. Not likely others. Once a court moves beyond the question whether a guarantee against unreasonable searches and seizures implies an exclusionary rule, the other questions all involve cost-benefit analyses of one sort or another. Who should be doing this complicated weighing: the courts or legislatures? If courts, are we better off with one national weighing for all jurisdictions or many such weighings of the benefits and burdens? With one imperfect solution? With many imperfect solutions?

Recall that five States have dealt with the issue through legislation. One can fairly ask if that is the best venue for balancing these ineffable considerations and for reweighing them over time. No justice from *Weeks* to *Mapp* to *Leon* has concluded that federal or state legislatures lack the capacity to make these choices. Just as Congress could enact an exception-free federal exclusionary rule applicable to federal officers and prosecutions without contradicting *Leon*, so the state legislatures could do the same. Nothing in *Leon* or the Court's earlier decisions in this area precludes such a legislative approach to the issue, and indeed a premise of the *Weeks/Mapp* critics is that this is what should have happened in the first place.

Before dismissing the option of a *legislative* remedy too quickly, it's worth remembering another Fourth Amendment case. In 1971, the National Supreme Court ruled that victims of an illegal search by a federal officer had an *implied* right of action to sue the offending officers for money damages.[238] The implied *Bivens* remedy stood in contrast to the explicit remedy provided for victims of constitutional violations caused by state officials. Since the mid-nineteenth century, a federal statute, 42 U.S.C. § 1983, has authorized money-damages actions against state officials who violate Fourth Amendment and other federal constitutional rights. While it is easy to conclude that citizens should be able to bring money-damages actions against state *and* federal officials for federal constitutional violations, it is not obvious that *Bivens* took us down the right road for correcting that imbalance. After the decision, the Court extended the implied remedy to some Fifth Amendment violations in 1979[239] and to some Eighth Amendment violations in 1980.[240] But it has rejected *every* other *Bivens* claim since 1980, "more than a dozen" by one court's count.[241] That means that, in telling contrast to the ready availability of § 1983 actions against state

officials for nearly *all* constitutional violations, the victim of a constitutional violation by a federal official has a remedy for just a few rights.
Suppose *Bivens* had rejected the request for an implied right of action
in 1971. Is it not possible, is it not likely, that Congress over the last
nearly half century would have corrected this disparity and enacted a §
1983–like remedy for *all* violations of the U.S. Constitution by federal
officials? Judicial solutions sometimes sap the zeal to develop legislative
solutions. And legislative solutions to policy problems sometimes beat
judicial solutions.[242]

Fifth, I have neglected so far another way of thinking about *Mapp*, one
best expressed by Justice Brandeis's dissent in *Olmstead v. United States*,
277 U.S. 438 (1928). At stake was a constitutional question prompted
by the (then novel) law enforcement technique of wiretapping. If governmental officials recorded a private telephone conversation, did that
amount to a "search and seizure"? In a 5–4 decision authored by Chief
Justice Taft, the Court held that the Fourth Amendment did not prohibit the use of surreptitiously taped conversations in a criminal prosecution. Justice Brandeis wrote a stirring dissent, one later vindicated
in *Katz v. United States*[243] and perhaps the writing for which he is best
known. (That's saying something.)

Both the majority and dissent, and Justice Holmes's dissent as well,
grapple with the meaning of many of the cases mentioned so far—*Boyd*,
Weeks, and *Silverthorne* included. As is so often the case, the question
was how far up the ladder of generalization each opinion would climb
in construing the terms "search and seizure" and, still more so, in
construing the Court's own opinions on that score. Justice Brandeis
went several rungs higher than Taft or Holmes did, and presumably
than Cardozo (who did not join this Court until 1932) would have.
You know you are in a difficult place when Cardozo, Holmes, Taft, and
Brandeis all see the same essential problem differently.

Here is how Justice Brandeis saw it. He described *Boyd* as "a case that
will be remembered as long as civil liberty lives in the United States."[244]
He "refused to place an unduly literal construction" on the language
of the Fourth Amendment,[245] as the Framers of the Constitution "undertook to secure conditions favorable to the pursuit of happiness,"
including "the right to be let alone—the most comprehensive of rights

and the right most valued by civilized men."[246] And independent of the constitutional question, he reasoned that the illegality of wiretapping by anyone prohibited the governmental agents from using the taped conversations, lest the government as prosecutor itself become a lawbreaker: "Decency, security, and liberty alike demand that government officials shall be subjected to the same rules of conduct that are commands to the citizen. In a government of laws, existence of the government will be imperiled if it fails to observe the law scrupulously. Our government is the potent, the omnipresent teacher. For good or for ill, it teaches the whole people by its example."[247]

One precedent invoked by Brandeis in the course of his dissent—*Buck v. Bell*, covered in the next chapter—deserves a brief explanation. It comes in the course of a paragraph, one central to his thesis, about the Constitution's capacity to meet change. The paragraph starts with an invocation of *McCulloch*'s dictum that "[w]e must never forget that it is a constitution we are expounding."[248] It then points out two areas in which the Court has exercised restraint in reviewing legislative efforts to address new problems. One was that "the Court has repeatedly sustained the exercise of power by Congress . . . over objects of which the Fathers could not have dreamed."[249] The other was that the "general limitations on the powers of Government, like those embodied in the due process clauses of the Fifth and Fourteenth Amendments, do not forbid the United States or the States from meeting modern conditions by regulations which 'a century ago, or even half a century ago, probably would have been rejected as arbitrary and oppressive.'"[250] After that windup, he delivers the central analytical pitch in his opinion, one that shifts from the Court restraining itself to halt legislative responses to the Court imposing new limitations on government to account for change: "Clauses guaranteeing to the individual protection against specific abuses of power, must have a similar capacity of adaptation to a changing world."[251]

Even if one explanation for this approach, *Buck v. Bell*, has not fared well, Justice Brandeis's explanation for a changeable Constitution to meet a changing world has fared well, at least as measured by its acceptance by the Court in many areas of the law and in many non-originalist decisions. Anyone who thinks that approach is wrong would do well to read his *Olmstead* dissent and answer it, as it seems to have generated considerable influence on the judicial mindset, for better or for worse, more so even than footnote 4 of *Carolene Products*.

Why, then, isn't the Brandeis perspective one that justified *Mapp* in 1961 and justifies it today? Perhaps it does for non-originalist judges. But anyone who wishes to embrace the deep sensitivity to individual freedom and skepticism of governmental power conveyed in that opinion, indeed especially someone so inclined, should want to know that the *Mapp* approach would work and has worked. That is not clear.

Sixth, in view of two central themes of this book—the importance of state court judges and the benefits of state and federal interaction—two state court opinions deserve special mention. Both come down on the no-exclusionary-rule side of the debate. But that's not why they deserve note. The first is Judge Cardozo's opinion in *Defore*. What matters is not that the opinion was thoughtful, well-reasoned, and well-expressed. As indeed it was. It's that the U.S. Supreme Court felt the need to address the reasoning of the decision—one premised on New York law—so carefully in *Mapp*. That's a sign of a healthy system of judicial federalism when federal judges engage the reasoning of their sister courts. And it stands in marked contrast to *Buck v. Bell*, where Justice Holmes (as you will soon see) never mentioned, much less tried to distinguish or engage with, the many state court decisions going the other way. It's possible that Justice Clark devoted so much time to *Defore* because Cardozo later joined the U.S. Supreme Court. Maybe so. But I doubt any serious court, state or federal, could address this issue without taking on the reasoning of such a forceful opinion. Since *Mapp*, regrettably, federal decisions that refer to the reasoning of state court decisions (not under review) are too few and too far between.

The other decision, briefly mentioned above, is Justice Lee's concurrence in *Walker*. Long after *Mapp*, the Utah Supreme Court faced a dispute about whether its constitution offered broader protections than the Fourth Amendment. Writing separately, Justice Lee pointed out that the inquiry made no difference because a thorough review of the relevant history showed that the Utah Constitution did not include an exclusionary rule in the first instance. Taking the independent status of state constitutions seriously does not inherently favor the government or the individual. What it does do is respect the sovereign status of each State and provide a two-way dialogue about the meaning of generally worded guarantees. Just as federal interpretations of the National Constitution may inform interpretations of a state constitution, so too state interpretations of their charters may inform interpretations of the federal charter.

Seventh, and last of all, it's worth considering the setting of the American exclusionary rule story: criminal procedure. Skeptics of state constitutionalism tend to be particularly skeptical of its utility in this area. They worry about the manner of picking nearly 90 percent of state court judges: elections. And they worry that elected judges can't be trusted to resolve such disputes in an even-handed fashion. But the state court backlash to *Leon* confirms that these complaints are overstated or at least should be more nuanced. In point of fact, the state track record on this issue is about the same pre-*Mapp* and post-*Mapp*. Nearly half of the States adopted an exclusionary rule on their own before *Mapp*, and close to half of the States have rejected *Leon* since.

Nor is this the only instance in which the States have filled a perceived criminal-procedure gap left by a U.S. Supreme Court decision. There are others, many others indeed. In *California v. Hodari D.*, 499 U.S. 621 (1991), the Court adopted a narrow rather than a broad definition of "seizure." Since then, at least fifteen States (Alaska, Connecticut, Delaware, Hawaii, Kentucky, Louisiana, Massachusetts, Minnesota, Montana, New Hampshire, New York, Oregon, Pennsylvania, Tennessee, and Washington) have adhered to a broader definition of seizure under their state constitutions.[252] So too in *Illinois v. Gates*, 462 U.S. 213 (1983). In overruling the *Aguilar-Spinelli* test for determining the sufficiency of an affidavit to support a search warrant, the Court left a gap that many States opted to fill. At least eight States have kept the old test as a matter of state law: Alaska, Hawaii, Massachusetts, New Mexico, New York, Oregon, Tennessee, and Washington.[253] Or consider state-court rulings over whether disclosure of business records, telephone calls, emails, and other information to third parties eliminates a reasonable expectation of privacy with respect to that information. The States have used a wide variety of approaches in this evolving area of the law, many of them more liberty protecting than federal law.[254] There are countless other areas, too many to mention here, that confirm that one should pause before accepting the too facile assumption that life-tenured federal judges will invariably provide greater protection for suspects of crime than elected state court judges.[255]

5

Compelled Sterilization

AMERICAN GOVERNMENTS MAY ASK a lot of the people. They may force them to part with their money through taxation. They may tell them how fast they can drive and when they can drink and smoke. And they may require them to submit to all manner of other regulations. One of our governments even may force individuals to take up arms for the country and, if need be, to die for it. All of this is said to be for the public good, and usually it is—to the utilitarian end of maximizing a group objective through individual sacrifice and occasionally to the paternalistic end of dictating what is good for us, whether we think so or not.

But some public ends are less essential than others, and some individual sacrifices are greater than others. That is why, for some deprivations of liberty and property, the traditional gauge of public utility—democratic support—will not alone sustain the policies in a system of limited and divided government power.

One remarkable illustration of this forever-young debate grows out of an effort at the beginning of the twentieth century to curb increases in the mentally ill, the immoral, and the criminally inclined. Catch a conservative on a bad day, and you may be asked who has caused more harm: the well-intentioned or the out-and-out scoundrels? Anyone who thinks this is an easy debate to win never met the eugenics movement.

Greek for "good genes," eugenics is "the science of improving a population by controlled breeding to increase the occurrence of desirable heritable characteristics."[1] An interest in controlled breeding sprang from good intentions: scientific and medical developments coupled with efforts to improve society in the face of social ills exacerbated by industrialization in the late 1800s and early 1900s.[2] What would become the eugenics movement started as a breakthrough in biology and proceeded through a series of stages, a mixture of scientific advancement, medical innovation, and social reform. If ever there were a time for divided government, a time for placing constitutional limits on federal *and* state governmental action, this was it.

The Roots of the Eugenics Movement

In the 1860s, an Austrian monk named Gregor Mendel undertook a series of genetic experiments by crossbreeding different types of garden peas.[3] Observing that some "parental" traits manifested themselves in the young plants and others did not, Mendel discovered what scientists now call dominant and recessive genes.[4] With this insight, Mendel created ratios to describe and predict when physical traits of the peas would reappear.[5] Through his research, Mendel described "the basic laws of inheritance" and "creat[ed] the foundation for the science of genetics."[6]

If it fell to a monk to lay the cornerstone of genetic understanding, it fell to a half cousin of Charles Darwin, Francis Galton,[7] to apply nature's principles of heredity to human propagation. From the 1860s until his death in 1911, Galton took genetic inheritance beyond what all could see—the passing of physical traits from one generation to another—to the broader idea that mental and psychological traits as well, even character traits, could be inherited. Much of his work focused on "good" genes, as the titles of several of his articles and books suggest: *Hereditary Talent, Hereditary Genius: An Inquiry into Its Laws and Consequences*, and *English Men of Science: Their Nature and Nurture*.[8] Responding to criticism that his work understated the role of environment, his last piece studied the lineage of members of the Royal Society, a collection of eminent British scientists.[9] Unrelenting in his claim that all men *are not* created equal, Galton refused to dance around the stark premise of his work:

> I have no patience with the hypothesis occasionally expressed, and often implied, . . . that babies are born pretty much alike, and that

the sole agencies in creating differences between boy and boy, and man and man are steady application and moral effort. It is in the most unqualified manner that I object to pretensions of natural equality. The experiences of the nursery, the school, the university, and of professional careers, are a chain of proofs to the contrary.[10]

This undisguised idea was not difficult to grasp. Or to promote.

If there is such a thing as good genes, eugenicists thought, there must be such a thing as bad ones. Industrialization in late Victorian England and the beginning of the second American century, together with the population growth and urbanization facilitated by it, gave social scientists ample reasons to consider what produced individuals ill-equipped to handle the new challenges of a fast-changing world. One cause, one explanation for the mentally ill and the wayward in their world, was genetics. Or so some reformers thought. Dissonant as it may sound to the modern ear, the message of many a well-meaning reformer was that heredity was the source of the country's strengths—and ills:

> [N]early all the happiness and nearly all the misery of the world are due, not to environment, but to heredity; that the differences among men are, in the main, due to differences in the germ cells from which they are born; that social classes, therefore, which you seek to abolish by law, are ordained by nature; that it is, in the large statistical run of things, not the slums which make slum people, but slum people who make the slums; . . . that if you want artists, poets, philosophers, skilled workmen and great statesmen you will also have to give nature a chance to breed them.[11]

Imprinted with this outlook, eugenicists before long would "ascribe almost every symptom of social disorganization to heredity."[12] Once eugenics moved beyond inheritable *physical* traits, all bets were off. All manner of intellectual and psychological traits could be attributed to genetic steering. The catchword was "feeblemindedness," a word that to the modern ear bespeaks a lack of intellectual capacity, say a low IQ. But to many eugenicists, intellectual capacity went not just to powers of reason but to being "normal," to being able to fit in, as it "linked intelligence to morals, virtue, and social adequacy."[13] This linkage had serious implications, as it potentially covered a wide range of people and a wide range of ailments: the mentally ill, the insane, epileptics, criminals, prostitutes, alcoholics, to name the most frequently, but not exclusively, mentioned.

Before puzzling over *what* the eugenicists were thinking, it is well to pause over *who* was doing the thinking. This was not a fringe group. Many leading figures of the day—Theodore Roosevelt, John D. Rockefeller, Mrs. Mary Harriman, David Starr Jordan (a biologist and the first president of Stanford University), to name some—were fervent eugenicists, putting their money, their power, their time, and their research behind the effort.[14] Theodore Roosevelt wrote that he "'wish[ed] very much that the wrong people could be prevented entirely from breeding,'" adding "that 'feebled-minded persons' should be 'forbidden to leave offspring behind them.'"[15] Galton was no slouch either. More than just a relative of Charles Darwin, he was a leading English scientist in his own right. Nor did this work come out of left field. It seemed to represent a natural outgrowth of what passed for the enlightened social and scientific thinking of the day: Darwin's development of the theory of natural selection;[16] Malthus's burgeoning work on the inevitability of, and risks caused by, overpopulation;[17] and Herbert Spencer's survival-of-the-fittest philosophy.[18] To Spencer, individuals came into a world in which they won or lost a gladiator-like competition with nature: "If they are sufficiently complete to live, they do live, and it is well they should live. If they are not sufficiently complete to live, they die and it is best they should die."[19] In many ways, eugenics was an establishment movement, holding "a special appeal for people at the top of society's hierarchies . . . who were convinced they belonged there."[20]

What these people were thinking had serious implications not just for understanding how the ill-equipped came to be but also for what to do about it. If bad genes were the cause of so-called degenerates, limiting reproduction of them was a potential solution, as many eugenicists came to believe. One way to limit procreation was to move affected men and women into institutions and to segregate them from each other, an answer first used in Victorian England and initially favored in this country as well. Homes for the mentally ill and prisons for the convicted were segregated by gender, preventing the feeble-minded from breeding and passing on this or that purportedly degenerate strain.

Yet perpetual institutionalization is expensive, and life sentences are not handed out for most crimes. Cost became a concern, as population growth and accompanying increases in the mentally ill strained the capacity of state homes—colonies as they were sometimes called—for the feebleminded. Even the most ruthlessly reformist leaders could not accept, or, if they could accept, could not obtain traction for, the one medically available procedure available for men through 1900: castration. This approach not only eliminated the possibility of reproduction. It also removed the means and desire for reproduction, bringing with it other physical and psychological consequences, too many for most eugenicists and citizens to stomach in the name of good-genes reform alone.[21]

At the turn of the century, doctors learned to cut and tie the vas deferens in men (a vasectomy) and eventually to do the same for women's fallopian tubes (a salpingectomy). The procedure divorced the procreation-causing part of sex from the pleasure-seeking part of it through a relatively minor operation that not only stimulated voluntary sterilizations but facilitated involuntary ones as well.[22] If castration was perceived as "too brutal" for addressing these issues, it "provided a foil against which sterilization seemed humane and politically more palatable."[23]

A leading "candidate for sterilization was the feebleminded person in an institution who could lead a productive life in society, but had to be segregated to prevent the spread of feeblemindedness through reproduction."[24] With this procedure in hand, states could "release the institutionalized person without the risk" of creating more so-termed degenerates—a solution that was seemingly compassionate (freeing the person from the institution) and cost-effective (freeing the State from having to house them).[25]

The First Wave of State Eugenics Laws

All that remained to put this eugenic solution in place was the passage of state laws that would allow it. While some doctors at some state institutions performed involuntary sterilization procedures in the early 1900s under their general authority to care for their patients,[26] most were unwilling to do so in the absence of state authority for the procedure. Indiana passed the first sterilization law, and a doctor named Harry Sharp was the key reason. A surgeon at a state reformatory, Dr. Sharp performed vasectomies on dozens of inmates.[27] Based on his experience, he wrote a leading paper, what one scholar calls a "virtual manifesto for a sterilization movement,"[28] that explained that the procedure was relatively noninvasive, simple, painless, and inexpensive, and through which he called on others to use the procedure as a "humane tool for eugenic control."[29] What moved Sharp was not just the good-genes/bad-genes outlook of the eugenicists but also concerns about the increasing number of criminals and increasing number of individuals who could not care for themselves. The census data, he thought, showed an alarming trend:

> [I]n 1850 there were 6,737 criminals in the United States, or one to each 3,442 of the population; while in 1890 the penal population is shown to be 83,329 or one to each 957 of the population. This is of the criminal alone. If all dependents were considered, such as inhabit public and private insane hospitals, almshouses and institutes for the feeble-minded we should find the proportion to be in the neighborhood of one to three hundred of the population.[30]

As Dr. Sharp and others saw it, the problem was not just a growing population of criminals and others incapable of taking care of themselves but that the proportion of the population with these "traits" was accelerating.

Thanks in large part to Dr. Sharp's advocacy, Indiana became the first state to enact a sterilization law in 1907. It read in full:

> AN ACT to prevent procreation of confirmed criminals, idiots, imbeciles, and rapists; Providing that superintendents or boards of managers of institutions where such persons are confined shall have the authority and are empowered to appoint a committee of experts, consisting of two physicians, to examine into the mental condition of such inmates.

WHEREAS, heredity plays a most important part in the transmission of crime, idiocy, and imbecility:

THEREFORE, BE IT ENACTED BY THE GENERAL ASSEMBLY OF THE STATE OF INDIANA, that on and after passage of this act it shall be compulsory for each and every institution in the state entrusted with the care of confirmed criminals, idiots, rapists and imbeciles, to appoint upon its staff, in addition to the regular institutional physician, two (2) skilled surgeons of recognized ability, whose duty it shall be, in conjunction with the chief physician of the institution, to examine the mental and physical condition of such inmates as are recommended by the institutional physician and board of experts and the board of managers. If in the judgment of this committee of experts procreation is inadvisable, and there is no probability of improvement of the mental and physical condition of the inmate, it shall be lawful for the surgeons to perform such operation for the prevention of procreation as shall be decided safest and most effective. But this operation shall not be performed except in cases that have been pronounced unimproveable. Provided that in no case the consultation fee be more than three dollars to each expert, to be paid out of the funds appropriated for the maintenance of such institution.[31]

Dr. Sharp was not alone in encouraging the States to enact sterilization laws. Harry Hamilton Laughlin, a high school biology teacher, became interested in eugenics first through friendships with members of a group acutely called the American Breeder's Association and eventually by leaving teaching to work full time for the Eugenics Research Office, a private body founded in 1910 to promote the study of eugenics and to collect eugenics data.[32] As the experiences of Sharp and Laughlin showed, the eugenics effort was less a "popular crusade" and more a movement spearheaded by medical, scientific, and social "specialists."[33] As Phillip Reilly puts the point: "The history of efforts to secure the involuntary sterilization of defective persons is the history of actions taken by a small but dedicated group of persons who were convinced that the future of the United States depended on protecting the 'race.' At the center of this group stood Harry Hamilton Laughlin."[34]

Through the efforts of Laughlin, Sharp, and others, fifteen States enacted sterilization laws between 1907 and 1918.[35] Here are the States: Indiana (1907); Connecticut (1909); Washington (1909); California (1909); Iowa (1911); New Jersey (1911); Nevada (1912); New York (1912); North Dakota (1913); Michigan (1913); Kansas (1913); Wisconsin (1913); Nebraska (1915); Oregon (1917); South Dakota (1918).[36] Had the choice been left to their legislatures alone, three other States (Pennsylvania, Vermont, and Idaho) would have joined the list. But the governors in each State vetoed the measures.

Not all of these laws were of a piece. As modified in 1913, the California law differed from the Indiana law in two ways. Once the relevant state agency found that individuals had an identified mental illness, the institution would discharge them if they agreed to be sterilized first.[37] And the law authorized the sterilization of intellectually disabled individuals (labeled "idiot[s] or "fool[s]" in the medical terminology of the day), without regard to whether they were leaving the institution, *if* the parents or a guardian consented.[38] In contrast to the Indiana law and most others, the California legislation thus did not permit involuntary sterilizations—at least not sterilizations initiated without some input from the patient, a guardian, or a family member.

Nor did all of these States use the authority granted by these laws to the same degree. From 1907 to 1921, the fifteen States sterilized a total of 3,233 individuals.[39] Just four States sterilized more than one hundred individuals during the period, with California overwhelmingly leading the group (2,558), followed by Nebraska (155), Oregon (127), and Indiana (120)[40]—and followed after that by Wisconsin (76), Kansas (54), Iowa (49), and New York (42).[41] Several of the States (Nevada, New Jersey, South Dakota) performed no surgeries during the period, and two performed just one (Michigan and Washington).[42] Not a single State from below the Mason-Dixon line passed such a law until 1919,[43] and the vast majority of the operations were performed in a handful of western and midwestern states. One other statistic of note: The States performed the procedure on more males (1,853) than females (1,380), a distinction attributable to the later development of the salpingectomy, the relative ease and relatively low price of a vasectomy, and "the immediacy of the (male) criminal problem."[44]

Why did many of the States that took the trouble to pass these laws opt not to use them? One answer was executive branch reticence. Some governors came reluctantly to the cause, and, as shown, some never supported the cause and vetoed the proposed laws.[45] And some state agencies, above all some superintendents of the state institutions, remained skeptical of sterilization as a legitimate solution to any of these problems.[46] Another answer was the courts, an explanation that shifts the conversation from the medical and social underpinnings of the laws and their halting implementation to the validity of them.

Constitutional Challenges to State Eugenics Laws

From 1912 to 1921, individuals or their guardians filed constitutional challenges to the laws in eight States—and won seven of them.[47] Most of the constitutional challenges were filed in state court, and most of them relied on one of three theories (or some combination of them): due process; equal protection; and cruel and unusual punishment. Even though virtually all state constitutions contain due process clauses and equal protection clauses (or at least clauses that operate like them),[48] the litigants generally favored reliance on the federal guarantees found in Section 1 of the Fourteenth Amendment, which apply directly to the States: "[N]or shall any State deprive any person of life, liberty or property, without due process of law; nor deny to any person within its jurisdiction the equal protection of the laws." When litigants in this era relied on prohibitions against "cruel" and/or "unusual" punishment, they necessarily relied on the state constitutional guarantees. It would not be until 1962 that the U.S. Supreme Court would make the Eighth Amendment's prohibition against "cruel and unusual punishment," originally applicable only to the federal government, applicable to the States as well.[49]

Two of the initial cases arose from criminal convictions and involved challenges to the "cruel" or "unusual" nature of the punishment imposed after them. The first challenge to an involuntary sterilization arose from a rape conviction against Peter Feilen in the State of Washington.[50] About forty years old at the time of the arrest, Feilen was the constable of Kirkland (a town not far from Seattle) and was perceived as "a man of family, and respected in his community."[51] The state law provided that, in the case of statutory rape of a girl under ten, or if the defendant is determined to be a "habitual criminal," the court "may, in addition to such other punishment or confinement as may be imposed, direct an operation to be performed upon such person, for the prevention of procreation."[52] The state judge imposed a sentence of life imprisonment on Feilen and, as the victim was younger than ten, exercised his discretion to require Feilen to submit to a vasectomy—"carefully and skillfully performed," he kindly added.[53] Feilen claimed that the involuntary vasectomy violated the state constitution's prohibition against "cruel" punishment.[54]

The Washington Supreme Court rejected Feilen's argument, establishing a victory for the eugenicists in the first reported case about the validity of these laws. The crime was "brutal, heinous, and revolting," the Court explained, one for which "death would not be held a cruel punishment," suggesting that "any penalty less than death, devoid of physical torture, might also be inflicted."[55] (The Court had ample grounds for characterizing the crime in this way but fewer grounds over time for its anything-less-than-death flourish.[56]) Nor should the "discretion of the Legislature" be second-guessed by the courts, "except in extreme cases."[57] This, the Court thought, was not such a case: "[M]odern scientific investigation shows that idiocy, insanity, imbecility, and criminality are congenital and hereditary" and that many States (Indiana, Connecticut, California, Iowa, New Jersey) as a result have required sterilization, making vasectomy a "common operation."[58] Nor was the operation particularly complicated. One doctor, indeed, characterized it as "less serious than the extraction of a tooth."[59] Easy for him to say, Feilen might have demurred. The Court even invoked newspaper articles, including one from the *Chicago Tribune* that said this: "The sterilization of defectives and habitual criminals is a measure of social economy."[60] The court did not mention any opposing views on the topic. The Court concluded that the procedure did not rise to the level of "extreme" and" barbarous" punishments prohibited by the state constitution.[61] The decision was unanimous, 4–0 to be exact, and authored by Justice Herman Crow.

The State of Washington nonetheless repealed the law one year later (1913) and replaced it eight years later (1921) with a law that did not cover convicts.[62] Phillip Reilly claims that "Feilen may be the only convicted rapist ever sterilized under a punitive statute."[63] I have my doubts. True or not, Feilen was the only person sterilized under the 1909 Washington law.[64] Feilen, as it happens, did not fit the eugenics profile. He had no criminal record, no relatives who were criminals, no indication of any "degeneracy" in his family.[65] The State, as it also happens, may not have convicted the right man. The governor pardoned Feilen in 1916 due to "grave doubt as to Feilen's guilt," an act that undid the conviction[66] but at the time could not undo the operation.[67] All in all, the State of Washington sterilized just one individual under the 1909 law, and, if Reilly is correct, the only rapist sterilized under a punitive statute in that State or the country as a whole was likely the wrong man. If this was a victory for the eugenicists, it's easy to wonder what losing would look like.

They had a chance to see, as they would lose most of the cases over the next fifteen years. Before turning to the civil cases, it's worth mentioning the last criminal case of this era. In 1918, six years after *Feilen*, a federal district court considered a forced-sterilization order arising from another rape conviction, and invalidated it under the State of Nevada's prohibition on "cruel or unusual punishment[]."[68] Why this federal district court was directly reviewing this state court criminal sentence under the Nevada Constitution is not clear. In modern times, that is not the norm.[69] No mention is made of a habeas petition. No mention is made of the fact that criminal defendants do not usually seek habeas relief on the basis of a violation of state law.[70] And the only reference to jurisdiction in the opinion is to say, again against the grain, that "[a]ll questions as to jurisdiction have been expressly waived."[71]

Be all that as it may, the Nevada law gave trial judges discretion to order a vasectomy on individuals convicted of rape or statutory rape (of females under the age of ten) as well as on "habitual criminal[s]."[72] Pearley Mickle pled guilty to rape and was given an indeterminate sentence of not less than five years, to which the trial court added a vasectomy for good measure. In requiring the vasectomy, the state trial judge "accorded considerable weight" to the fact that Mickle was an epileptic.[73] At sentencing, Mickle admitted to ten epileptic fits in the previous four years but maintained that nobody in his family, save one cousin, suffered from epilepsy.[74]

In reviewing the constitutionality of the sentence, the federal trial judge began by mentioning several "considerations" that "are beside the issue," though apparently not so beside the issue as to escape mention. "Possibly in the exercise of its police power," Judge Farrington proceeded to say, "it may be lawful for the Legislature to adopt reasonable measures, adequate and sufficient to prevent degenerates and persons afflicted with transmittable mental defects, physical disease, or criminal tendencies from begetting children; but legislation of that character must operate alike on all unfortunates of the same class, and the classification must operate reasonably with relation to the end sought to be accomplished."[75] If the goal is to "prevent the transmission of criminal tendencies," he added, the law does not apply to all such offenders but only to those that the judge in his "discretion" opts to sterilize.[76] Many judges are opposed to such "mutilation" and thus will not further this objective of the law.[77] And some "brute[s] guilty of rape . . . might regard it as an advantage . . . to be sterilized," as the operation eliminates only one of the potential effects of future rapes but leaves the convict "physically capable of committing the offense" again.[78]

Moving to "the issue" raised by Mickle, the court noted that the state and federal decisions on what amounts to "cruel" or "unusual" punishments "are not altogether harmonious"[79]—true then, perhaps true now. In construing the Nevada disjunctive guarantee, part of the original 1864 Nevada Constitution, the court noted that "mutilation" has never been used in the State for punitive purposes.[80] While it concluded that a "[v]asectomy in itself is not cruel," it reasoned that, "when resorted to as punishment, it is ignominious and degrading, and in that sense is cruel"—and "unusual in Nevada."[81]

That left rehabilitation as a potential saving explanation. "Reformation of the criminal is a wise and humane purpose of punishment, to be disregarded only when the death penalty is inflicted."[82] Yet a "degrading and humiliating punishment is not conducive to the resumption of the upright and self-respecting life."[83] For the criminal and "for society, a fair opportunity to retrieve his fall is quite as important as the eugenic possibilities of vasectomy," the latter of which amounts to a "brand of infamy."[84] It matters not that the death penalty could (then) be inflicted for rape, as the reality "that the extreme penalty is not exacted is evidence that the criminal is considered worthy to live"—and to be reformed.[85] So far as the record shows, the State of Nevada did not appeal this decision.

Judge Farrington, educated at Amherst College in the East and Hastings College of Law in the West, was not a likely candidate to invalidate the Nevada eugenics law in one sense.[86] He was the fifth judge appointed to the District of Nevada, then with just one seat,[87] and was appointed to the seat by President Theodore Roosevelt.[88] At the time, he thus was the only federal trial judge in Nevada, and he held the seat only because a leading eugenicist nominated him.

In the first fifteen years of constitutional challenges to eugenics laws, just two of the reported cases involved criminal applications of the laws. Neither case boded well for the long-term prospects of the eugenics movement. In the first case, the State convicted the wrong man but won the case, a pyrrhic victory for the State and a disfiguring loss for the defendant. In the second case, the State convicted the right man but lost the case. Not until *Skinner v. Oklahoma* in 1942, as we will see, would the criminal law side of this story be finally laid to rest.[89] But for now, it's worth benchmarking the early results: An elected state governor reversed the one conviction upheld under the law, and an unelected federal trial judge invalidated the law's application in the only other case during this period.

The rest of the challenges in this initial period arose outside the criminal setting, thus implicating the paternalistic objective, as opposed to the punitive goal, of the eugenics movement. First up was the New Jersey Supreme Court. The case arose from the actions of a New Jersey agency, the title of which—"The Board of Examiners of Feeble-Minded (including idiots, imbeciles, and morons), Epileptics, Criminals and other Defectives"—gives acronyms a good name. After consulting with the chief physician of the New Jersey State Village for Epileptics, the agency ordered Alice Smith to undergo a salpingectomy in 1911.[90] It found that Smith was an epileptic (though she had been attack-free for the previous five years), that she had been in the home since 1902, that "procreation by her is inadvisable," and that there is "no probability" that her condition would improve.[91] As the first decision assessing the constitutionality of a sterilization law under the Equal Protection Clause of the Federal Constitution, and as the first decision of any kind to assess the validity of these laws against a known innocent not charged with any crime, the New Jersey Supreme Court's unanimous decision rises to the occasion.

Justice Charles Garrison ably sets the stage. At one end, the state legislature has the "inherent" power to pass "whatever regulations are in its judgment demanded for the welfare of society at large in order to secure or to guard its order, safety, health, or morals."[92] That's accurate, by the way, because the States, unlike the national government, have inherent rather than enumerated legislative powers. At the other end, "the artificial enhancement of the public welfare by the forceable suppression of the constitutional rights of the individual is inadmissible."[93] The case, he said, falls "[s]omewhere between these two fundamental propositions," raising the "novel" question "whether it is one of the attributes of government to essay the theoretical improvement of society by destroying the function of procreation in certain of its members who are not malefactors against its laws."[94]

As if laying the groundwork to say that the entire topic of legislation is off limits—a groundbreaking idea at the time—the opinion sets off on a discussion about the "far-reaching" consequences of upholding the law.[95] "For the feeble-minded and epileptics are not the only persons in the community whose elimination as undesirable citizens would, or might in the judgment of the Legislature, be a distinct benefit to society."[96] If "such a power exists in the case of epileptics, the doctrine . . . cannot stop there."[97] What of "pulmonary consumption or communicable syphilis"?[98] What of "[r]acial differences," which "might afford a basis for such an opinion in communities where that question is unfortunately a permanent and paramount issue"?[99] "Even beyond" all that, "it might be logically consistent to bring the philosophic theory of Malthus to bear upon the police power to the end that the tendency of population to outgrow its means of subsistence should be counteracted by surgical interference of the sort we are now considering."[100]

After offering this bait for a far-reaching decision, he switches back to a narrower ground. Observing that "these illustrations" serve the "purpose of indicating why we [make] the decision of the present case upon a ground that has no such logical results or untoward consequences," the court proceeds to explain why the law suffers from a narrower means-ends "classification" problem, one that violates the Equal Protection Clause of the U.S. Constitution.[101] The key problem is that, even if you take the legislature at its word, even if you give eu-genics the benefit of the doubt, the risk of propagation applies just as readily—more readily in reality—to epileptics who live outside of institutions than to epileptics housed inside of them. The "principle of selection" of those involuntarily sterilized thus "bears no reasonable re-lation to the proposed scheme for the artificial betterment of society."[102] "For not only will society at large be just as injuriously affected by the procreation of epileptics who are not confined in such institutions as it will be by the procreation of those who are so confined, but the former vastly outnumber the later, and are, in the nature of things, vastly more exposed to the temptation and opportunity of procreation, which in-deed in cases of those confined in a presumably well-conducted public institution is reduced practically to nil."[103]

Nor, the court added as an aside, would "the classification . . . be sufficient" if the institution allowed the institutionalized individuals to go free once they were sterilized, thereby saving the State money.[104] That option, the court concluded, was not "deserving of serious consid-eration": "The palpable inhumanity and immorality of such a scheme forbids us to impute it to an enlightened Legislature that evidently enacted the present statute for a worthy social end, upon the merits of which our present decision upon strictly legal lines is in no sense to be regarded as a reflection."[105]

The New Jersey Supreme Court's decision in *Smith* marked a path that might well have stopped the eugenics movement in it tracks. The classification problem identified by the Court—if inheriting bad genes is the concern, why sterilize the one group of people, the institution-alized, least able to procreate—revealed the limits of eugenic zeal. No law to my knowledge urged any State to round up epileptics, the men-tally ill, or anyone else living innocently and happily in society (often presumably with their families or in private institutions), and coer-cively sterilize them. No "infrastructure" for such a law existed.[106] Even the option of offering sterilization as the price to be paid for freedom, which some institutions required, did not explain away this means-end problem.

Smith also deserves note as a federal equal protection case. Early in the opinion, the Court explains that the law "possibly" "threatens" "the liberty" of Smith "in a manner forbidden by both the state and federal Constitutions."[107] For reasons all its own, however, the Court resolved the case on the broader ground—the federal one—even though it could have decided the case on the state ground and in the process insulated it from U.S. Supreme Court review.[108] The State of New Jersey never sought review of the *Smith* decision in the U.S. Supreme Court, perhaps suggesting executive branch reticence about the policy behind the law. More than two decades *after* the *Smith* decision, the New Jersey Supreme Court construed Article I, paragraph 1 of the New Jersey Constitution, language dating from the 1844 Constitution ("All men are by nature free and independent, and have certain natural and unalienable rights, among which are those of enjoying and defending life and liberty, acquiring, possessing, and protecting property, and of pursuing and obtaining safety and happiness."), as containing an equal protection guarantee.[109]

Of consequence for federal *and* state equal protection purposes, the Court used "reasonable" fit language.[110] This language foreshadowed the U.S. Supreme Court's *City of Cleburne* decision, discussed in more detail later, which applied a heightened form of rational-basis review in another disability-rights case toward the end of the century.[111]

Justice Garrison was a promising candidate to write this path-setting decision in some ways but not in others. He came from a prominent New Jersey family, and two features of his background may have sensitized him to the issues. As a matter of ethics, his father was a prominent Episcopal minister,[112] and he himself served as Chancellor of the Southern Diocese of the Protestant Episcopal Church of New Jersey for roughly thirty-five years.[113] As a matter of medicine, Justice Garrison (like his father) was trained first as a doctor and practiced medicine for several years.[114] Only later did he become a lawyer and judge. On the other hand, his family was acquainted with Woodrow Wilson, another New Jerseyan, who as governor of the State signed the eugenics legislation that was almost used to sterilize Alice Smith.[115] Confirming the close connections between the two New Jersey families, Wilson as president appointed one of Justice Garrison's brothers, Lindley Garrison, to be his secretary of war from 1913 to 1916.[116]

Alice Smith was said to present "an ideal eugenic history" for a test case.[117] In 1902, the State had committed her to the New Jersey Village for Epileptics, the "objects of which are to 'secure the humane, curative, scientific, and economical care and treatment of epilepsy.' "[118] For five years before the 1911 decision to sterilize her, she had been epilepsy-free,[119] though that feature of her medical history may show how little such a diagnosis had to do with many coerced-sterilization orders.

Her medical history, as compiled by caseworkers and summarized by Harry Laughlin, went well beyond concerns about epilepsy. "Going back three generations," the caseworkers "documented feeblemind-edness, epilepsy, illegitimacy, sexual immorality, drunkenness, con-sumption, criminality, dropsy, and virtually any other negative 'unit character' imaginable."[120] "The patient's family is well known in the town, as they are generally spoken of as being half-witted. They have always lived in the poorer parts of the town, for the most part in the vicinity of the railroad, in an alley known as 'Washerwoman's Alley,' where the houses are in poor condition and are occupied by negroes."[121] "The father's paternal interest in this patient, as well as all his children, was directly in proportion to their earning capacity. Many times, in fits of anger, he would turn his daughters out of his house, and they would seek refuge among the negroes about the neighborhood."[122] Four of Alice's five living siblings resided in similar state institutions, and both parents were considered "feebleminded and/or epileptic, as were several of their siblings."[123] Alice claimed to have been raped, the file adds, at which point she became pregnant and gave birth to a child who died at six months in an orphan asylum.[124] While caseworkers described her as "ignorant and uneducated," they added that "she is a young woman with a pleasant facial expression, very kind and obliging in manner and a very good and steady worker. She has a special fondness for her children."[125] There was one other perceived defect: She "possessed none of the normal aversions of a white girl to a colored man, who was per-haps nice to her."[126] Laughlin described Smith as an ideal case, not even "borderline," due to "the persistence throughout [her] pedigree of de-generative human qualities from which the race must purge itself, if it is to endure."[127] Alice Smith had much in common with Carrie Buck, the subject of the U.S. Supreme Court case fourteen years later.

Until 1927, the New Jersey Supreme Court's *Smith* decision would influence other courts. It was *the* case when it came to the first wave of lawsuits challenging involuntary sterilizations of innocents. The Michigan Supreme Court faced a similar challenge in 1918 and, prominently invoking the New Jersey Supreme Court's decision, reached a largely similar result.[128] Confined at the Michigan Home and Training School at Lapeer, Nora Reynolds was deemed "insane" and ordered to undergo a salpingectomy. She was twenty-seven at the time, and the State committed her at nineteen.[129] She was said to have the mental capacity of a ten-year-old. She repeatedly escaped from the institution and gave birth to two illegitimate children.[130] The night watchman not only helped her escape but "was guilty of having had carnal relations with her."[131] Her guardian challenged the constitutionality of the sterilization law on equal protection grounds (the opinion does not indicate whether on state or federal grounds) because the law applied only to the mentally ill and insane housed in institutions, not those outside of them. The Michigan Attorney General in an amicus brief apparently conceded that the law was unconstitutional.[132]

Relying on *Smith*, the Court in a 7–0 decision written by Justice Steere concluded that the law violated the "constitutional prohibition against class legislation."[133] The problem, as in *Smith*, was this: "[T]he legislature selected out of what might be termed a natural class of defective and incompetent persons only those already under public restraint, leaving immune from its operation all others of like kind to whom the reason for the legislative remedy is normally and equally, at least, applicable, extending immunities and privileges to the latter which are denied to the former."[134] After a long block quotation from *Smith* to the same effect, the Court was done. And so was the Michigan law.

Michigan returned to the drafting board in 1923. The new law solved some of these problems but created others. The act cast the net more broadly by including some people living outside of institutions as well as in: It authorized sterilizations for two classes of potentially sexually active "defective persons"—those likely to have mentally defective children and those likely to burden the State with their children because of an inability to support them.[135] In 1925, *Smith v. Wayne County Probate Judge*[136] blessed some of these changes but not others in rejecting the proposed sterilization of Whillie Smith, a sixteen-year-old, "feeble-minded" boy, whose father, with the mother's consent, filed a petition to have Whillie sterilized under the new law. Although the court rejected his general challenges to the law—e.g., due process and cruel and unusual punishment—it found that the law still amounted to unconstitutional class legislation because it applied only to those who could not afford to provide for their offspring.[137] It also found that the probate court had failed to follow all of the state procedural protections required before a sterilization order could become valid:

> No more important duty devolves on a probate judge than that imposed on him under this act. The responsibility of determining that a surgical operation shall be performed on a human being who is mentally defective "for his own welfare or the welfare of the community" rest[s] upon him, and it may properly be discharged by him only on the most painstaking and thorough investigation of the facts disclosed upon the hearing.[138]

Justice Wiest dissented from the parts of the decision that upheld the law.[139] Wiest never graduated from high school and never attended law school and was a machinist before apprenticing as a lawyer.[140] "Paradoxical as it may appear, although Justice Wiest was time without number called upon to decide questions of great magnitude directly relating to scientific and economic progress, he was personally slow to accept changing time and the external expression of them."[141] To Justice Wiest, the law "invite[d] atavism to the state of mind evidenced in Sparta, ancient Rome, and the Dark Ages, where individuality counted for naught against the mere animal breeding of human beings for purposes of the state or tribe."[142] Not only did the law draw unconstitutionally irrational lines,[143] but it also counted as cruel and unusual punishment,[144] and exceeded the scope of state power in its potentially far-reaching effects.[145] What remained of the Michigan eugenics law was almost invalidated one year later in *In re Salloum*.[146] A change in the composition of the Michigan Supreme Court, however, created a 4–4 deadlock,[147] permitting the lower court order to sterilize Agnes Salloum to stand.[148]

The New York law met a worse fate in 1918 in the *Osborn* case, though in this instance not through the work of the State's highest court (the New York Court of Appeals) but of its lowest court of general jurisdiction (the Supreme Court).[149] The New York law, like the others, dealt with "the inherited tendency to crime, insanity, feeble-mindedness, idiocy or imbecility."[150] But unlike many of the other laws, it allowed the individual subjected to a sterilization order to seek review by the Supreme Court or any justice of the court.[151]

What makes the case significant is that Justice William Rudd put together a thorough record about the benefits and burdens of the law and the extent to which medical evidence supported it. Rudd was the first president of the Albany County Bar Association,[152] and was described at his death as "a leader in civic movements at Albany for most of his Life."[153] Notably, the superintendent of the institution that housed Frank Osborn, Dr. Bernstein, opposed the sterilization order and said he could not think of one person in the 1,300-person institution who would benefit from it. As paraphrased by the court, "it would not help the boy, and it would not help society"; he still would have to be supervised, and a vasectomy will not alter his sexual interests; and if "this legislation" is meant to be "in advance of our enlightenment," "we don't know today what we are dealing with."[154] Most of the other experts, including several leading eugenicists, such as Dr. Davenport and Mr. Van Wagenen, also testified *against* the order—with Dr. Davenport saying that, while he wholeheartedly supported the eugenics work of Dr. Sharp and others, he preferred segregation over vasectomy, and with Van Wagenen saying (as paraphrased by the court) he would not recommend such an operation "except upon those who consented."[155] One other doctor, a Dr. Coakley, pointed out another problem: The vas deferens potentially can be "reunited," so that "nothing is accomplished."[156] Based on this "practically uncontradicted" record, Justice Rudd found that the order of the board of examiners was "not justified either upon the facts as they today exist or in the hope of benefits to come."[157]

Having removed the existence of any live controversy between Osborn and the board of examiners on nonconstitutional grounds, Justice Rudd nonetheless proceeded to invalidate the statute on federal equal protection grounds.[158] No such ruling would have been possible in federal court, as Article III of the U.S. Constitution extends the power of the federal courts only to "cases and controversies."[159] The same is not true of most state courts, many of which have authority to issue the ultimate in decisions not grounded in a case or controversy: advisory opinions.[160]

In invalidating the statute, the court followed the increasingly well-tread path set by the New Jersey Supreme Court. "Can it be said,"

Justice Rudd rhetorically asked, "that the law can direct the physical mutilation of the bodies of those who are in the state's care, and not be concerned with the same class of persons who are in the world at large?"[161] As other features of his lengthy opinion make clear, Justice Rudd found the case not only doctrinally easy but morally so as well. Consider: "Frank Osborn is not a malefactor. He is mentally deficient. He is defective without personal responsibility for such defect";[162] "if turned out into the world" with or without the operation, Osborn "could not care for himself or make a living," defeating the supposed cost-saving objective of the law and leaving him alike in all respects to a "mentally deficient" individual cared for by his family at home, save that one would be sterilized while the other would not be;[163] the law seems "almost inhuman in its nature";[164] and "why sterilization by vasectomy of patients in a hospital, who are grouped as a class with rapists in a state prison, strikes an awakening note in a new era . . . is beyond the comprehension of this court and is not enlightening."[165]

The Appellate Division of the Supreme Court unanimously affirmed Justice Rudd without an opinion.[166] An appeal was filed to the New York Court of Appeals in 1919. But before the court could rule on the case, the New York legislature voted unanimously to repeal the law.[167]

Laughlin was not happy about the New York case, claiming it "set back eugenical progress among the state's institutions more than ten years."[168] "The test case," he added, "was selected well after the legal challenges to the New Jersey statute had become clear (1915). Without amending the laws, prior to selecting a test case, the New York authorities virtually guaranteed the statute's failure in court."[169]

The New York case would not end Laughlin's disappointment. Taking fewer pages but coming to the same end was *Cline v. State Board of Eugenics*.[170] The Oregon Board of Eugenics ordered the sterilization of Jacob Cline, a sixty-five-year-old preacher convicted of raping his twelve-year-old daughter.[171] The order implicated the validity of two Oregon laws, one from 1917, one from 1919. The first one, the court held, violated the state and federal guarantees "prohibiting class legislation" because "it is confined in its operation to the inmates of certain state institutions"—the same equal protection theory that doomed the New Jersey law in *Smith*.[172] The second law, the court held, did not amount to class legislation but violated the federal due process guarantee. As to that, the court reasoned that a vasectomy amounted to a deprivation of life, as opposed to liberty, invoking Justice Field for the idea that due process "extends to all those limbs and faculties by which life is enjoyed."[173] The court explained that the law left in doubt the extent of the procedural guarantees in place to satisfy the "strict rules of procedure" needed in such a setting, as it was "silent" about the amount of evidence needed to support (or protest) an order, how it could be appealed and where, and other rules of procedure for ensuring that the "deprivation of life" was properly implemented.[174]

The other cases from the period sound many of these themes. *Davis v. Berry*[175] offers a grab bag of constitutional rulings. An Iowa law, according to the court, required sterilization of "idiots, feeble-minded, drunkards, drug fiends, epileptics, syphilitics, moral and sexual perverts" and those "twice convicted of a felony."[176] When the warden of an Iowa penitentiary sought to enforce the law against a man named Davis, the attorney general issued an opinion that the procedure would violate the ex post facto clause, and the warden opted not to follow through with the vasectomy. Nonetheless, the three-judge federal court opted to address the constitutionality of the Iowa law, noting that a future attorney general might take a different view of the validity of the law and that at all events the opinion (the attorney general's, that is) was advisory.[177] Of course, what should have mattered was that the warden was not planning to enforce the statute against Davis. The court proceeded anyway, opting to disagree with the attorney general's ex post facto analysis but finding that the law violated a host of other guarantees—due process and cruel and unusual punishment—and amounted to that rarest of creatures: a bill of attainder.[178] The author of the opinion, Judge Smith McPherson, conveying no shortage of contempt for the law, did not unite his passion with analytical rigor. Saying that the law "belongs to the Dark Ages," he asked, "Must the marriage relation be based and enforced by statute according to the teachings of the farmer in selecting his male animals to be mated with certain female animals only?"[179] But, in continuing, he seemed not to appreciate the distinction between a vasectomy and castration. After devoting considerable space to explaining why castration was a form of medieval cruelty, he reasoned that "the purpose *and result* of the two operations are one and the same."[180] Not everyone would agree. And it is the rare law that amounts to a bill of attainder—basically a legislative decision to punish one individual alone for an act done before the law is passed—and I venture to guess that this was the only law in history treated as a bill of attainder but found *not* to be ex post facto. Bills of attainder would seem to be subsets of ex post facto laws.[181] All of this may explain why one of the judges on the panel, Judge Smith (not to be confused with Judge Smith McPherson), concurred separately, relying solely on the due process problems with the statute: no opportunity for a public hearing, and no opportunity for the inmate to introduce any evidence about whether he indeed had been twice convicted of a felony.[182] The State appealed to the U.S. Supreme Court. Soon after, the State repealed the law, and the Court through a unanimous opinion by Justice Holmes reversed the decision of the three-judge court and sent the case back to dismiss the complaint (and presumably vacate the court's decision[183]), as "[a]ll possibility or threat of the operation has disappeared now, if not before, by the act of the state."[184]

The remaining decision from this era takes us back to the first State to enact a eugenics law: Indiana. In *Williams v. Smith*,[185] the Supreme Court of Dr. Sharp's home State refused to permit doctors at the Indiana Reformatory to perform a vasectomy on one Warren Wallace Smith. The law, recall, permitted two surgeons to consult with the chief physician of the institution to determine which recommended inmates and institutionalized individuals should be sterilized because "procreation is inadvisable" and there is "no probability" of change in the mental capacity of the inmate.[186] The trial court refused to allow the vasectomy. Relying on the due process ruling of *Davis v. Berry*, the Iowa federal court case, the court, in an opinion by Justice Howard Townsend, found a federal due process violation: "[T]he prisoner has no opportunity to cross-examine the experts who decide that this operation should be performed upon him. He has no chance to bring experts to show that it should not be performed; nor has he a chance to controvert the scientific question that he is of a class designated in the statute."[187]

As 1921 came to a close, one might have thought that one of the most aggressive chapters of the eugenics movement—involuntary sterilization—was on its last legs and would soon come to an end through the repeal of some laws, the invalidation of some others, and the lapse into unenforced desuetude of what remained. Had this happened, the heroes of the story would have been the state courts and the state and federal constitutions. That was not because the state courts precluded the possibility of a constitutional eugenics law but because they placed a series of daunting procedural road blocks in front of them. In an era when the concept of "substantive due process," in so many words, did not exist, it should come as no surprise that the constitutional decisions did not reject the eugenic premises of the laws as beyond the authority of the legislature, except in fleeting and vague *dicta*. But they did raise obstacles that, if accepted elsewhere, likely would have doomed the broadest civil conceptions of the laws. The equal-protection, class-legislation theory of invalidity, established by the New Jersey Supreme Court, left little practical room for further legislation, as the States largely were unwilling to follow eugenics premises to their natural end—by requiring sterilization of *all* members of the class, whether institutionalized or not, whether causing problems in society or not. And arguably the due process rulings could have come to the same end. As some of the decisions from the era showed, the premises of eugenics were far from proven, and many well-respected doctors rejected them entirely. Vague scientific-sounding generalities about potential and probable births of future "degenerates" would have had a hard time surviving as-applied evidentiary challenges to each subject of this remarkable set of experiments.

What might have happened did not. Instead of retreating, the eugenicists launched a masterful counteroffensive. Much of the credit goes to Harry Laughlin and other like-minded (and like-impassioned) eugenicists who flooded the social, scientific, and popular literature with studies and data purporting to show the escalating risks of allowing nature to take its course. His 1922 study *Eugenical Sterilization in the United States* surveyed 160 institutions with sterilization programs, reviewed the successes of the programs, and proposed a model sterilization law that purported to correct the constitutional defects in earlier laws.[188] Facilitating his advocacy was an increasing focus on the relationship of eugenics and immigration, the idea that social engineering of this sort had to contend not just with defective individual genes but with purportedly defective racial genes as well. While immigration slowed during World War I, it increased significantly after the war.[189] Before long, Laughlin was testifying and writing about a correlation between the growing number of defective individuals and the growing number of immigrants. Add a dose of anti-miscegenation concerns, and the mentally ill had become one among many reasons for motivated thinkers to take eugenics legislation seriously.

All of this led to a new wave of state sterilization laws. By 1925, seventeen States had such laws,[190] a significant uptick given that from 1907 to 1921 six of the fifteen state laws had been invalidated in one way or another. One other thing happened during this second wave: A few States below the Mason-Dixon line enacted eugenics laws.

Buck v. Bell

Passage of the Virginia law in 1924 and its vindication in the U.S. Supreme Court three years later in *Buck v. Bell* contributed mightily to the rebirth of the eugenics movement.[191] The case marked a shift in litigation strategy from trying to avoid constitutional losses in fifty state supreme courts to trying to win one constitutional battle in the National Court—a litigation strategy used in *Buck v. Bell* and many times since, whether in trying to uphold state laws (as here) or in trying to invalidate them. And a strategy used to great effect in *Buck v. Bell*. The case not only ended at the one Court that the state courts could not contradict—at least on matters of federal law—but the decision also was penned by Oliver Wendell Holmes, perhaps the most prominent Justice to serve on the Court.

First things first, however. Any lawsuit at a minimum takes two parties. And what started as the Bell side of *Buck v. Bell* is as interesting as what became the Buck side of the case. The Virginia legislature authorized funds for the Virginia Colony for Epileptics and Feebleminded, approving its charter in 1910.[192] Albert Priddy became the Colony's first superintendent and before long advocated segregated residential space for many residents of the Colony and, not long after that, sought legislative authority to perform involuntary sterilizations on feebleminded residents. Through the assistance of Aubrey Strode, a senator in the Virginia General Assembly, the legislature amended the Colony's charter in 1916. "[T]he new law expanded Priddy's medical authority to treat inmates. With his board's approval, Priddy could now impose whatever moral, medical, and surgical treatment he felt was appropriate for his patients."[193] Not long after the legislature amended the charter, Priddy sought approval from the Colony's Board to sterilize several patients.[194] The Board contained three members, one of whom was Irving Whitehead, and they approved Priddy's request.[195]

The Board approved several more such requests, and Whitehead participated in all of them, at least until he left the Board in 1917.[196] One request led to litigation and sought money damages from Dr. Priddy.[197] According to Professor Lombardo, this litigation, embarrassing as it was to Priddy and the Colony, prompted efforts to pass additional legislation that explicitly authorized therapeutic, yet still involuntary, sterilizations.[198] A combination of Dr. Priddy's advocacy and eugenic views, the steadfast lobbying of Harry Laughlin, Strode's influence with the legislature, and state fiscal challenges all allowed Virginia to pass such a law in 1924. In drafting the law, Strode used some of the language from the Model Eugenical Sterilization Law put together by Harry Laughlin.[199]

As Dr. Priddy well knew, the new law did not eliminate the possibility of a new lawsuit, particularly since most of the constitutional challenges to eugenics laws had succeeded up to 1924. "Haunted by the humiliation of the *Mallory* lawsuits," Priddy proposed that, " 'as a matter of precaution[a]ry safety,' " the Colony should create " 'a test case of the constitutionality of the Sterilization Law . . . before any operation is performed.' "[200] Priddy died before the litigation ended, and the new superintendent, J. H. Bell, was substituted in his place.[201]

That's where the Buck side of *Buck v. Bell* comes in. Carrie Buck was a resident of the Colony. Then eighteen, she was Priddy's choice for the test case. Why? According to the Colony, not only was Carrie feebleminded but so also was her mother, Emma Buck, who resided in the Colony as well. One thing more: Carrie had an out-of-wedlock daughter, who, at least according to the Colony,[202] showed signs of mental disability.

Priddy petitioned the Board of the Colony to sterilize Carrie involuntarily.[203] After appointing Carrie a guardian, the Board held a hearing, after which it concluded:

> Carrie Buck is a feebleminded inmate of this institution and by
> the laws of heredity is the probable potential parent of socially

inadequate offspring, likewise afflicted, that she may be sexually sterilized without detriment to her general health, and that the welfare of the said Carrie Buck and of society will be promoted by such sterilization.[204]

Under the Virginia law, her guardian was required to hire a lawyer to appeal the order to the state trial court. He chose Irving Whitehead, the one-time director of the Board who had approved many earlier sterilizations and a friend of Strode and Priddy.[205] The Colony and Priddy asked Strode to defend the order. That's not as strange as it sounds. Why not have the legislative sponsor of a law defend its constitutionality in court, an approach potentially useful to the legislature and to the court (if the lawmaker is up to the task)?

As a search for the truth, the trial was a sham. While others found that Whitehead performed " 'ineffective[ly],' " Professor Lombardo claims that was not all. Whitehead, he says, "did not fail in his advocacy of Carrie Buck simply because he was incompetent; Whitehead failed because he intended to fail."[206] Professor Lombardo has marshaled considerable support for his thesis, and more recently Adam Cohen came to a similar conclusion in his equally impressive book about the case. The evidentiary record, for one, was remarkably one-sided. Whitehead made no effort to challenge the hereditary premises of eugenics and made no effort to challenge the Colony's assumptions that Carrie, her mother, and her daughter were themselves all feebleminded or particularly at risk of procreating.[207] Sixty years after the fact, it is remarkable what Professor Lombardo and Adam Cohen were able to find, as opposed to what Whitehead was able to find, even though Whitehead was on the scene at the relevant period of time and knew just where to look (had he wanted to look). How indeed, one might ask, could Whitehead have represented Buck in seeking to overturn the sterilization order? There is no evidence that he, as a former member of the Board, sought the permission of the Colony to represent Buck *against* it. That may be because he never stopped working *for* the Colony's interests. One of the Colony's many witnesses was the ubiquitous Harry Laughlin. Based solely on information provided by Dr. Priddy (Laughlin never met Carrie Buck), Laughlin opined that Carrie had a record "of immorality, prostitution and untruthfulness"; had never been self-sustaining;

and had one illegitimate child "supposed to be mentally defective."[208] As for her mother and the family, Priddy said that Carrie's mother was "divorced from her husband on account of infidelity," that she had three illegitimate children, including Carrie, and that "[t]hese people belong to the shiftless, ignorant, and worthless class of antisocial whites of the South."[209] Not unlike the New Jersey *Smith* case, Laughlin thought the Colony had found "an ideal eugenic history" for a test case, even better this time with supposedly "three generations" of feeblemindedness. [210]

Much that the trial record purported to show was not true. As it turns out, Carrie was not illegitimate. Her parents remained married at the time of her birth.[211] Nor was it clear that Carrie was weak-minded. "Carrie's school records indicate that she was a normal child: She attended school for five years and was promoted to sixth grade. The year before she left school, her teacher recorded the comment 'very good—deportment and lessons' and recommended her for promotion."[212] As for the claim she had mothered a child out of wedlock, Professor Lombardo has produced evidence suggesting "Carrie [was] pregnant . . . because she had been raped"—raped indeed by the nephew of the family with whom she was staying before being institutionalized, the same family that moved Carrie to the Colony, not implausibly to cover up the crime.[213] Whitehead did not call the family with whom Carrie had stayed for fourteen years. Nor, as it happens, was the evidence about Vivian, Carrie's child, accurate. All that the evidence at trial showed was that Vivian, according to one nurse, was "not quite normal."[214] Whitehead never challenged this vague comment either, and while Vivian lived just eight more years, she did well in two years of school, at one point "earn[ing] a spot on her school's honor roll."[215] And of course, as many state court cases had already shown, the premises of eugenics were not beyond reproach. Yet Whitehead did nothing to put this evidence in the record, even though the New York case had laid it all out.

If the uneven introduction of evidence suggests a collusive trial, one other reality seems to confirm it. Remarkably, Strode *and* Whitehead made a presentation to the Board about the case. According to the Board minutes, they "outlined the present status of the sterilization test case . . . , their advice being that this particular case was in admirable shape to go to the court of last resort, and that *we could not hope to have a more favorable situation than this one.*[216] If Whitehead was not guilty of misconduct in this regard, he at least seems to have been guilty of motivated thinking—motivated by the reality that he was a former Board member, a building at the Colony was named in his honor, he had authorized many sterilizations as a Board member (indicating he believed in the premises of the good-breeding movement), and he and Strode were close friends, so close that Strode delivered the eulogy at his funeral.[217]

It is easy to think that Whitehead's half-hearted advocacy by itself caused the decisions of the Virginia Supreme Court (then called the Supreme Court of Appeals of the State of Virginia) and the U.S. Supreme Court to uphold the Virginia law. The uneven record and the false impression left by it—that three generations of Bucks had inherited a weak-minded genetic trait, bolstering the worst fears of eugenicists—created as "favorable" a "situation" for upholding the law, to use Whitehead's and Strode's words, as could be hoped for. And if zealous advocacy goes a long way to helping courts resolve legal questions correctly, the reverse must occasionally be true as well. Still, in view of the raft of state court decisions (and two federal ones) in existence before 1927 that cogently explained the potential constitutional pitfalls of such a law and in view of the reality that *Buck v. Bell* presented a legal and constitutional question, it is hard to excuse the courts based on the claim that Whitehead and Strode had "orchestrated a judicial charade."[218] The U.S. Supreme Court from all appearances was a willing participant.

Justice Holmes's decision for the Court is five paragraphs long. His legal reasoning took two paragraphs, a sum of fifteen sentences. It is worth quoting his reasoning in full. After explaining the (purported) procedural protections in the law, he dispatches the due process argument with one sentence:

> There can be no doubt that, so far as procedure is concerned, the rights of the patient are most carefully considered, and, as every step in this case was taken in scrupulous compliance with the statute and after months of observation, there is no doubt that, in that respect, the plaintiff in error has had due process of law.

He then rejects the equal protection challenge in the last two paragraphs:

> The attack is not upon the procedure, but upon the substantive law. It seems to be contended that in no circumstances could such an order be justified. It certainly is contended that the order cannot be justified upon the existing grounds. The judgment finds the facts that have been recited, and that Carrie Buck is the probable potential parent of socially inadequate offspring, likewise afflicted, that she may be sexually sterilized without detriment to her general health, and that her welfare and that of society will be promoted by her sterilization, and thereupon makes the order. In view of the general declarations of the legislature and the specific findings of the Court, obviously we cannot say as matter of law that the grounds do not exist, and, if they exist, they justify the result. We have seen more than once that the public welfare may call upon the best citizens for their lives. It would be strange if it could not call upon those who already sap the strength of the State for these lesser sacrifices, often not felt to be such by those concerned, in order to prevent our being swamped with incompetence. It is better for all the world if, instead of waiting to execute degenerate offspring for crime or to let them starve for their imbecility, society can prevent those who are manifestly unfit from continuing their kind. The principle that sustains compulsory vaccination is broad enough to cover cutting the Fallopian tubes. *Jacobson v. Massachusetts*, 197 U.S. 11. Three generations of imbeciles are enough.
>
> But, it is said, however it might be if this reasoning were applied generally, it fails when it is confined to the small number who are in the institutions named and is not applied to the multitudes outside. It is the usual last resort of constitutional arguments to point out shortcomings of this sort. But the answer is that the law does all that is needed when it does all that it can, indicates a policy, applies it to all within the lines, and seeks to bring within the lines all similarly situated so far and so fast as its means allow. Of course, so far as the operations enable those who otherwise must be kept confined to be returned to the world, and thus open the asylum to others, the equality aimed at will be more nearly reached.[219]

The Colony sterilized Carrie Buck on October 19, 1927.[220]

This was not Justice Holmes's finest hour—or the Court's. Eight Justices supported the Virginia law, and Justice Butler alone dissented. In the absence of an opinion by Justice Butler, we can only guess why he parted ways with his colleagues—whether out of due process concerns, equal protection concerns, or something else. (Some speculate that, as a practicing Catholic, Butler was unwilling to support eugenic social engineering,[221] even if he was unwilling to explain why.) That Justice Butler did not explain himself, in truth not unusual in those days, is our loss, and his. He had a lot to work with, as much as, if not more than, what Justice Harlan had to work with in *Plessy*.

It is useful to put *Buck* in the context of the many state and federal court decisions that preceded it. Notions of cruel and unusual punishment had little to do with this civil case. And Carrie Buck did not rely on any Virginia constitutional guarantees in the state or federal courts, perhaps unsurprising given Whitehead's half-hearted advocacy. As for federal due process, the procedural kind, the Virginia legislature had fixed many of the problems identified in earlier cases. Laughlin and Strode had indeed improved upon the earlier laws, guaranteeing individuals hearings, opportunities to create a record, a right of appeal, and so forth. In the abstract, Justice Holmes may well have been right in one sense that, as a matter of process, the Virginia law met the constitutional minimum on paper. Of course, in view of what Professor Lombardo, Adam Cohen, and others have discovered about the litigation, an as-applied due process challenge by Carrie Buck—premised on what we now know was Whitehead's hopelessly conflicted loyalties in the case—would have won. Whitehead's main due process argument was that Virginia was depriving Carrie of her life by sterilizing her, apparently in view of the risks of the surgery. In pointing out that there must be some due process limit on a legislature's capacity to take a person's "life," he complained that otherwise "judicial trials" over a sterilization order "are a farce."[222] Whitehead would know.

No substantive due process argument was made, at least not in so many words. But neither had one been made in the earlier cases. By 1927, the Court had decided *Pierce v. Society of Sisters* (1925),[223] arguably creating a substantive limit on legislative intrusions on liberty—telling the State of Oregon it had no right to require parents to send their children to public schools. If the Fourteenth Amendment's liberty guarantee barred a legislative directive about *how* a parent raised a child, it would not have been a sizeable stretch to argue—at least to argue—that the guarantee likewise barred a legislative direction about *whether* one could produce a child.

The heart of the debate in *Buck* turned instead on equal protection and legislative classifications—the same debate that preoccupied most of the earlier courts, the same debate most of the prior claimants had won, the same debate that produced the New Jersey Supreme Court's landmark decision in *Smith*. Yet Holmes, a former state high court judge, gave the back of the hand to the arguments and never mentioned the considerable state court authority in support of Buck. While the *Buck* factual record, inaccurate though it was, suggested a heredity problem, the other cases showed that the heredity of these traits was not well established as a matter of science or medicine. The record of the New York case proved the point. Plus, Holmes never answered why the classification was a rational one, why involuntary sterilization should apply only to those too poor to live outside a state institution. If the benign purpose of the law was to allow the resident to return to society, that did not mean she had to be sterilized involuntarily. Give her the choice instead, as was true in California.

How Holmes wrote the opinion, however, is what turns the head and what is the most unforgivable feature of *Buck v. Bell*. His emphatic endorsement of eugenic thinking undermined the most conceivable ground for upholding the law: judicial restraint. As the author of one of the iconic judicial-modesty opinions in American law—the *Lochner* dissent—Holmes's instinct to uphold the Virginia law was consistent with his general judicial philosophy, that the job of a judge was not to take sides on the policy debates of the day or even to save the citizenry from foolish legislation. Consider this passage from *Lochner*:

This case is decided upon [a] . . . theory which a large part of the country does not entertain. If it were a question whether I agreed with that theory, I should desire to study it further and long before making up my mind. But I do not conceive that to be my duty, because I strongly believe that my agreement or disagreement has nothing to do with the right of a majority to embody their opinions in law. It is settled by various decisions of this court that state constitutions and state laws may regulate life in many ways which we as legislators might think as injudicious, or if you like as tyrannical. . . . The 14th Amendment does not enact Mr. Herbert Spencer's Social Statics.[224]

Holmes could have said much the same in *Buck*. If the validity of Herbert Spencer's laissez-faire, survival-of-the-fittest theories did not bear on the constitutionality of legislation capping the number of hours bakers could work, it is hard to see why the validity of Spencer's theories should bear on the constitutionality of compelled-sterilization legislation. To uphold the Virginia eugenics law did not require Holmes to endorse it any more than upholding the wage-and-hours law had required him to endorse that. Perhaps the difference between the two opinions reflects the difference between a young Justice who knows he has not seen it all and a mature Justice who thinks he has. "[S]ooner or later," Holmes wrote Harold Laski after the decision came out, "one gets a chance to say what one thinks."[225] That occurred later in this instance: Holmes penned his *Lochner* dissent in 1905, just three years after joining the Court, and his *Buck* majority in 1927, just five years before he left the Court. Whatever the cause, the reasoning of *Buck* is not the reasoning of judicial restraint and the writing of *Buck* is not that of a mere "judicial spectator."[226]

Conspiring against Carrie Buck was a double dose of conventional progressive thinking, circa the 1920s: (1) the courts should allow legislatures to experiment with and learn from new social policies without interference from the judicial branch; and (2) eugenics provided a way to improve the human race. Holmes committed his judicial career to the former, and he became an enthusiast for the latter. "One decision that I wrote gave me pleasure," he crowed to a friend, "establishing the constitutionality of a law permitting the sterilization of imbeciles."[227]

That enthusiasm apparently got the best of Holmes. Instead of writing the opinion in a laboratories-of-experimentation sort of way— shocking but consistent—and instead of saying there is preliminary evidence to support the premises of eugenics and preliminary evidence that undermines them, all of which would make it inappropriate for the judiciary to interfere, he wrote a paean to eugenics. From the vantage point of 2018, it's easy to mock "Three generations of imbeciles is enough." But from the vantage point of 1927, the most damning feature of the line is that Holmes, the exemplar of judicial modesty, enthusiastically takes one side in the debate. The opinion reads not as the hard case it was—surely true in view of the many state court (and federal court) decisions going the other way and in view of Butler's dissent—but as a Madison Avenue endorsement of further legislation. That language is not the language of restraint and indeed is not unlike the flowery patriotic language of Frankfurter's majority opinion in *Gobitis*, the first flag-salute case, which (as we will see in the next chapter) extolled the need to support the country in war and unleashed a war of its own on Jehovah's Witnesses.

The Rebirth of Eugenics Legislation

As an advertisement for eugenics, *Buck v. Bell* worked. The stamp of federal constitutional—and policy—approval on Virginia's law, by Justice Holmes no less, changed the direction of the movement. Eugenics must be a good idea, one could forgive a citizen for thinking, because eight members of the Supreme Court had just said so. Instead of adopting the New Jersey Supreme Court's incremental federal law decision and making *it* the law of the land—to the effect that equal protection precludes sterilizing a class of the mentally disabled (just those in public homes) to the exclusion of all others (even those living in circumstances that made procreation more likely)—the Court casually dismissed the challenges to the law, suggesting that other challenges to the law would fall short too. In the words of Harry Laughlin, the ruling took the eugenics movement beyond the "experimental period" and meant that "eugenical sterilization will be looked upon by the American people as a reasonable and conservative matter."[228] And in the words of Adam Cohen, the ruling "breathed new life into the sterilization movement."[229] Within two years of the decision, twelve more States enacted sterilization laws.[230] Four years after the decision, twenty-two States had "introduced" new sterilization legislation.[231] By 1931, twenty-eight States had enacted such laws.[232]

Two measures of *Buck*'s impact are the roads taken by Indiana (the first State to pass a eugenics law) and by New Jersey (the first State to consider the constitutionality of the law) after Holmes's decision. The New Jersey legislature never revisited the concept of forced sterilization after its High Court's decision in *Smith*. After the Indiana High Court's *Williams* decision in 1921, however, the Indiana legislature tried several times to enact eugenics legislation, passing one law in 1927 (the year of *Buck*) and expanding it in 1931.[233] The Indiana law remained on the books until 1974.[234] Indiana ultimately performed almost 2,500 sterilizations,[235] while New Jersey never performed one.[236] The Indiana experience turned out to be more representative of other state experiences. In contrast to the dwindling number of States with eugenics legislation before *Buck*, twenty-eight States would adopt (or maintain) such laws after the decision, with some States re-enforcing and reinvigorating dormant laws.[237]

Unlike the state courts' nearly uniform resistance to eugenics legislation before *Buck*, most of the state courts fell in line after *Buck*, even when it came to their independent, uniquely sovereign, and *final* authority to construe their own constitutions. A few cases illustrate the trend. The Supreme Court of Kansas rejected the challenge of Emil Luthi to a forced sterilization in 1928, one year after *Buck v. Bell*. Even though the challenge was premised on state and federal grounds, the decision does not acknowledge the court's independent power to impose greater liberty protections under the Kansas Constitution. It relies on *Buck* in quickly rejecting the federal challenge, as of course it had to. But it seems to build on the eugenics enthusiasm of *Buck* in rejecting the state challenge, arguably even outdoing Holmes in the process. After acknowledging that the individual's liberty "interest" is "of the highest order," it "reduc[es]"

> reconciliation of personal liberty and governmental interest to its lowest biological terms; the two functions indispensable to the continued existence of human life are nutrition and reproduction. Without nutrition, the individual dies; without reproduction, the race dies. Procreation of defective and feeble-minded children with criminal tendencies does not advantage, but patently disadvantages, the race. Reproduction turns adversary and thwarts the ultimate end and purpose of reproduction. The race may insure its own

perpetuation and such progeny may be prevented in the interest of the higher general welfare.[238]

The one region of the country least likely to enact eugenics legislation remained the South. With the exception of Virginia and a few other States, the movement never caught on below the Mason-Dixon line. Even Virginia came late to the effort. It did not enact a law during the first wave of eugenics laws and would not do so until 1924. That law, of course, would produce *Buck v. Bell*, and the State eventually would perform roughly 8,000 forced sterilizations.[239] But the southern norm ran largely in the other direction. Several States in the region—Florida, Kentucky, Louisiana, Texas—never established forced sterilization programs.[240] And most of the States that did enact such programs used them relatively infrequently: Alabama (224), Mississippi (683), South Carolina (277), and West Virginia (98).[241] The two exceptions, beyond Virginia, were Georgia (3,284) and North Carolina (6,851).[242] Edward Larson offers several plausible explanations for this geographic distinction: Strong family ties prompted many families to keep disabled children at home rather than send them to institutions; one of the key pushbacks against eugenics proponents came from faith-based groups, and religion played a not-inconsequential role in Southern customs and culture; and the political-party patron of the eugenics movement (progressivism) held little sway in the South.[243]

What of the rest of the country? What of the present? Today, even outside the South, we do not have public proponents of eugenics. And sterilization as an involuntary civil remedy or criminal punishment no longer occurs. What bridges the gap between *Buck v. Bell* and the end of compelled sterilizations? One answer is time, no friend of grand yet half-baked public policy initiatives. Another answer is science, which exposed many of the shaky premises and promises of the eugenics movement.[244] The surprise is not that the eugenics movement ended but that it lasted as long as it did. To have any impact, the idea required legislation (1) that did not violate the federal *or* state constitutions, and (2) that the superintendents of institutions, criminal and civil, would utilize. Emblematic of the last point is that many States with laws on the books permitting involuntary sterilizations rarely, if ever, embraced the procedure, such as Nevada (0), Arizona (30), Idaho (38), and New York (42).[245]

Some parallels, gradually perceived, between America and Europe in the 1930s did eugenics no favors. The Nazis did not see any advantages to a melting-pot culture, and neither did many American eugenicists.[246] In trying "to save the nation from the looming threat of hereditary disaster,"[247] American supporters of eugenics cast a wide net. Laughlin thought "northern European stock . . . was superior to other nationalities," and he and other American eugenicists were instrumental in limiting immigration from southern and eastern European countries. New restrictions in the Immigration Act of 1924 put these considerations into law. After it, immigration from southern and eastern Europe dropped from two-thirds of immigrants in 1920–21 to 10 percent, and Jewish immigrants dropped from "190,000 in 1920 to 43,000 in 1921, and just 7,000 in 1926."[248] Nor were concerns about "heredity disasters" limited to immigration. Note what else happened in 1924. That's not only the year in which the Virginia legislature enacted the eugenics law upheld in *Buck v. Bell*; it's also the year—indeed it happened on the same day—that the Virginia legislature enacted the Racial Integrity Act, which significantly increased restrictions on interracial marriage.[249] According to Adam Cohen, American and German eugenicists competed with each other in improving "the national stock," with the "German eugenicists . . . becoming worried that their American counterparts were surpassing them."[250]

Just as the Third Reich would give a bad name to compelled raised-arm flag salutes, so too it would eventually lead Americans to second-guess the promises, scientific underpinnings, and morality of eugenics. In Nazi Germany, more than 400,000 forced sterilizations occurred in a country with a much smaller population than the United States and over a much shorter period of time.[251] Nazi scientists at the Nuremberg trials, notably, defended their use of involuntary sterilization based in part on *Buck v. Bell*.[252]

Skinner v. Oklahoma

The rise of the Third Reich also may have affected the decline of the eugenics movement in another way: the courts. In 1942, soon after

America entered the war, the U.S. Supreme Court decided *Skinner v. Oklahoma*.[253] At issue was the 1935 Oklahoma Habitual Criminal Sterilization Act, which required the sterilization of anyone convicted of two or more felonies "involving moral turpitude," making them a "habitual criminal."[254] The act exempted some felonies, such as embezzlement, political offenses, and tax crimes.[255] Skinner met the recidivism requirement through convictions for stealing chickens (1926), robbery with a firearm (1929), and robbery with a firearm once more (1934). The only question at trial was whether he was a "habitual criminal" and whether making him "sexually sterile" would be "without detriment to his . . . general health."[256] A jury found both to be true, and the Oklahoma Supreme Court affirmed the involuntary vasectomy order by a 5–4 vote, what seems to be a narrow margin given the existence of *Buck v. Bell* but that may have signaled shifting views about eugenics.

Writing for the U.S. Supreme Court, Justice Douglas warms up to the task with this opening: "This case touches a sensitive and important area of human rights. Oklahoma deprives certain individuals of a right which is basic to the perpetuation of a race—the right to have offspring."[257] He then acknowledges, but refuses to consider, several of Skinner's constitutional claims: The law amounted to an improper use of the police power "in view of the state of scientific authorities respecting inheritability of criminal traits"; the law violated due process because, unlike the law upheld in *Buck v. Bell*, "the defendant is given no opportunity to be heard on the issue as to whether he is the probable potential parent of socially undesirable offspring"; and the law amounted to cruel and unusual punishment under the yet-to-be-incorporated Eighth Amendment.[258]

The Court instead invalidated the law on equal protection grounds. The key flaw was the irrationality of bringing some prior crimes, but not others, within the definition of a criminal who repeatedly, "habitual[ly]" in the words of the Court, commits crimes of "moral turpitude." The legislative distinction that the Court could not let pass was between grand larceny and embezzlement. Larceny became grand when it involved more than $20. Yet for reasons the legislature never explained and the Court could not justify, a clerk's embezzlement of more than $20 was not covered. As a result, "the clerk is not subject to the pains and penalties of the Act no matter how large his embezzlements nor how frequent his convictions," while the thrice-convicted chicken thief may be sterilized so long as the value of the chickens exceeds $20 each time.[259] The distinction had nothing to do with the premises of eugenics legislation and risked converting fine common law distinctions between trespass and other crimes into "a rule of human genetics."[260]

In reaching this conclusion, the Court acknowledged that *Buck* and other police-power cases give the States broad discretion to make classifications in their civil and criminal laws—that the equal protection clause indeed is "the usual last resort of constitutional arguments."[261] Even giving Oklahoma the "large deference" that *Buck* and other cases require, the Court could not uphold the law. Part of the problem was the irrationality of the classification: "We have not the slightest basis for inferring that that line has any significance in eugenics, nor that the inheritability of criminal traits follows the neat legal distinctions which the law has marked between those two offenses."[262] And part of the problem, the greater part of the problem for which the case has come to be known, was the effect of the classification:

> We are dealing here with legislation which involves one of the basic civil rights of man. Marriage and procreation are fundamental to the very existence and survival of the race. The power to sterilize, if exercised, may have subtle, far-reaching and devastating effects. In evil or reckless hands it can cause races or types which are inimical to the dominant group to wither and disappear. There is no redemption for the individual whom the law touches. Any experiment which the State conducts is to his irreparable injury. He is forever deprived of a basic liberty.[263]

All of this was relevant, the Court explained, "not to reexamine the scope of the police power of the States" but to explain why "strict scrutiny of the classification which a State makes in a sterilization law is essential, lest unwittingly, or otherwise, invidious discriminations are made against groups or types of individuals in violation of the constitutional guaranty of just and equal laws."[264]

Chief Justice Stone concurred in the result, preferring not to rely on the Equal Protection Clause. "If," as he put it, the State could sterilize criminals "on the assumption that their propensities are transmissible to future generations by inheritance," it was "doubt[ful] that the equal protection clause requires it to apply the measure to all criminals in the first instance, or to none."[265] He would have invalidated the law on the due process ground that Oklahoma did not give Skinner a hearing to determine whether "his criminal tendencies are of an inheritable type."[266] Thus, "while the state may protect itself from the demonstrably inheritable tendencies of the individual which are injurious to society, the most elementary notions of due process would seem to require it to take appropriate steps to safeguard the liberty of the individual by affording him, before he is condemned to an irreparable injury in his person, some opportunity to show that he is without such inheritable tendencies."[267]

Justice Jackson concurred with the Chief Justice that the state-provided hearing was too limited to satisfy due process and with the majority opinion that the classification failed equal protection. Justice Jackson added that, notwithstanding *Buck v. Bell*, "where the condition had persisted through three generations and afforded grounds for the belief that it was transmissible and would continue to manifest itself in generations to come," "[t]here are limits to the extent to which a legislatively represented majority may conduct biological experiments at the expense of the dignity and personality and natural powers of a minority."[268] As to that, he "reserve[d] judgment."[269]

Skinner is striking on many levels. Fifteen years after *Buck v. Bell*, at a time when many premises of constitutional law were changing, there remained an unwillingness to question the decision, perhaps because Justice Holmes was its author, and at least one member of the 1942 Court (Justice Frankfurter) was a protégé of Holmes. Save for Justice Jackson, no member of the Court suggests a substantive limit on a State's ability to sterilize its citizens involuntarily, and even Jackson does so reticently by reserving judgment on the point. What today is perceived as one of the great missteps in constitutional history was in 1942, even with the Nazi enthusiasm for eugenics and even with no consensus about the scientific validity of eugenics, still a precedent worth distinguishing rather than burying, perhaps because all members of the Court had known, and in some instances idolized, Holmes.

Of special interest here, *Skinner* invoked several state court decisions on this and related points, while *Buck* had ignored them all. And *Skinner* invoked them even though these pre-*Buck* decisions largely were inconsistent with *Buck*. Justice Douglas mentioned *Davis v. Berry*, *Williams v. Smith*, *State v. Feilen*, *Mickle v. Henrichs*, and *Smith v. Wayne Probate Judge*, and relied on the last of them to support the proposition that "[t]he equal protection clause would indeed be a formula of empty words if such conspicuously artificial lines could be drawn."[270] The *Skinner* Court may have been unwilling to overrule *Buck*, but it was not unwilling to invoke the state court (and lower federal court) decisions ignored in *Buck* and inconsistent with it.

The Gradual Decline and Fall of Eugenics

Skinner left *Buck* on the books. It thus did not outlaw eugenics legislation, even in the criminal context. All it demanded was a better explanation for placing some prior convictions and not others in the recidivism basket. But the language and reasoning of *Skinner*—its description of procreation as a fundamental right, its insistence on more rigorous means-end scrutiny, its invocation of the state court decisions— undermined eugenics laws. If nothing else, *Skinner* eliminated the anything-goes impression left by *Buck*, transforming the U.S. Supreme Court from a proponent of eugenics legislation into a skeptic of it.

Perhaps because *Skinner* was a criminal case and surely because *Buck* remained on the books, 1942 does not mark a notable change in the fortunes of eugenics legislation. Forced sterilizations continued through the end of the 1940s. In most States, the number of forced sterilizations began to decline between 1949 and 1959.[271] Even then, the change was not uniform. In some States, the rate of surgeries increased: North Carolina performed more than 3,500 sterilizations, Georgia about 2,500, and Virginia about 1,885 during this period.[272]

Not until the 1960s did most States repeal their mandatory-sterilization laws.[273] Even when it came to interpreting their own state constitutions, the state courts rarely interfered with the enforcement of these laws. As late as 1972, the Oregon Court of Appeals upheld a sterilization order against a seventeen-year-old girl with a history of emotional challenges, indiscriminate sex, and brain damage.[274] The North

Carolina Supreme Court reached a similar decision in 1976, holding that the State's sterilization law for the mentally disabled amounted to a valid exercise of the police power.[275] In doing so, it relied on *Buck* to show that the right to procreate contained limits and that the law did not violate the equal protection guarantee.[276]

The last known involuntary sterilization apparently took place in Oregon in 1981.[277] Efforts after that point were blocked in some cases by state court decisions and more likely by state and federal legislation. In 1983, the Georgia Supreme Court rejected a forced-sterilization petition, reasoning that it was analogous to an irreversible end to parental rights and required greater evidence to support it.[278] The court sidestepped the question whether the order violated the individual's substantive right to privacy.[279] So too for the Minnesota Court of Appeals in 1985 and the Colorado Supreme Court in 1990.[280] The most recent state court decision occurred in 1991, when the Arkansas Supreme Court invalidated a forced-sterilization law that did not have sufficient judicial oversight.[281]

Yet the federal and state courts and the federal and state constitutions were minor, not major, causes of the demise of eugenics in American history. The state legislatures became the eventual heroes of their own story. An indispensable early feature of the eugenics movement was the passage of legislation designed to give mental health institutions the authority to order forced sterilizations when they saw fit. Those laws, as we have seen, did not fare well in the courts in the first decade and a half after they were passed. When the U.S. Supreme Court enthusiastically gave the States the green light to continue to enact such laws in *Buck v. Bell*, the spotlight returned to the States where the state courts could have exercised their sovereign authority to construe their own constitutions differently from the federal constitution and followed the many state courts that, between 1913 and 1925, had blocked forced-sterilization orders. By and large, that did not happen. In the near term, the state courts fell in line, corrected course, and set sail with Holmes. If any branches of state government would write the last chapter of the eugenics movement, it would have to be the executive and legislative branches of state government.

From the outset, some governors and some superintendents of the institutions had shown reticence in implementing eugenics legislation.

What may have been easy for some legislatures in 1920 to enact in the abstract was not as easy for some superintendents to implement in the concrete. When it came time to apply the cost-benefit analysis of eugenics legislation to the sterilization of individuals, some executive branch officials hesitated and some affirmatively blocked the implementation of the laws. That is one reason, presumably the main reason, why the States varied so widely in the number of forced sterilizations they ordered from 1907 to 1981. But just as executive branch resistance to eugenics legislation in some States only partially slowed the pace of involuntary sterilizations from the beginning, it only partially led to the movement's demise.

What might have happened immediately on the legislative front did not. Much as the reformist legislative efforts of the early 1900s were blocked by the state court decisions of that era, the ruthlessly reformist zeal of *Buck* could have been blocked by the state legislatures after 1927. That did not happen, or at least it did not happen in the near term. In what surely counts as a maddening feature of democracy, especially democracy divided along fifty-one vertical and horizontal lines, the death of the eugenics movement through the legislative process came slowly. And it almost assuredly came more slowly than it otherwise would have due to Holmes's and the U.S. Supreme Court's clanging endorsement of eugenics policy.

What ultimately made involuntary sterilizations a thing of the past was not the legislative repeal of some laws, though that of course helped, but the States' across-the-board enactment of legislation that protected the disabled from discrimination in general. Antidiscrimination laws protecting the disabled were a twentieth-century innovation, and a state innovation at that. Not until the 1940s did the first laws come into existence. They were state laws known as "white cane" laws and initially were designed to provide access to public services and accommodations. Authored by Jacobus tenBroek, blind since age fourteen, the founder of the National Federation of the Blind and a prominent professor of political science at the University of California at Berkeley,[282] the laws applied only to the visually impaired at first. Missouri, to my knowledge, became the first State to enact such a law in 1941, when it provided that "[a]ny blind person . . . shall . . . be entitled to any and all accommodations, advantages, facilities and privileges of all public conveyances and all places of public accommodations."[283] Other States followed Missouri's example and before long extended the protections to other disabilities. In 1965, Wisconsin raised these measures by one. Rather than merely ensuring access, it enacted a general antidiscrimination law applicable to private and public employers.[284] By 1980, more than thirty States had similar measures. And by 1990, when Congress enacted the Americans with Disabilities Act (ADA), all States in the country had enacted disabilities-rights legislation of their own.[285] At least one member of Congress confirmed that the States had been the leaders in this area. "[T]his is probably one of the few times where the States are so far out in front of the Federal Government," he noted, "it's not funny."[286] The state laws, much like the ADA, generally contained two features, then and now: an antidiscrimination mandate, prohibiting governmental entities and the private sector from discriminating against the disabled, and an accommodation mandate, requiring governmental entities and the private sector to make reasonable accommodations for individuals with disabilities.[287]

These laws became increasingly inconsistent with the eugenics laws still on the books. How could a prohibition against treating the disabled differently than able-bodied and able-minded individuals be consistent with the forced sterilization only of individuals with disabilities? To honor the one would demean the other. Even in States with some eugenics laws still on the books, the passage of antidiscrimination laws made their enforcement a near legal impossibility.[288]

What starts as a legislative story ends as a legislative story. That's the good news. In a democracy, there is something to be said for allowing the gravitational forces of representative government to cure problems of its own making—and, by learning from the experience, to become better equipped to resist the next ill-begotten policy urge of the moment. Between the seventy-five years from start to finish of the eugenics movement, however, the States carried out more than 60,000 forced sterilizations.[289] That is the bad news, which prompts a few observations.

First, judicial restraint ought to be restrained. There's nothing wrong with crediting a *legislature's* explanations for a law and with allowing governmental experiments of one sort or another to continue until the empirical evidence comes in. That's what it means to give the legislature the benefit of the doubt, particularly at the outset of a policy initiative. Yet when the courts place their stamp of approval on the policy bona fides of a law, and do so before the evidence is in, that trespasses the line between legislating and judging. From today's vantage point, it is easy to see that, when Justice Holmes "erred," the "lucidity of his reasoning" showed that his explanation was "'wrong clearly.'"[290] If Holmes, to say nothing of two other prominent members of the Court (Chief Justice Taft and Justice Brandeis), could not see the perils of eugenics, it suggests the virtue of modesty to all judges, whether in inculpating or exculpating the policy virtues of a law. No one taught that lesson better than Holmes in *Lochner*. And few have failed to follow that lesson to worse effect than Holmes (and seven of his brethren) in *Buck*. Even very good judges can have very bad ideas.

Second, as a matter of judging *and* legislative policy, the *Buck* story confirms the virtues of caution when it comes to the next great advance, whether from scientific, medical, or technological quarters. The eugenics movement and other claimed advances of the past all show the ease with which time can make yesterday's progressives look like today's reactionaries. Looking back on the early stages of the movement, ample warnings existed that eugenics might not live up to its promises and that many of the threats that prompted it were overwrought. Just as there were scientific reasons to take eugenics seriously, there were scientific reasons to question it.[291] Early on, the New York Supreme Court provided ample reasons for hesitating before accepting the claims of eugenics laws—or at least couching opinions upholding the laws in the language of dispassion—particularly when it came to allowing the States to carry out involuntary sterilization orders as opposed to procedures chosen by the individual, a family member, or a guardian.

Third, while there is much to lament about the pace with which the country ended the eugenics experiment, there is nothing to lament about a feature of American government that prevented matters from being worse. When state democracies force compassionless laws into desuetude and later into repeal, and do so after withstanding judicial review no less, that is a plus, not a negative. Yes, it took longer than it should have, unfairly easy as that is to say from the blur-free eyes of the twenty-first century. But the kind of divided government that prevented a swifter change may have avoided a swift nationalization of eugenics legislation. Separation of powers, as the Framers well understood, guards against the reality that men and women are not angels and perhaps protects us best when government leaders come to think of themselves as angels.[292]

Consider Germany in the 1930s. When that country caught the same eugenics bug that captivated U.S. progressives in the teens and twenties, few separation of powers problems stood in its way. No state courts or state constitutions blocked the initiative. No state governors or state superintendents declined to implement the law. And no National Constitution limited the powers of the national government to reach the topic.

Eugenics leaders in the United States, notably, wanted Congress to enact and a federal agency to administer a "federal eugenics statute."[293] But no serious lawyer then, and none presumably now, thinks our national government could have imposed eugenics legislation on the entire country as a unified solution to problems associated with mental disabilities, criminality, and immoral behavior.[294] In this country, the national government remains one of limited and enumerated powers. And only a most pernicious and unbounded interpretation of Congress's power to "regulate Commerce . . . among the several States" would have permitted a national eugenics law. Not so in Germany. It faced no comparable limitations on national power, offering one reason why it would order 400,000 forced sterilizations over twelve years,[295] and the United States would order 60,000 over seventy-five years in a much bigger country.

Fourth, a comparison between the effects of the first state high court decision (*Feilen*) and the first Federal High Court decision (*Buck*) reveals the risks when the National Court resolves a complicated national debate. When the Washington Supreme Court enthusiastically upheld that state's eugenics law in 1912, it had little effect. Other state courts did not follow the decision. Not even Washington followed it, as the state legislature repealed the law the next year. *Buck* was another matter. It necessarily shut down further debate about the legitimacy of such legislation under the Federal Constitution. That is no surprise in view of the Supremacy Clause, and perhaps a fifteen-year delay between the first state court decision and *Buck* suggests the Court did not move too quickly in resolving that point. But the credibility of the National Court and the epigrammatic certitude with which Holmes dispatched anti-eugenic arguments carried great influence, perhaps more than it should have in a federal system with dual limitations on state power. As a result, the state courts for the most part refused to take seriously arguments under their own constitutions after *Buck*—forcing a legislative, rather than a judicial, solution to the eugenics efforts—even though excellent state court decisions remained on the books. Decisions of the U.S. Supreme Court sometimes carry more weight than they should.

Fifth, as a matter of doctrine, how might the rise of the eugenics movement have been slowed and its fall expedited? Using the conventional tools of late nineteenth- and early twentieth-century constitutional law, the state courts deployed two approaches in restricting the implementation of eugenics legislation. The most widespread, the least ebullient, and perhaps the most effective approach was to insist on honoring all state and federal *procedural* guarantees. In the context of an involuntary sterilization, the individual's liberty interest nears its apex, making it imperative to ensure that the process due *before* the State undertakes the operation is individual specific, record supported, and thorough. That kind of approach stopped many a proposed sterilization in the States in the first two decades of the movement, and one wonders what would have happened had the States continued to review such orders vigorously and rigorously to ensure their compliance with due process.

There is scant basis for wondering how Carrie Buck's case would have ended had the Colony provided fair process to her. It would have taken little effort to discover plenty of contrary evidence about each generation of alleged imbecility. Vivian was "perfectly normal" and had finished the second grade before dying at age eight.[296] Carrie had completed the sixth grade until her adopted family prevented her from continuing; she was not "immoral" but had been raped, which is apparently why she ended up, seven months pregnant, being committed to the Colony; she was merely "an undereducated woman of perfectly normal intelligence"; her court-appointed guardian did not look after her interests, and indeed she did not know the procedure was designed to sterilize her.[297] The intelligence tests on Emma likely overstated her mental deficiencies, and the assumption that she gave birth to Carrie out of wedlock was wrong.[298] Harry Laughlin at one point said he could not think of a situation in which "feeblemindedness" appeared in a parent, child, and grandchild.[299] That was true before *Buck v. Bell*. And it was true after the decision, as all participants to this saga should have realized. On top of that, as the New York case confirmed, the scientific underpinnings of the eugenics laws were sketchy and unproven.[300] Had the Colony provided the process due under state and federal law, Carrie Buck's case in Virginia would have ended up like Alice Smith's case in New Jersey.

The other approach placed limits on what was called "class legislation."[301] State courts first began to use the phrase during the antebellum era to condemn "partial or special laws," laws that "singled out certain persons or classes of persons for special benefits or burdens."[302] By the Civil War, nearly every state constitution had restricted legislative power to enact "class legislation."[303] The prohibition targeted laws that suffered from a means-end disconnect, a theory that resonated with early state courts faced with challenges to the constitutionality of eugenics legislation, including the New Jersey Supreme Court, because the laws turned on the risk that the "feebleminded" would reproduce but applied only to those least able to procreate: institutionalized individuals. *Buck v. Bell* began the gradual relaxation of the means-end-fit requirements of the federal equal protection clause, and the state courts for unimaginative reasons of their own followed the federal lead. One can fairly wonder what would have happened had the state courts held to their position. They would have foreshadowed and perhaps laid the foundation for *City of Cleburne*, a 1985 U.S. Supreme Court decision in which the Court applied a more rigorous form of rational basis review to invalidate a local zoning regulation that inhibited the location of a group home for the disabled in the community.[304]

Sixth, one sometimes hears advocates in the disabilities-rights community regret that the best they could do from the U.S. Supreme Court was *City of Cleburne*, that they never got their *Brown v. Board of Education*. They have a point. Rational basis review, even rational basis review with a tooth or two, does not equal strict scrutiny. No disabilities-rights case equals *Brown* in compelling change. And if *Dred Scott* and *Plessy* warranted a response like *Brown*, it's perhaps hard to understand why the same was not true of *Buck*. But the reality is that the stars of this story were initially state court judges and eventually the people, who insisted that their representatives right these wrongs. From time to time, that can be a fitting, hopeful, sometimes even more promising, way to end an individual rights story.

6

Free Speech, Free Exercise of Religion, and Freedom from Mandatory Flag Salutes

IT IS ONE THING for a constitution to guarantee that individuals may *think* what they wish and *believe* what they want. It is another for a constitution to ensure that individuals may *do* as they wish or *practice* their religion in whatever way they wish. Most school days in this country used to begin with a pledge of allegiance to the nation and our flag. Before and during World War II, disputes arose over whether local school boards could compel Jehovah's Witnesses to salute the flag in a raised-arm salute and to recite the pledge of allegiance. The Witnesses thought the salute and pledge amounted to compelled blasphemy, the worship of a false idol. The school boards, in the midst of World War II, thought the Witnesses were being insufficiently patriotic and expelled dissenting children if they refused to participate in the ceremony. In response, Witnesses filed scores of cases in the state and federal courts challenging the authority of the school districts to compel them to participate in these ceremonies even when their faith told them to desist. The cases relied on the federal and state constitutions and the freedom of speech and freedom of religion guarantees in each.

On the federal side, the First Amendment to the U.S. Constitution says that "Congress shall make no law respecting an establishment of religion, or prohibiting the free exercise thereof; or abridging the freedom of speech." The U.S. Supreme Court has made both of the guarantees pertinent to this chapter—the free speech guarantee[1] and the free exercise guarantee[2]—binding on the States.

On the state side, all States have free speech and free exercise guarantees of one sort or another, and some of the early state guarantees provided the blueprint for the federal guarantee. As for the free speech guarantees, the Pennsylvania Constitution provides an early example: "The free communication of thoughts and opinions is one of the invaluable rights of man; and every citizen may freely speak, write and print on any subject, being responsible for the abuse of that liberty."[3] The New York guarantee is similar to many others: "Every citizen may freely speak, write, and publish his or her sentiments on all subjects, being responsible for the abuse of that right; and no law shall be passed to restrain or abridge the liberty of speech or of the press."[4] Indiana offers a variation on these themes: "No law shall be passed restraining the free interchange of thought and opinion, or restricting the right to speak, write, or print freely on any subject whatever; but for the abuse of that right, every person shall be responsible."[5] And the South Carolina guarantee parallels the federal one: "The General Assembly shall make no law . . . abridging the freedom of speech or of the press."[6]

As for the free exercise guarantees, some mirror the to-the-point language of the National Constitution and indeed were the model for it. The Massachusetts Constitution is a good example: "No law shall be passed prohibiting the free exercise of religion."[7] Most of the state protections, however, are longer and cover more topics. Take New York: "The free exercise and enjoyment of religious profession and worship, without discrimination or preference, shall forever be allowed in this state. . . ."[8] Or Texas, longer still:

> All men have a natural and indefeasible right to worship Almighty God according to the dictates of their own consciences. No man shall be compelled to attend, erect or support any place of worship, or to maintain any ministry against his consent. No human authority ought, in any case whatever, to control or interfere with the rights of conscience in matters of religion, and no preference shall ever be given by law to any religious society or mode of worship. But it shall be the duty of the Legislature to pass such laws as may be necessary to protect equally every religious denomination in the peaceable enjoyment of its own mode of public worship.[9]

The Federal Story

West Virginia Board of Education v. Barnette,[10] as some civics students remember and as most first-year law students learn, is the flag-salute case. It starts as a tale of two cases, not one, as the story must account for the astonishing about-face between the Supreme Court's rejection of a challenge to compelled flag salutes in 1940 (*Minersville School District v. Gobitis*[11]) and the Court's embrace of the identical claim in 1943 (*Barnette*). Yet it becomes a tale of many cases, as the story must account not just for the turnaround between the two well-known federal cases but also for a slew of lesser-known state cases that tried at the same time to come to grips with the tension between each State's interest in promoting patriotism and in allowing individuals to speak and worship as they choose.

First this is a story about people, about American families, starting with the Gobitas and Barnett families. When people lend their names to landmark cases, the credit is fleeting, save for the lingering acclaim that goes with attaching the family name to the constitutional principle for which the case stands.[12] Not only did time soon forget the sufferings of the Gobitas and Barnett families, but the U.S. Supreme Court added the indignity of misspelling their names, forever linking the principle against compelled speech to families that do not exist.[13] Although it would be difficult to conclude that *both Gobitis* and *Barnette* were wrongly decided, I must start by acknowledging that both were wrongly captioned.[14]

Gobitis

As for the two families, let's begin with the Gobitas clan—spelled with an *a*, not with a second *i*. Walter Gobitas held a common job and practiced an uncommon religion. He owned a local grocery store in a Pennsylvania town known as Minersville—yes, a community with a fair share of miners—and raised six children with his wife, Ruth.[15]

At the beginning of each school day, the Minersville school board required all teachers and children to pledge allegiance to the American flag.[16] The pledge was not a new idea. It started in 1892 as a patriotic way to celebrate the four hundredth anniversary of Columbus's discovery of America.[17] Congress declared the day a national holiday (hence Columbus Day) and authorized the first pledge, the familiar words of which are: "I pledge allegiance to the flag of the United States of America and to the Republic for which it stands, one Nation indivisible, with liberty and justice for all."[18] Congress added "under God" to the pledge in 1954.[19] As initially conceived, the pledge was verbal and physical. While the students recited the words, they extended their right hand from their heart outward and up toward the flag.[20]

By the 1930s, this ceremony posed a problem for Jehovah's Witnesses, an evangelical Christian faith started in Pennsylvania in the 1800s.[21] In 1935, the leader of the Witnesses, Joseph Rutherford, a lawyer, gave a speech at the Witnesses' national convention encouraging Witnesses not to participate in flag-salute ceremonies.[22] As he saw it, the Bible is "the Word of God" and "is the supreme authority,"[23] and three of the Ten Commandments precluded flag salutes: "Thou shalt have no other gods before me"; "Thou shalt not make unto thee any graven image"; "Thou shalt not bow down thyself to them, nor serve them."[24] Pledging fealty to anything but God, whether the object was a country, a leader, or a secular symbol, violated these commandments. As a spiritual leader and lawyer, Rutherford had no problem urging followers to stand on principles of faith and law.

Consistent with Rutherford's teachings, the Gobitas parents directed their children not to participate in the flag-salute ceremony required by the Minersville school board.[25] When two of the Gobitas children, Lillian (12) and William (10), followed their parents' instructions, the school board expelled them.[26] The father sued the school board, its members, and the superintendent in federal district court.[27] The district court[28] and the Third Circuit[29] granted the Gobitas family relief, invoking the free exercise guarantee of the First (and Fourteenth) Amendment, and permitted the children to return to school.

The Supreme Court was another matter. All nine justices voted to reject the claim after oral argument, with just Chief Justice Hughes and Justice Frankfurter explaining their thinking in any detail at the justices' conference.[30] Frankfurter circulated an opinion for the Court, and three days before its release, Justice Stone circulated a dissent.[31] No one else joined the Stone dissent.

The *Gobitis* decision caused problems for the Gobitas family and worse problems for other Jehovah's Witnesses across the country. Before and after the decision, many Minersville residents led a boycott of the Gobitas grocery store.[32] Thanks to the willingness of a police officer to guard the store, no violence or destruction of the store occurred.[33] After several months, business for the most part returned to normal.[34]

The same was not true for Witnesses in other communities. As school boards across the country enacted mandatory flag-salute requirements,[35] Witnesses were put to the choice of sending their children to the local public schools or of compromising their religious beliefs. Making matters more difficult for Witnesses was the first peacetime draft in American history. Launched by President Franklin D. Roosevelt in September 1940 and ramped up after Pearl Harbor in December 1941, the draft put male Witnesses in a difficult position.[36] They sought exemptions from conscription on the ground that proselytizing was a central tenet of the faith and a full-time job, leaving no time for war efforts.[37] Although the draft exempted conscientious objectors, it exempted them only from combat, not from other war-related services, which Witnesses claimed to have no time to perform in view of their duties to proselytize for the faith.[38] The Witnesses' response to conscription did not sit well with draft boards across the country or with many Americans. Over the course of World War II, the government imprisoned 10,000 men who resisted conscription.[39] Forty percent of them were Witnesses.[40]

The Witnesses' resistance to the flag salute and to the wartime draft, combined with the Supreme Court's stamp of constitutionality on compelled flag salutes in *Gobitis*, unleashed a wave of persecution with few rivals in American history. *Gobitis* was decided on June 3, 1940. In the first three weeks after the decision, there were hundreds of attacks against Witnesses across the country.[41] Between May and October 1940, the ACLU reported to the Justice Department that vigilantes attacked 1,488 Witnesses in 335 communities, covering all but four States in the country.[42] The American Legion led as many as one-fifth of the attacks.[43]

A few examples give a flavor of what happened:

• June 9–10, 1940: A mob ransacked and burned the Witnesses' church in Kennebunk, Maine. The mob went from town to town in southern Maine dragging Witnesses from their houses and demanding they salute the flag.[44]

- June 16, 1940: Witnesses came to proselytize in Litchfield, Illinois, and rioters pulled them out of their cars, beat them severely, and forced them to salute the flag.[45]
- June 28–29, 1940: Witnesses came to proselytize in Richwood, West Virginia, after which the police arrested them and took them to the county jail, where vigilantes tied them together with rope and forced them to drink pints of castor oil. The vigilantes led the Witnesses on a forced march to an American Legion rally and beat them when they refused to salute the flag.[46]

While *Gobitis* undoubtedly accelerated the mistreatment of Witnesses, it would overstate things to conclude that the decision alone caused the problem. Witnesses faced plenty of violence before the decision. In April 1940, just months before the Court handed down *Gobitis*, one Witness described this incident:

> This Mr. Bowman . . . carried this flag in a spear-like position, and he came forward and gave a terrific lunge to plunge me through. I avoided this blow, and as he came by he pushed me into the gutter against an automobile standing there. And he walked by to the corner and offered the flag to a man standing there. . . . And he came back toward me and caught me by the collar and said, "You son of a bitch."[47]

Did these attacks and others deter Witnesses from proselytizing? Apparently not. If anything, the attacks and threats seemed to invigorate them. A yearbook from the period says this:

> Daily suffering cruel persecution at the hands of religious fanatics, Jehovah's Witnesses are not in the least bit discouraged or dismayed. On they joyfully go performing their God-given commission. They know that the persecution which they suffer is indisputable proof that they are the children of God and that nothing can befall them except by the permission of Almighty God and that all things shall work together for the ultimate good of them because they love God and are called according to his purpose.[48]

At the same time that the attacks did not discourage Witnesses from continuing to proselytize, the attacks did not encourage local law enforcement to deter as many of them as one might have hoped. Some officers did not help at all. When a reporter asked one sheriff why he didn't stop an attack, he answered, "They're traitors—the Supreme Court says so. Ain't you heard?"[49]

From the outset, *Gobitis* was not a popular decision in the press or the legal academy. One hundred and seventy newspapers editorialized against it, and few favored it.[50] *The New Republic* and the ACLU criticized the decision fiercely, a noteworthy development because Frankfurter, the author of *Gobitis*, had helped to found both organizations.[51] How, they thought, could one of their own, one of the great civil libertarians of the day, the defender of Sacco and Vanzetti, write such a decision?

The director of the ACLU, Roger Baldwin, wrote a letter to Joseph Rutherford, the Witnesses' leader, promising to help limit or over-rule the decision, noting his "shock" that the Court had swept "aside the traditional right of religious conscience in favor of a compulsory conformity to a patriotic ritual."[52] "The language" of the decision, he added, "reflects something of the intolerant temper of the moment."[53]

The New Republic was harder on the Court. It observed that the "country is now in the grip of war hysteria," creating the risk "of adopting Hitler's philosophy in the effort to oppose Hitler's legions."[54] The magazine even compared the decision to one by a German court punishing Witnesses who refused to honor the Nazi salute, saying it was "sure that the majority members of our Court who concurred in the Frankfurter decision would be embarrassed to know that their attitude was in substance the same as that of the German tribunal."[55] Ouch.

Barnette

That brings us to the second family, the Barnett family, whose name ends with a *t*, not an *e*.[56] Inspired by the *Gobitis* decision and perhaps by the bombing of Pearl Harbor one month earlier, the West Virginia Board of Education in January 1942 required all teachers and students in all West Virginia schools to participate in flag-salute ceremonies.[57] "[R]efusal to salute the Flag," the state board said, would "be regarded as an Act of insubordination, and shall be dealt with accordingly."[58] The "accordingly" was expulsion with readmission permitted only after the student agreed to salute the flag.[59] In the interim, the student would be treated as "unlawfully absent" and a delinquent, permitting the State to prosecute, if not persecute, the parents for truancy and to send the children to reformatories for juvenile delinquents.[60] The only way out of this bind was for the affected families to send their children to private schools, a remedy that most could not afford.[61]

In 1942, the same year that the West Virginia Board of Education passed its compulsory flag-salute requirement, Congress for the first time adopted a federal flag code, distinct from the law with respect to the pledge of allegiance.[62] Before 1942, various patriotic organizations, such as the American Legion, had published codes about how to handle the American flag. Notably, this initial federal legislation, enacted in June 1942, was a collection of recommendations, not mandates accompanied by sanctions.[63] The law from the outset did not require hand gestures of any kind:

> That the pledge of allegiance to the flag, "I pledge allegiance to the flag of the United States of America and to the Republic for which it stands, one Nation indivisible, with liberty and justice for all[,]" be rendered by standing with the right hand over the heart; extending the right hand, palm upward, toward the flag at the words "to the flag" and holding this position until the end, when the hand drops to the side. However, civilians will always show full respect to the flag when the pledge is given by merely standing at attention, men removing the headdress. Persons in uniform shall render the military salute.[64]

The one sentence—"civilians will always show full respect to the flag when the pledge is given by merely standing at attention"—appeared to accommodate Witnesses who did not object to standing during the pledge.[65] After Congress passed this law, the Department of Justice sent messages to local school districts drawing their attention to this part of the law.[66] The ACLU did the same.[67] Later that year, in December 1942, Congress removed the raised-hand salute component of the ceremony due to the parallel between it and the Nazi salute, recommending that the pledge "be rendered by standing with the right hand over the heart."[68] Yet many school districts continued to require salutes anyway.[69]

Marie and Gathie Barnett, aged 9 and 11, attended Slip Hill Grade School, an elementary school outside Charleston, West Virginia.[70] The school was not big. Just twenty to twenty-five students attended it. And the school was not wealthy. It could afford only a picture of a flag, not the real thing.[71] In the spring of 1942, the principal of the school stopped Marie and Gathie, and asked them whether they would recite the pledge and salute the flag that day.[72] Answering "no," they explained that "pledging allegiance to a flag was an act of worship, and we could not worship anyone or anything but our God Jehovah."[73] The principal sent them home.[74]

Led by Hayden Covington, the same lawyer who worked on the *Gobitis* case, the Barnetts sought an injunction in federal court against enforcement of the law, and a three-judge court was formed to hear the case. Notwithstanding the 8–1 *Gobitis* decision, the three-judge court *granted* the injunction in favor of the parents in a 3–0 decision.[75] And notwithstanding the *Gobitis* decision, the West Virginia Board of Education did not ask for a stay pending its appeal to the U.S. Supreme Court.[76] Marie and Gathie Barnett returned to school.[77]

Later that school year, the Supreme Court returned to its senses. On June 14, 1943—Flag Day, as it happened—the Court held that compelled flag salutes could not be reconciled with the free speech requirements of the First Amendment.[78] The 6–3 majority opinion was authored by one of the Court's new appointees, Robert Jackson. Jackson is the last individual appointed to the U.S. Supreme Court who did not graduate from law school.[79] He attended Albany Law School for a year and never attended college.[80] In spite of all this (or, horror of horrors, because of it), his *Barnette* opinion is a gem. It explains how compelled speech cannot be reconciled with "free" speech.[81] And it contains one of the most memorable lines in American constitutional history: "If there is any fixed star in our constitutional constellation, it is that no official, high or petty, can prescribe what shall be orthodox in politics, nationalism, religion, or other matters of opinion or force citizens to confess by word or act their faith therein."[82]

Justice Frankfurter was not happy. Instead of making a tactical retreat from *Gobitis*, he dug in, using a form of confession and avoidance. He confessed to agreeing with the underlying policy of the majority opinion—that it is not the government's job to coerce faith in the country. But he avoided the conclusion that might flow from that premise by reminding the majority of the progressives' critique of conservative jurists over the last thirty-plus years—that they had no business importing their preferred policies into the Constitution. The first five sentences of his opinion capture the point, invoking the familiarity of members of his own faith (Judaism) with religious persecution:

> One who belongs to the most vilified and persecuted minority in history is not likely to be insensible to the freedoms guaranteed by our Constitution. Were my purely personal attitude relevant I should wholeheartedly associate myself with the general libertarian views in the Court's opinion, representing as they do the thought and action of a lifetime. But as judges we are neither Jew nor Gentile, neither Catholic nor agnostic. We owe equal attachment to the Constitution and are equally bound by our judicial obligations whether we derive our citizenship from the earliest or the latest immigrants to these shores. As a member of this Court I am not justified in writing my private notions of policy into the Constitution, no matter how deeply I may cherish them or how mischievous I may deem their disregard.[83]

The Path from *Gobitis* to *Barnette*

The path from *Gobitis* to *Barnette* is a story in itself. The speed with which the Court changed its mind between the two decisions is startling and unprecedented. What starts as an 8–1 ruling against the First Amendment claim in *Gobitis* becomes a 6–3 ruling in favor of it in *Barnette*. That is a shift of five votes in just three years, almost two lost votes per year. No issue of federal constitutional law to my knowledge has seen a greater shift of votes in a shorter period of time.[84]

The shift comes so fast that it is tempting, almost three-quarters of a century later, to make light of the *Gobitis* majority, to wonder indeed what it was thinking. How could the Court think that, in the midst of an epic struggle against fascism, it was a good idea to expel twelve-year-old children from school when their only offense was a choice to stand respectfully and silently as the pledge was recited? The only thing more head snapping would be a law compelling salutes to the First Amendment before civics class.

At the time, however, *any* First Amendment claim against a State was a relative novelty, as the Free Exercise Clause had been incorporated against the States through the Fourteenth Amendment just fourteen *days* before *Gobitis* and the Free Speech Clause just fifteen years before that.[85] At the time, Justice Frankfurter was perceived as a leading, if not the leading, progressive thinker on constitutional law, and his vote was consistent with years of advocacy *against* using the U.S. Constitution and the federal courts as a means of trumping the winners of the policy debates of the day.[86] In 1940, with Chief Justice Hughes, the leading conservative, aligned against the claim, and Justice Frankfurter, the leading liberal, aligned against the claim, the Gobitas family faced what appeared to be a long and steep climb.

The war also may explain things. Remember that *Gobitis* was handed down just months after the fall of France in World War II, perhaps unduly sensitizing the Court to the need for the kind of patriotism that likely would be required before long to sustain American's entry into the war.[87] Within the Court, Frankfurter's opinion was called the "Fall of France" opinion.[88] In a letter to Justice Stone on May 27, 1940, Frankfurter suggested that the war affected his position.[89] Wartime circumstances, Frankfurter wrote, required the Court to make the delicate "adjustment between legislatively allowable pursuit of national security and the right to stand on individual idiosyncrasies."[90] The letter echoes Justice Holmes, one of Frankfurter's heroes. In rejecting a First Amendment challenge to criminal convictions of socialists who discouraged Americans from entering the draft during World War I, Justice Holmes wrote for the Court: "When a nation is at war many things that might be said in time of peace are such a hindrance to its effort that their utterance will not be endured so long as men fight and that no Court could regard them as protected by any constitutional right."[91]

Just as the war may explain the thinking of the *Gobitis* majority, however, it may do the same for the *Barnette* majority. How, Jackson thought, could the country use the fight against fascism as a basis for compelling unwilling children to pledge allegiance to the flag?[92] It is sometimes said that the law sleeps during war. If the law slept through *Gobitis*, it woke up in time for *Barnette*.

Also explaining the rapid switch in votes were the public criticism of *Gobitis* and the impact of the decision on Witness persecutions. The *Barnette* story proves that flawed judicial restraint is occasionally just as dangerous as flawed judicial activism. If forced to generalize, I would propose that, in a close federal constitutional case, one in which the language and history of the provision do not answer the question, the National Court should err on the side of deference to the elected branches, on the side of judicial restraint. More often than not, the Court poses a greater risk to the country by invalidating laws than by letting the political processes oversee them. And the American people are more likely to accept the resolution of difficult social and economic issues when they have a say in the matter.

While democracy is flexible, judicial review at the federal level is not. While democracy is designed to adjust to new circumstances, judicial review generally is not. And while all legislative and judicial decisions will have unintended (and unknown) consequences, the elected branches are far better equipped to respond to them than life-tenured judges. In close cases unanswered by text or precedent, it thus makes sense for courts to err on the side of democracy, to allow the elected branches of government to monitor, adjust to, and ultimately to solve difficult social and economic problems.

Yet *Gobitis* illustrates the risk of generalization. The decision took a bad situation (needless persecution of Jehovah's Witnesses) and made it worse through inaction (by prompting greater violence against Witnesses). As Hayden Covington, the Barnetts' lawyer, pointed out during the *Barnette* oral argument, with only some hyperbole, *Gobitis* facilitated a "civil war against the Jehovah's Witnesses."[93] Judges, like doctors, should first be mindful that they do no harm, that they do not make a bad situation worse. The Court did not heed this lesson in *Gobitis*, which is surely one of the reasons the Court overruled it as quickly as it did. Every now and then, there can be real harm in inaction, something that *Plessy*[94] demonstrated before *Gobitis* and that *Korematsu*[95] reaffirmed after it.

The turnabout from *Gobitis* to *Barnette*, somewhat paradoxically, occurred *after* President Roosevelt had remade the Court with

Democratic appointees. By 1943, none of the Four Horsemen, the four conservatives on the Court—Justices Van Devanter, Sutherland, Butler, McReynolds—remained. They had either "hung up their spurs" or had left for the "Great Ranch in the sky."[96] Just two appointees put on the Court before Roosevelt's presidency remained, and both were relatively congenial to Roosevelt's policies.[97] Chief Justice Stone was not appointed to the Court by Roosevelt, but Roosevelt elevated him to the Chief Justiceship.[98] And Justice Roberts had voted several times to uphold New Deal programs, casting (some say) the fabled switch-in-time vote that preserved nine.[99]

With this set of seemingly like-minded justices, one might have expected a unified Supreme Court. It did not turn out that way. They remained unified, it is true, in permitting virtually unlimited exercises of the Commerce Clause Power by Congress,[100] and in agreeing that the Court should not second-guess state and federal economic regulations.[101] But when it came to civil liberties, unanimity disappeared.

A little history helps to explain why. Strange though it may sound to modern ears, the first promoters of frequent and aggressive judicial review were conservatives. In the first four decades of the twentieth century, a conservative-dominated Supreme Court invoked liberty of contract, the impairment of contract, and the limits on congressional power to invalidate roughly 290 state and local laws and fifty federal laws.[102]

The progressives responded to these decisions with growing skepticism about the utility and legitimacy of judicial review. The leading judicial progressives of the day—Holmes, Hand, Brandeis, Frankfurter—all decried what they perceived as an activist Court.[103]

Once Roosevelt had remade the Court with New Dealers like Black and Douglas and progressives like Frankfurter, the question arose as to which way the new Court would go. Should they stand by the Holmesian view of judicial restraint? Or should they treat judicial review differently, depending on the type of constitutional guarantee at issue?

In 1938, with footnote 4 of *Carolene Products*,[104] then-Justice Stone, the author of the solo dissent in *Gobitis*, proposed a way to retain a progressive critique of conservative judicial activism but permit some liberal judicial activism—by distinguishing between economic rights on the one hand and civil liberties on the other.[105] In addition to Stone, many of the Roosevelt appointees—Black, Douglas, Murphy, Rutledge—embraced this approach. Frankfurter was an exception, and so usually was Justice Jackson. Noah Feldman captured the point well in *Scorpions*: "As the other liberals on the Court shifted ground, Frankfurter—to his astonishment—found himself transformed into a conservative. Frankfurter's critics, then and later, have tried to explain how it could be that the country's best-known liberal became its leading judicial conservative. But the source of the change was not Frankfurter, whose constitutional philosophy remained remarkably consistent throughout his career. It was the rest of liberalism that abandoned him and moved on once judicial restraint was no longer a useful tool to advance liberal objectives."[106] *Gobitis* is the seed, *Barnette* the first fruit, of that division.

To this day, a struggle lingers over what a progressive or liberal jurisprudence should look like. Judicial conservatives face a similar dilemma. Many of today's conservative justices came of age and defined themselves in opposition to what they perceived as an unrestrained Warren Court. Now they must decide what their theory of judicial review is and what it should be. The same is true for today's judicial liberals. Through all of this, Judge Frank Easterbrook reminds us that even a Court filled with nine like-minded individuals, indeed nine clones, eventually will splinter, whether along lines currently known or yet to be imagined.[107] The Stone Court is exhibit A in proving his point, and the *Barnette* story illustrates it.

A discerning reader might wonder why Chief Justice Stone assigned the *Barnette* opinion to Justice Jackson. Stone wrote the solo dissent in *Gobitis*. Jackson was a newcomer to the Court. And of course Stone was the Chief Justice, the first among equals on the Court and the first among nonequals when it comes to opinion assignments. I do not know the answer, but I have a few suspicions.

Justice Jackson was the weakest link in the majority. As time would show, Jackson's inclinations about judicial review were closer to Frankfurter's than to Stone's.[108] No less important, the majority faced a doctrinal dispute that lingers with us to this day. Was *Barnette* (and cases like it) a case about religious liberties or a case about free speech? To Stone and the others, *Barnette* was a case about the free exercise of religion.[109] Yet to Jackson, *Barnette* was a case about compelled speech.[110] Jackson, it seems to me, could not get over two realities: (1) the Free Exercise Clause had only recently—just two weeks earlier—been made applicable to the States through the Fourteenth Amendment; and (2) Jackson found it difficult to understand why *anyone* should be required to salute the flag, whether over faith-based objections or not.[111] If the *Barnette* principle applied to spiritual *and* secular objections to the pledge, it must be a free speech case. To this day, the Supreme Court struggles with whether to review general laws that restrict speech and faith, such as the pledge requirement, under the Free Exercise Clause or the Free Speech Clause.[112]

Because Jackson premised *Barnette* on free speech grounds, the Court has continued to invoke *Gobitis* in free exercise cases. In perhaps the most important free exercise case since then, the Court invoked *Gobitis* in rejecting a challenge to a neutral, generally applicable law that allegedly infringed religious liberties:

> We have never held that an individual's religious beliefs excuse him from compliance with an otherwise valid law prohibiting conduct that the State is free to regulate. On the contrary, the record of more than a century of our free exercise jurisprudence contradicts that proposition. As described succinctly by Justice Frankfurter in *Minersville School Dist. Bd. of Ed. v. Gobitis*, 310 U.S. 586, 594–95 (1940): "Conscientious scruples have not, in the course of the long struggle for religious toleration, relieved the individual from obedience to a general law not aimed at the promotion or restriction of religious beliefs. The mere possession of religious convictions which contradict the relevant concerns of a political society does not relieve the citizen from the discharge of political responsibilities."[113]

In the eyes of today's Court, *Barnette* is a free speech case.

Justice Frankfurter and Judicial Review

For most, the path from *Gobitis* to *Barnette* is a story about Justice Jackson's triumph and the lively and vivid way in which he penned this classic rights-protective decision and Justice Frankfurter's loss and

the pained and personal way in which he expressed his disappointment at the unwillingness of his colleagues to exercise judicial restraint.
The winners indeed write the history. What of the possibility, rarely
taken up these days, that Frankfurter was right in *Gobitis*? The defense
requires advocacy skills I do not possess. But a few points complicate
the picture.

Start with the possibility that democracy, if given a little more time,
might have solved the problem. The Justice Department, it is true, was
not helpful in responding to the widespread vigilantism prompted by
Gobitis.[114] But Congress did respond. Between *Gobitis* and *Barnette*,
Congress passed a law, quoted above, that established that standing
silently at attention during the flag salute is all that local governments
could ask of their citizens.[115] The law was designed to soften local
practices, and it was a law the Witnesses were willing to live with.[116] In
Barnette, the Court mentioned the law and had a chance to rely on it.[117]
But the Court did not.

In civil liberties debates, it sometimes is worth asking this
question: Would citizens rather live in a country in which a majority
of a nine-member Supreme Court protects the rights of dissenters or a
country in which a majority of its citizens do so? To be concrete, what
is more important to the protection of racial and religious minorities
in this country: Court decisions such as *Brown*[118] or legislation such as
the 1964 Civil Rights Act?[119] There is something to Frankfurter's insight
that civil liberties are best protected when they become part of our
political culture and part of what we Americans do for each other, not
part of what the Court does for us.[120] Every time the Court protects us
from our own mistakes, we cheapen self-government and undermine
its capacity to steel us against the next ill-conceived policy urge of the
moment.

Frankfurter's views had deep roots. Fourteen years before he joined
the Court, Frankfurter wrote an unsigned editorial in 1925 for *The New
Republic* about the role of the Supreme Court in advancing liberal
policies. The title of the editorial hints at his point: "Can the Supreme
Court Guarantee Toleration?"[121] The contents of the editorial confirm
his answer. He offers two perspectives, one favorable, one not, on the
Court's decision in *Pierce v. Society of Sisters*, 268 U.S. 510 (1925), which
invalidated an Oregon law that mandated attendance at public schools.

From one vantage point, the decision "gives just cause for rejoicing. The Supreme Court did immediate service on behalf of the essential spirit of liberalism."[122]

But from another vantage point, his vantage point, the case "raises a new consideration of the Supreme Court's function in the American political scheme. It calls for a more rigorous appraisal of the actual encouragement to liberalism afforded by judicial nullification of anti-liberal legislation,"[123] for a "full accounting of the gains and losses to our national life due to the Supreme Court's control of legislation by the States."[124] "In rejoicing" over the *Pierce* decision, he warns, "we must not forget that a heavy price has to be paid for these occasional services to liberalism," namely, Supreme Court decisions that lock in place a more conservative perspective on the meaning of "due process."[125] Those "vague words" ultimately "hold the power of life and death over State action." And they "mean what the shifting personnel of the United States Supreme Court from time to time makes them mean," which leads to the reality that "[t]he inclination of a single Justice, the tip of his mind—or his fears—determines the opportunity" for two distinct possibilities: the death "of a much-needed social experiment" or the perceived death "of intolerance."[126] The "real battles of liberalism are not won in the Supreme Court."[127] "Only a persistent, positive translation of the liberal faith into the thoughts and acts of the community," he ends, "is the real reliance against the unabated temptation to straightjacket the human mind."[128]

No one can fairly doubt that Frankfurter's opinions in *Gobitis* and *Barnette* went against his policy preferences. Before joining the Court, he had devoted his career to protecting civil liberties.[129] Yet, as he appreciated, no judicial philosophy is worth its salt if it does not sting from time to time, if it does not force the judge to rule against the cause he would prefer to side with. Frankfurter may have been wrong in *Gobitis*, but he was right to bury his policy preferences. We do not have a judiciary filled with blue-robed judges and red-robed judges, and Frankfurter was surely correct to resist any suggestion to the contrary and indeed to devote a professional lifetime to proving it need not be so. In a world in which the public too often sees good policy and constitutional rights as one and the same, that calling is not an easy one. For Frankfurter, it meant receiving praise he did not want in *Gobitis* (for upholding patriotic ceremonies) and criticism he did not deserve in *Barnette* (for being insensitive to the plight of Witnesses).

Consistency is a virtue, not a vice, when it comes to judicial philosophy. Having spent his formative years as a lawyer and a professor writing about and criticizing conservative justices for imposing their economic and political views on the country, he was not about to do the same for a Court suddenly dominated by liberals. He was rightly skeptical of the idea that constitutional rights could be fairly divided into economic and liberty rights, and indeed there is some support for this point in the modern era. Is it really true, for instance, that the Supreme Court's *Kelo*[130] decision—permitting the use of eminent domain over a middle-class family's home solely for the purpose of economic development by a large corporation—is a case about property rights as opposed to liberty rights? A case about money or about freedom? To most eyes, and assuredly the eyes of Susette Kelo, that was a case about liberty and freedom. One may fairly disagree, indeed quite fairly disagree, with Frankfurter's application of this philosophy in *Gobitis*, but it is hard to criticize his attempt at principled consistency on the appropriate role of judicial review in American government.

Frankfurter's judicial career calls to mind the story, likely apocryphal, of the young lawyer who worked for an elected official. The lawyer asked his boss how he handled matters that involved patrons who had helped support him along the way, whether with financial contributions, promotions, introductions, or other forms of support. The answer was straightforward: "I must follow the law where it takes me, whether it takes me in the direction of my political friends or not." It came with one caveat: "Of course, if it is a 50-50 call, I will side with my friends." That sounded reasonable enough, the young lawyer thought at the time. But after looking back on several years of service with the elected official, the young lawyer noticed a lot of fifty-fifty calls. Say what you will about Justice Frankfurter, whether about his opinions in *Gobitis* and *Barnette* or about his tenure on the Court, he did not rationalize himself into making a lot of fifty-fifty calls. No political party or interest group kept a halter on Frankfurter once he joined the Court.

Frankfurter nonetheless erred in *Gobitis* and should have admitted as much in *Barnette*. Not even James Bradley Thayer and Holmes, the two people most responsible for shaping Frankfurter's thinking, thought judicial review had no role to play.[131] They thought instead that the same restrained theory of judicial review applies to *all* provisions in the text of the Constitution.[132] All rights. All structure. Frankfurter never took the position that there was no role for judicial enforcement of civil liberties. He embraced the Holmes and Brandeis dissent in *Abrams v. United States* (1919),[133] in which the majority upheld criminal convictions for distributing antiwar literature. He joined *Brown v. Board of Education*.[134] And he later joined, and wrote, many other such decisions as a justice.

Judges are not known for admitting their mistakes, and perhaps that is a tradition that should change. In any given year, I sit on roughly ten to twenty cases that reverse decisions of district court judges. Is it not possible that appellate judges and justices on the state and federal courts have similar rates of error? It of course helps that we sit in groups (often three, seven, or nine), a form of decision-making that diminishes the risk of error. But it does not eliminate that risk.

As one Justice of the U.S. Supreme Court aptly put the point: "Wisdom too often never comes, and so one ought not to reject it merely because it comes late." The appellate courts might be well served to follow that advice. The source of this advice was Frankfurter himself.[135]

But even if Frankfurter did not learn the right lesson from *Gobitis* by the time of *Barnette*, he did not, to his credit, remain rigidly opposed to judicial review thereafter. Wisdom may indeed have come late for Frankfurter, but it did come. One wonders what would have become of Frankfurter's legacy if the insight had come earlier—if he had been the first member of the Court to realize the misstep in *Gobitis*, if he had written the *Barnette* majority, if he had used the opinion to explain how and why judicial restraint need not mean judicial abdication, and if he had begun *that* opinion by talking about the law's and wisdom's delays.

So ends one chapter of the flag-salute story.

The State Story before *Gobitis*

So begins another. Just as the federal courts wrestled with the validity of state-compelled flag salutes, bookended by the *Gobitis* and *Barnette*

decisions, so did the state courts, sometimes under federal law, sometimes under state law. In a system of dual sovereigns, it should startle no
one that the cascade of intimidation and violence aimed at Witnesses
led to state court challenges under the federal and state constitutions.[136]
The results in the state courts, like the results in the federal courts, were
mixed from the perspective of the Witnesses. Not unlike the federal
story, some early state supreme court decisions set damaging precedents
for the Witnesses' claims. In the years between *Gobitis* and *Barnette*,
however, the state courts began to provide relief to Witnesses. In some
cases the relief was complete, as when courts interpreted their state
constitutions to protect Witness students' right to refuse the flag salute.
The U.S. Supreme Court, as shown, has no power to review state court
decisions that turn on state law. In other cases, state courts avoided the
constitutional question or allowed *Gobitis* to control it, choosing to resolve the cases on other grounds.

Before turning to the state cases, it's worth pausing over one twist. If
the source of the pledge and if the rules about how to respect the flag
during the pledge arose from federal statutes, how was there any possibility that the state constitutions (or for that matter any state law) could
protect steadfast Witnesses? Wouldn't the Supremacy Clause of the U.S.
Constitution, which prioritizes federal law over state law in any conflict
between the two, have required the school boards to follow the federal
laws? Yes and no. Yes, the Supremacy Clause would have required local
school boards to follow any such federal law (assuming Congress had
the power to enact the law) if a conflict arose between the state and
federal law. But, no, there was no conflict. The federal laws were not
mandatory and did not impose any sanctions for noncompliance.

It was the state and local school boards that took these statutes (and
practices recommended by the American Legion) and made them mandatory on pain of expulsion for noncompliance. And it was the state
and local school boards that kept the raised-hand and pledged-heart
components of the ceremony even after Congress said that "civilians
will always show full respect to the flag when the pledge is given merely
by standing at attention." In retrospect, the flag-salute story shows local
governments giving too much respect to one component of federal law
(the pledge and flag statutes), too little respect to another (the First
Amendment), and too slow an appreciation of their own authority over

the matter (the free speech and free exercise guarantees in their own constitutions).

The state cases follow a general pattern: an unwillingness to take the claims of Witnesses seriously (whether under the federal or state constitutions) before *Gobitis* and a willingness to treat them quite seriously after *Gobitis*, even after the U.S. Supreme Court gave state courts the go-ahead to reject such claims under the Federal Constitution. Before 1940, the year *Gobitis* was decided, several state courts failed to come to grips with the nature of the Witnesses' constitutional theories.

One of the first cases, *Hering v. State Board of Education*, decided in February 1937, involved the expulsion of two children, 5 and 7 years old, who refused to salute the flag. The Supreme Court of New Jersey rejected the idea that the expulsion violated the constitutional and statutory guarantees of "free schools for all the people."[137] It then reached, and rejected, the focal point of their claim, holding that "[t]he performance of the [flag salute] could, in no sense, interfere with religious freedom."[138] The Court's one-paragraph analysis gives a sense of how off the wall these claims seemed to the courts, at first. "It is little enough," the Court said, "to expect of those who seek the benefits of the education offered in the public schools of this state that they pledge their allegiance to the nation and the nation's flag. The pledge of allegiance is, by no stretch of the imagination, a religious rite. It is a patriotic ceremony which the Legislature has the power to require of those attending schools established at public expense."[139] The Court ended the opinion by observing that there is no requirement that children attend public schools, only that they attend some school: "A child of school age is not required to attend the institutions maintained by the public, but is required to attend a suitable school. Those who do not desire to conform with the commands of the statute can seek their schooling elsewhere."[140] Missing from the Court's decision is any appreciation of the difficulty this approach might pose. Not everyone can afford private schools. If the local community pool did not permit Jehovah's Witnesses (or some other religious or racial group), could a claim of discrimination be rejected on the ground that the victims could join a private country club? To ask is to answer.

Of a piece with this ruling is one by the Supreme Judicial Court of Massachusetts two months later. In 1935, the same year Joseph

Rutherford first urged Witnesses not to salute the flag, an eight-year-old student in the Lynn public schools resisted the "[c]ourteous requests," as the court put it, of the teacher and principal that he participate in the flag ceremony.[141] The Court did not doubt the State's authority to require such a ceremony, seeing it as "clearly designed to inculcate patriotism and to instill a recognition of the blessings conferred by orderly government under the Constitutions of the State and nation."[142] Nor did it see a problem with compelling the ceremony in view of the Massachusetts Constitution's religious freedom guarantees. According to one of those guarantees, "no subject shall be hurt, molested, or restrained, in his person, liberty, or estate, for worshipping God in the manner and season most agreeable to the dictates of his own conscience; or for his religious profession or sentiments; provided he doth not disturb the public peace, or obstruct others in their religious worship."[143] According to the other, a model, by the way, for the federal guarantee: "No law shall be passed prohibiting the free exercise of religion."[144]

Writing for the Court, Chief Justice Rugg rejected the Witnesses' claims on several grounds. Even though "a deep reverence for religion permeates" the Massachusetts Constitution and even though the parents' and child's "statement of beliefs" are "assumed" to be "genuine and true," he concluded that "[t]he flag salute and pledge of allegiance here in question do not in any just sense relate to religion."[145] They are instead "wholly patriotic in design and purpose," "an acknowledgment of sovereignty, a promise of obedience, a recognition of authority above the will of the individual," something that "has nothing to do with religion."[146] The salute and pledge, the Court continued, "do not go beyond that which . . . is due to government" and "exact nothing in opposition to religion."[147] It then invoked two National Supreme Court decisions in support: *Reynolds v. United States*, an 1878 decision that upheld antipolygamy laws in the face of a federal free exercise challenge and reasoned that "[l]aws are made for the government of actions, and while they cannot interfere with mere religious belief and opinions, they may with practices,"[148] and *Hamilton v. Regents of University of California*, a 1934 decision that upheld a law conditioning enrollment in a state university on taking military training, once more drawing a distinction between laws that govern belief and action.[149]

In the next two years, supreme courts in three more States—Georgia, New York, and Florida—for the most part walked down the same trail, denying state and federal constitutional protection, though in all cases taking the claims more seriously and in one case finding an alternative ground for granting relief to the family.[150] In July 1937, the Georgia Supreme Court dealt with the federal and state claims of a twelve-year-old student from the Atlanta public schools who failed to follow a 1935 law requiring the salute and pledge. Consistent with the earlier cases, the First Amendment came to naught as the free exercise guarantee had yet to be incorporated into the Fourteenth Amendment.[151] The claim under the Georgia Constitution—"All men have the natural and inalienable right to worship God, each according to the dictates of his own conscience, and no human authority should, in any case, control or interfere with such right of conscience"—came to a similar end, though only after more elaboration than the earlier decisions.[152] If the greater imposition on free exercise of daily required Bible readings (from the King James Version) and prayer for all did not violate this guarantee, the court reasoned, neither did the pledge and salute.[153] "[T]hose choosing to resort to the educational institutions maintained with the funds of the state," the Court explained, "are subject to the commands of the state."[154] Here, too, the Court did not think that the pledge and salute amounted to "a religious rite."[155]

Almost two years later, little seemed to have changed. In January 1939, the Court of Appeals of New York rejected similar claims. Of note, the Witnesses were represented by Arthur Garfield Hays, the one-time general counsel of the ACLU who participated in the Scopes, Sacco and Vanzetti, and Scottsboro cases. Joseph Rutherford also filed an amicus brief in the case. This able team scored a victory of sorts and prompted a concurrence by Judge Lehman that belongs in the orbit of Justice Jackson's *Barnette* opinion. Grace Sandstrom, 13 years old and a "recalcitrant scholar," refused to salute the flag, and the State punished her parents for keeping her from attending public school.[156] At the hearing, the State asked Grace: "What do you think would happen to you if you salute the flag contrary to your conscience?" Her answer was stark: "When the battle of Armageddon comes, I would be slain. Because the flag is an image and it says in the Bible not to bow down to images."[157] The family claimed that the mandatory pledge violated the New York Constitution's religious freedom guarantee:

> The free exercise and enjoyment of religious profession and worship, without discrimination or preference, shall forever be allowed in this State to all mankind; and no person shall be rendered incompetent to be a witness on account of his opinions on matters of religious belief; but the liberty of conscience hereby secured shall not be so construed as to excuse acts of licentiousness, or justify practices inconsistent with the peace or safety of this State.[158]

The Court determined at the outset that the educational authorities had punished the wrong people: the parents. "The procedure" in this setting "has always been to expel the student, not to punish the parents unless they in some way have disobeyed the law."[159] Rather than leaving it at that and rather than leaving the impression that the Court thought "that this young girl [should] be summarily dealt with," the Court proceeded "to consider the case a step further," what became a several-page assessment of the constitutional issues and what to do about them.[160]

Picking up on the theme of earlier courts, Chief Judge Crane explained that "[s]aluting the flag in no sense is an act of worship. . . . The flag has nothing to do with religion, and in all the history of this country it has stood for just the contrary, namely, the principle that people may worship as they please or need not worship at all."[161] He then went further, developing the patriotism/prospect-of-war theme that Frankfurter would feature in *Gobitis*. "The State," he wrote, "cannot reasonably be required to defer the adoption of measures for its own peace and safety until revolutionary utterance and acts lead to actual disturbance of the public peace or imminent and immediate danger of its own destruction; but it may, in the exercise of its judgment, seek to prevent evil in its incipiency."[162] No doubt sensitive to the possibility of war, he wrote that "[t]here is another strength which is necessary to preserve the government besides military force, and that is the moral strength, or public opinion of its citizens. Public opinion is as vital to the maintenance of good government as an army or a navy; in fact these latter can be destroyed [more] quick[ly] by public opinion than by the attacks of an enemy. . . . The State, therefore, is justified in taking such measures as will engender and maintain patriotism in the young."[163]

But, the Court pivoted, "[t]hese are ponderous truths to flash upon this little girl who in all conscientiousness cannot, at her time of life, grasp them," prompting it to "re-examine this statute which the Legislature has adopted."[164] "Surely," the Court continued, "it was never intended to force patriotism upon children by a militaristic order. It seeks to teach, to enlighten, to reveal, to lead the mind, to understand and appreciate what our government really is and what the flag stands for."[165] "The emphasis . . . must be placed more upon instruction than mere blind obedience. . . . [S]aluting a flag, even an American flag, is of little vital force to the nation unless behind it there is a love and reverence for the things it represents."[166]

All of this became the windup for an unexpected pitch. At the same time the Court acknowledged that the pledge and salute did not violate "any rights preserved by the [state or federal] Constitution," it queried, "May there not be . . . a better way for accomplishing the purposes of this law than immediate resort to disciplinary measures?"[167] "Faith in our fine educational system and its corps of efficient teachers leads one to believe that with a little more patience and some tact, as the child grows in knowledge a reverence for our flag will develop, and she will be glad that it is still here to salute."[168] After all, it concluded, this provision of New York statutory law has "been upon the statute books since 1898," and "[t]his is the first time that any trouble has arisen regarding its enforcement."[169]

This was not the approach of a purist. Chief Judge Crane started out on a theme of constitutional avoidance—that the State punished the wrong people—and could have reversed the conviction then and there. But instead of *avoiding* the constitutional issue, he proceeded to offer a detailed analysis about the validity of flag salutes. He then suggested a way to avoid the burdens on Jehovah's Witnesses that would arise from upholding the pledge and salute, namely that the schools use "tact" and "patience" to find a way to avoid "forc[ing] patriotism upon children by a militaristic order." In what might be described as constitutional-avoidance avoidance, the Chief Judge suggested a form of tact and wisdom that offered a way to respect patriotism *and* liberty.

Judge Lehman concurred in the result but could not agree "that the defendants' daughter may, on pain of expulsion, be compelled to salute the flag though such salute be contrary to her religious convictions and her conscience."[170] The New York religious liberty guarantee, he concluded, applies to unabridged beliefs *and* reasonable practices consistent with those beliefs. "It includes the right of the individual to carry out every obligation which *he believes* has a divine sanction, *to practice any religious principle*, and to teach any religious doctrine which does not violate the laws of morality and property, and which does not infringe personal rights."[171] Worthy of full quotation is Judge Lehman's key point:

> Episcopalians and Methodists and Presbyterians and Baptists, Catholics and Jews, may all agree that a salute to the flag cannot be disobedience to the will of the Creator; all the judges of the State may agree that no well-intentioned person could reasonably object to such a salute; but this little child has been taught to believe otherwise. She must choose between obedience to the command of the principal of the school, and obedience to what she has been taught and believes is the command of God. She has chosen to obey what she believes to be the command of God. I cannot assent to the dictum of the prevailing opinion that she must obey the command of the principal, though trembling lest she incur the religious wrath of her Maker and be slain "when the battle of Armageddon comes."[172]

"The Legislature," he continued, "cannot authorize the school authorities to give an order which outrages the religious conscience of a child at least unless such order does in reasonable degree tend to promote the general health or welfare or is required for the orderly conduct of the school."[173] The salute may well be "an aid in teaching good citizenship—but surely not where a little child is compelled in fear and trembling to join in an act which her conscience tells her is wrong." And none of this hurts anybody: "She does not insist upon doing an act which might harm herself or others; she does not refuse to do an act which might promote the peace, safety, strength or welfare of her country."[174] Nor would the flag salute lose any "dignity or worth if she were permitted to refrain from joining in it. On the contrary, that would be an impressive lesson for her and the other children that the flag stands for absolute freedom of conscience except where freedom of conscience is asserted to justify practices inconsistent with the peace or safety of this State."[175] Concluding: "The salute of the flag is a gesture of love and respect—fine when there is real love and respect back of the gesture. The flag is dishonored by a salute by a child in reluctant and terrified obedience to a command of secular authority which clashes with the dictates of conscience. The flag 'cherished by all our hearts' should not be soiled by the tears of a little child. The Constitution does not permit, and the Legislature never intended, that the flag should be so soiled and dishonored."[176] As a case that did not require any judge on the New York Court of Appeals to reach the constitutional issues, *Sandstrom* generated two thoughtful opinions, which ably set the stage for *Gobitis* and *Barnette*.

Although most state court judges rejected this first wave of constitutional objections to compulsory salutes, not all did. In 1937, a nine-year-old girl, Charlotte Gabrielli, refused to salute the flag and disobeyed orders of the local school board along the way.[177] The school expelled her, after which she filed (with her father's help) a writ of mandamus to be readmitted. The trial judge in the Superior Court of Sacramento, Judge Peter J. Shields, granted the writ, critiquing the prevailing view that the flag salute was not a religious rite and thus could not curtail religious liberty: "[W]e are not to be the judges of the reasonableness of another's religious belief nor the merits of his conscientious convictions."[178] Although the yet-to-be-incorporated federal guarantees did not apply, Judge Shields decided that the California Constitution offered protection through its guarantee of "the free exercise and enjoyment of religious profession and worship."[179] In affirming, the Third District Court of Appeals avoided the constitutional issues and held the school board's decision unreasonable and arbitrary.[180]

Before the *Gabrielli* case reached the California Supreme Court, the U.S. Supreme Court dismissed two appeals of state flag-salute cases, *Leoles* and *Hering*, as lacking a substantial federal question.[181] On the strength of these dismissals, the California Supreme Court reversed.[182] Not only did the dismissals foreclose federal constitutional relief for Charlotte, but the Court also held that the California Constitution failed to provide protection. Despite the state constitution's independent "express guaranty of freedom of religion," worded differently from the "Free Exercise" Clause of the U.S. Constitution, and despite the California Supreme Court's independent duty to construe the state guarantee independently, the California Supreme Court deferred to federal law and elected to construe its own Constitution just like the federal model—an early form of lockstepping.[183]

The State Story after *Gobitis*

By 1940, when the U.S. Supreme Court decided *Gobitis*, every state supreme court to hear a flag salute case (and to address the issue) had found compulsory salutes constitutional. *Gobitis* confirmed the trend and resolved any doubts as to whether Witness children expelled from school could look to the Federal Constitution for redress. Yet in the flurry of expulsions that followed *Gobitis*, two state supreme courts and at least one trial court construed their own constitutions to grant protections denied by federal law. Only after the U.S. Supreme Court told the States that they could continue to expel "recalcitrant scholars" did some of their state courts refuse.

The first case, *State v. Smith*, decided on July 11, 1942, illustrates the lengths to which school officials would go in enforcing flag-salute laws.[184] On the first day of the 1941 school year in Lawton, Kansas, Artye Lee Smith, aged 8, and his sister Barbara, aged 9, children of Witnesses, turned up for class with the rest of their schoolmates. When teachers asked the children to participate in a flag salute exercise consistent with the State's "Manual of Patriotic Instruction," the two children refused.[185] Although patriotic exercises had been conducted at the school in previous years without rigorous enforcement and thus without incident, the school board decided that year to crack down on children unwilling to salute the flag. The school board demanded that the school's principal send Artye Lee and Barbara home.

When the parents hired a private tutor for the children, the school board found his out-of-state licensing credentials inadequate. The children attended a school fifteen miles away, until the school board met and required flag salutes at that school as well. The new school, like the old school, sent the children home. After some time, the parents enrolled the children in a school forty miles away, where they had to pay tuition and board. As the Smiths sought a way to educate their children in one location after another, a truant officer filed a lawsuit against the parents for failing to comply with the State's compulsory education law. A jury convicted them, and they appealed to the Kansas Supreme Court, which heard their case along with one brought by a like-treated family, the Griggsbys. Representing both families was Hayden Covington, who would argue *Barnette* at the U.S. Supreme Court nine months later.

Writing for the Court, Justice Harvey said three things about *Gobitis*. He described its holding and reasoning. He observed "without comment as to its effect" (and he might have added "without comment to its lack of effect") that three of the justices who joined *Gobitis* had since recanted their votes in *Jones v. City of Opelika*, 316 U.S. 584 (1942)—a free speech case about licensing fees imposed on Jehovah's Witnesses and others engaged in door-to-door solicitations.[186] And he noted with some effect that no one had thought to use the thirty-four-year-old compulsory education law to expel a student for failing to salute the flag until the U.S. Supreme Court decided *Gobitis*.[187] Even though *Gobitis* did not purport to *require* a flag-salute law, just as *Buck v. Bell* did not purport to require sterilization laws, *Gobitis* too had a catalytic effect in spurring States and local governments to enforce compulsory education and truancy laws in ways others had not enforced them before.

Even so, the Kansas Supreme Court continued, *Gobitis* did not govern the case because it had proceeded on the assumption that the law at issue complied with the Pennsylvania Constitution.[188] The Kansas Supreme Court faced an antecedent question: "whether regulations of the school boards in question are valid under the Constitution and laws of our state."[189]

> When our Constitution became effective, January 29, 1861, there was no federal constitutional provision applicable to the new state respecting the freedom of religious beliefs; hence, the framers of our Constitution wrote into our Bill of Rights (Sec. 7) the following: "The right to worship God according to the dictates of conscience shall never be infringed; nor shall any person be compelled to attend or support any form of worship; nor shall any control of or interference

with the rights of conscience be permitted, nor any preference be given by law to any religious establishment or mode of worship."[190]

This provision, the Court stressed, contains "much more . . . detail respecting religious freedom" than the First Amendment and is " 'more than a mere collection of glittering generalities.' "[191] "At no time in the history of our state," it added, "have the conscientious religious beliefs of people been restrained, prohibited, or penalized by any statute."[192]

The Court avoided a misstep made by many of the state court decisions up to then. Instead of saying that a compelled salute to a flag could not reasonably be construed as a religious act,[193] the Kansas Supreme Court took the Witnesses at their word: "It is enough to know that in fact their beliefs are sincerely religious."[194] "Perhaps," the Court acknowledged, "the tenets of many religious sects or denominations would be called reasonable, or unreasonable, depending upon who is speaking."[195] So long as their "beliefs are sincerely religious" and so long as they "are not of a kind which prevent them from being . . . law-abiding citizens," they must be respected.[196] The Court reversed both convictions, holding that the state statute on which the school districts relied was never intended to compel the expulsion of children under such circumstances, and any law so intending would be struck down by the religious freedom clause of the Kansas Constitution.[197]

The second victory came from the Washington Supreme Court in a case called *Bolling v. Superior Court* on January 29, 1943, a little more than five months before *Barnette*.[198] If the Kansas school board's actions inconvenienced the Smith family, the actions of state officials in Washington were potentially devastating for the four Witness families involved in that case. The Bolling family typified the situation. The school board expelled their three children, all under 16, for refusing to salute the flag, and the parents found no other way to educate them. Local officials filed delinquency charges against the children. The trial judge held a hearing to consider the children's welfare and ordered them removed from their parents' custody and placed in the care of a relative. To stop this state-imposed diaspora of their family, the parents sought relief from the Washington Supreme Court based on federal and state law. The relevant state constitutional guarantee, dating from 1904, says:

Absolute freedom of conscience in all matters of religious sentiment, belief and worship, shall be guaranteed to every individual,
and no one shall be molested or be disturbed in person or property
on account of religion; but the liberty of conscience hereby secured
shall not be so construed as to excuse acts of licentiousness or justify
practices inconsistent with the peace and safety of the state.[199]

Following many of the cairns laid down by *State v. Smith*, the Court
emphasized that its role was not to decide whether the Witnesses' beliefs
about the flag salute were reasonable but to decide whether, given those
beliefs, the State's Constitution demanded that this form of religious
freedom yield to the local policy.[200] Reversing the trial court's decision,
the Court grounded its holding on the value of religious toleration,
"[o]ne of the corner stones of our system of government."[201]

Writing for the Washington High Court, Justice Beals acknowledged
several points of federal law before relying on the state Constitution
to ground his decision. He acknowledged the federal statute enacted
in 1942 that said "civilians will always show full respect to the flag
when the pledge is given by merely standing at attention."[202] "In this
connection," he noted, the parents "state that they and their children honor and respect the flag, and that it accords with their religious views to stand at attention while others repeat the pledge of
allegiance."[203] Justice Beals then mentioned the *Gobitis* decision, on
which the trial court had relied in denying relief. The Justice did not
quote any of Justice Frankfurter's decision but found it "difficult to
refrain from quoting at length from Chief Justice Stone's dissent," so
difficult that he did not stop quoting until four paragraphs later.[204]
He then mentioned *Jones v. Opelika*, in which Justices Murphy, Black,
and Douglas renounced their votes in *Gobitis*.[205] He then mentioned
the three-judge decision in *Barnette*, in which "the questions presented
were exactly similar to those in the *Gobitis* case," and yet in which the
court did "not follow[] that decision."[206] The Court's agreement with
Chief Justice Stone's dissent in *Gobitis* and with Judge Parker's decision
for a three-judge panel in *Barnette* allowed the Court to say that *Gobitis*
"can scarcely be deemed to have become authoritative."[207] But that was
merely a stage-setting device.

"In any event," the Court turned, "it is for this court to construe and apply the portion of our state constitution above quoted."[208] Relying on the Washington Constitution's "guarantee[] to every individual" of "[a]bsolute freedom of conscience in all matters of religious sentiment, belief and worship," Justice Beals made a few essential points in invalidating the state law's flag-salute requirement. "One of the corner stones of our system of government is religious toleration," as the language of the state guarantee suggests.[209] What makes the guarantee more than a Potemkin barrier is judicial enforcement—the "duties of our courts to ever guard and maintain our constitutional guarantees of religious liberty."[210] What raises the risk of judicial dilution is a "supposed emergent situation" or that the claim of religious liberty is "of little consequence" because it "affect[s] only a few persons."[211] Rather than invoke a local history of religious tolerance to buttress his analysis, as state courts often do in independently construing their States' constitutional provisions, Justice Beals went further back in time and farther away in geography. "In the time of the Roman empire," he noted, "it was customary for the people to burn a pinch of incense before a statue of the emperor. The early Christians, while recognizing the sovereignty of the emperor, refused to perform this ceremony, deeming it idolatrous."[212] What was true of early Christians in trying to honor God's and Caesar's domains, he pointed out, may be just as true for others today: "A phrase, or the making of a gesture, which to most people may seem either right or possibly unimportant, may to others appear to be of great significance."[213] For these reasons, the families were "entitled to the protection of our constitutional guarantees of religious liberty."[214]

During this period, at least one state trial court took a similar state-constitutional path, indeed arguably marked that path, as the decision predated *Smith* and *Bolling*. On June 1, 1942, more than a year before *Barnette*, Judge J. Harold Brennan, a trial judge from the Circuit Court of Hancock County, West Virginia (the same State that would produce *Barnette*), invalidated a state law that had led to the indictment of five Jehovah's Witnesses. The setting, a State punishing parents for refusing to require their children to salute the flag, was familiar. The reasoning of Judge Brennan's unpublished opinion was not. He acknowledged the legitimate purpose of the pledge: "The pledge of allegiance is, by no stretch of the imagination, a religious rite. It is a patriotic ceremony which the Legislature has the power to require of those attending public schools established at public expense."[215] But that was not the end of the matter: "As an individual, I agree heartily with every word quoted. As the court, I cannot accept his conclusion that no religious question is involved simply because the judge of the court cannot stretch his imagination to cover it. The answer to his statement is that many imaginations have been stretched so as to construe this as a religious rite. The moment any court takes to itself the right to hold a religious view unreasonable, that moment the American courts begin to deny the right of religious freedom. The very purpose of our guarantees of freedom of religion is that unpopular minorities may hold views unreasonable in the opinion of the majorities."[216]

At the same time that Judge Brennan found the Witnesses' belief "completely beyond my comprehension," he could "think of many beliefs incorporated in religions in various parts of the world that are just as incomprehensible to me as this one is" and yet "[t]o all of these we guarantee freedom."[217] That by itself did not answer the question, however, as "[w]e do not tolerate human sacrifice or polygamy merely because we are told religion requires either."[218] The distinction, he reasoned, was that these examples involved "active violations of negative laws" while these criminal indictments involved "remaining passive when active participation is required."[219] Even though the West Virginia Constitution's protection of religious liberty had sometimes been treated as "merely a more elaborate wording" of the federal guarantees, he noted that it would "be difficult to read" the state guarantee's language—"nor shall any man be enforced, restrained" due to "his religious opinions or belief"—as inapplicable when a man is "imprison[ed] . . . because he will not force his child to do a positive act wholly inconsistent with the religious beliefs of both of them."[220] On that ground and with this coda, he invalidated the indictments: "[W]hat this court is asked to do is to force children . . . to do something against the consciences of both themselves and their parents. This has not been done in America hitherto; we shall not begin it here."[221]

The reader may wonder why just two state high courts and at least one state trial court extended state constitutional protections to Witnesses during this period. The answer is that, in the years between *Gobitis* and *Barnette*, courts tended to avoid addressing the constitutionality of the flag-salute laws by resolving the claims on other grounds.[222] There were plenty of expulsions and opportunities for state-centric rulings, as expulsions occurred in all of the States and "totaled more than 2,000 by 1943."[223] As *Smith, Bolling,* and *Mercante* demonstrate, state courts could still rule on state constitutional issues in such cases.[224] But they could also more easily rule on other grounds, avoiding a clash with the U.S. Supreme Court and mitigating the worst effects of postexpulsion punishments state and local officials sought for Witness children and their parents. Many courts took this path.

Two examples illustrate how many state courts opted to handle these cases.[225] In *State v. Lefebvre,* the New Hampshire Supreme Court reversed a number of orders committing children, who had been expelled and whose parents were too poor to provide private education, "to the Industrial School for the periods of their respective minorities."[226] Treating the constitutional issues as somehow moot, the Court stated that it could neither force the school to take the children back nor force the children to submit to the flag salute.[227] Without attempting a full resolution, the Court held that the children were better off in their homes, perhaps without any education, than they would be as wards of the State.[228] In *People v. Chiafreddo,* a jury in an Illinois county court sentenced the mother and father of a child who refused to salute to one of the harshest punishments associated with these cases.[229] The mother received a year in the Illinois Women's Reformatory and the father a year in the Illinois State Farm.[230] The Illinois Supreme Court put off questions of constitutionality and held that the State had provided insufficient evidence to prove its case.[231]

Barnette marked the end of this period. It not only ended the debate about the validity of compelled flag salutes under the First Amendment, but it also created a floor of federal rights that no State could ignore, making further debate about the meaning of the state guarantees in this setting less likely. Doubtless, the decision did not end all persecution or harassment of Witnesses. But it did provide Witnesses with a legal tool that would end the double insult of student expulsions and parent truancy charges.[232]

One post-*Barnette* case, *Zavilla v. Masse,* bears mention.[233] A school expelled student Witnesses under a Colorado compulsory flag-salute requirement, and the families sued for a writ of mandamus. The students relied only on the Colorado Constitution because, when they filed the lawsuit, *Gobitis* controlled the federal question.[234]

The Colorado Constitution, like most state constitutions, contains more detailed protections for freedom of religion and conscience. One of the relevant guarantees says in part: "[T]he free exercise and enjoyment of religious profession and worship, without discrimination, shall forever hereafter be guaranteed; and no person shall be denied any civil or political right, privilege or capacity, on account of his opinions concerning religion."[235]

The Colorado Supreme Court refused to second-guess the Witnesses' spiritual convictions. "We may not, and should not, determine by judicial pronouncement that their conclusion as to what they may not do without violating [their faith] is not a religious opinion."[236] And it reasoned that the denial of the Witnesses' free exercise rights was more likely to undermine than promote the patriotic goals of flag-salute ceremonies. "As a matter of elementary psychology, it is apparent that compelling the expression of a sentiment not felt or the doing of an act that it is feared will subject the actor to punishment hereafter, will not only fail to create and foster respect for the compelling authority, but will engender a sentiment of rebellion against it."[237] Even with the *Barnette* decision on the books, the Court did not hesitate to rely independently on the potentially more far-reaching protections of its own Constitution:

> We need not, and do not, rest our decision on the authority of the last pronouncement of the United States Court alone, for we are of the opinion that without reference to the federal Constitution or to either of the foregoing cases decided by the Supreme Court of the United States, the action of the school board here attacked, could not be sustained under our state Constitution.[238]

Should the U.S. Supreme Court change its mind yet again in this area, the state justices might have added, the citizens of Colorado would have nothing to fear.

Who are the heroes of this story? The relevant families—the Barnetts, the Gobitases, the Sandstroms, the Smiths, the Bollings, and many other Witness families—deserve considerable credit for holding fast to the faith-based principle behind their constitutional convictions. Threats of jail time for parents, school expulsions for children, and plenty of harassment for all Jehovah's Witnesses must have prompted many a family to wonder if it was worth it. As these federal and state cases suggest and as other cases confirm, the Jehovah's Witnesses played a remarkable role in developing free speech law and some free exercise law. The Witnesses' lead lawyer, Hayden Covington, who worked on the *Gobitis* brief, argued *Barnette*, and argued several state court cases, prevailed in twenty-four U.S. Supreme Court cases between 1938 and 1955, all on behalf of Witnesses. The Witnesses' objection to the flag salute, their zeal in spreading their faith, their willingness to do so in the most hostile environments, and their omnipresent distribution of pamphlets laid the groundwork for much of what we now take for granted as first premises of federal and state free speech and free exercise law.

On the federal side, we have these other landmark Witness cases:

- *Lovell v. City of Griffin*, 303 U.S. 444 (1938) (invalidating a city ordinance that banned the distribution of printed literature without a permit as a free speech violation);
- *Cantwell v. Connecticut*, 310 U.S. 296 (1940) (incorporating the Free Exercise Clause against the States and invalidating a state requirement that persons obtain a permit before soliciting religious contributions);
- *Chaplinsky v. New Hampshire*, 315 U.S. 568 (1942) (establishing the fighting words doctrine while affirming the conviction of a Witness who called a city marshal "a damned Fascist");
- *Murdock v. Pennsylvania*, 319 U.S. 105 (1943) (invalidating a municipal ordinance that required a permit (at a cost of $7 per week) to distribute or sell literature door to door);

On the state side, we have these significant cases, among others:

- *City of Gaffney v. Putnam*, 15 S.E.2d 130 (S.C. 1941) (reversing the conviction of a Witness whose expression of his religious views and distribution of literature instigated a fight);

- *State ex rel. Singleton v. Woodruff*, 13 So.2d 704 (Fla. 1943) (ruling that an ordinance requiring a license to distribute literature at an annual cost of $50 violated the state constitution);
- *Morgan v. Civil Service Commission*, 36 A.2d 898 (N.J. 1944) (holding that the state constitution prohibited the civil service from refusing to appoint a Witness to a government position because he would not salute the flag).

In this era, it was difficult to be a Witness and *not* be a free speech and free exercise scholar. Without the Jehovah's Witnesses, it's likely that these now-familiar principles of the U.S. and state constitutions would not be the same, and it's a certainty that they would have followed a different course.

Did one system, the federal or state courts, perform more admirably than the other in addressing these issues? There's no obvious answer. If one thinks, as I do, that the Witnesses were entitled to judicial protection but appreciates that the claims required new thinking about constitutional rights in a time of intense patriotic fervor, as I also do, the cases show two court systems stumbling toward a correct answer. Through 1940 and the *Gobitis* decision, it's fair to say that the high courts for each government fell short. Just as the lopsided 8–1 decision in *Gobitis* shows a Court membership that had failed to appreciate the liberty guarantees at stake, so too did all of the state court outcomes and most of the state court analyses, with *People v. Sandstrom* a happy exception. Not one of the state or federal high courts during this era granted relief on a constitutional claim.

Too often, the state and federal courts committed an error all too easy to make in freedom of religion cases. They second-guessed whether the individuals' faith required their action. Justice Frankfurter treated the Witnesses' beliefs as mere "idiosyncrasies," and many of the state court judges (not Jehovah's Witnesses themselves) doubted that the Witnesses' faith required them to refuse to salute the flag.

The lesson before *Gobitis* is a difficult one for a judge to acknowledge. Sad to admit, it's dangerous to place too much reliance on any of our courts, federal or state, high or low, to enforce some civil liberties claims in some settings at some times. But that reality reveals a truth and reinforces a central virtue of federalism. The truth is that, at some points in history, the citizens are the best and only protectors of our liberties—in how they behave in their communities and in how they work bravely (or not) to turn the court of public opinion in the right direction. The virtue of federalism is this: If history shows that it's perilous at times to place too much faith in judges to enforce constitutional guarantees, that only confirms the benefit—the salient benefit—of having two sets of court systems tasked with enforcing two sets of constitutional guarantees independently. While two sets of protections may fail us from time to time, as they largely did during the years leading up to 1940, one set of independent protections assuredly will fail us more often than two.

Oddly enough, the state courts' sensitivity to these rights grew after *Gobitis*, after the U.S. Supreme Court overwhelmingly rejected the federal claims. Here again is a variation on the lessons from the school-funding and exclusionary-rule chapters—that state court judges will not invariably linger in the shadows of the U.S. Supreme Court's assessment of core constitutional liberties. Under their own constitutions, several state courts granted relief after *Gobitis* and before *Barnette*. Perhaps the state courts responded to the criticism of *Gobitis*. Or perhaps they attended to the signals sent by various U.S. Supreme Court justices who had grown uncomfortable with *Gobitis*. Or perhaps they were influenced by other state court decisions dignifying these rights under their own constitutions. Whatever the reason, they opted not to march together with the National Court and vindicated the sovereign independence of their own constitutions in the process.

The lower federal courts, more unusually, did not march to the *Gobitis* tune either. Lost in every discussion of the flag-salute cases is a reality that only a middle-management judge would notice. In all three federal lower-court opinions from this era, the junior courts were vindicated, whether it was the (initially reversed) district court or the (initially reversed) court of appeals in *Gobitis* or the (affirmed) three-judge court in *Barnette*. The U.S. Constitution requires one Supreme Court and permits Congress in its discretion to create such "inferior" courts, as the Constitution painfully puts it, from time to time. One lesson from the flag-salute story is that "inferior" courts are not necessarily populated by "inferior" judges.

Lurking behind this observation is a question: How would lower federal court judges have authority to anticipate the overruling of a Supreme Court precedent, as the three-judge court did in *Barnette*? They have no such authority today. But that was not true in 1943. Ever since 1989, the Court has been clear that *it*, not the lower courts, should do the overruling.[239]

Notice that this problem does not exist for the state courts, so long as the plaintiff brings a claim under state law as well as federal law. Given their independent authority to construe their own constitutions beyond the protections provided by the federal sibling, they need not consider, they need not even mention, the federal ground, if they opt to provide independent relief to the plaintiffs on the state law ground. Such a ruling not only would provide the plaintiffs all of the relief they seek—an invalidation of the pledge requirement—but also would be insulated from review.[240] The Supreme Court does not have authority to review state court decisions that rest only on state law.

What of the performance of the *justices*, the federal and state high court justices? Much has already been said here and elsewhere about Justice Jackson's powerful writing and reasoning in *Barnette* and Justice Frankfurter's principled but anguished error in *Barnette*. Too little has been said about the state court judges who grappled with these same claims and who in several instances rose to the occasion. Deserving of special note are the thoughtful opinions of Chief Justice Crane and Justice Lehman of the New York Court of Appeals in *People v. Sandstrom*, in which they granted relief on procedural grounds—pre-*Gobitis*— but helped to set the stage for both U.S. Supreme Court decisions. So too of the California trial judge, Judge Peter Shields, who invoked the California Constitution to grant relief but was later reversed by a California Supreme Court unwilling to break from *Gobitis* and its interpretation of the U.S. Constitution. After *Gobitis*, there is much to admire in Justice Beals's decision for the Washington Supreme Court and Justice Harvey's decision for the Kansas Supreme Court—both independent-minded, both premised on their state constitutions, both in sum persuasive precursors to *Barnette*. Their opinions confirm that, in a federal system, nothing prevents the state courts from being path blazers.

Four of the state court decisions suggest that Justice Jackson may have missed one opportunity in writing his opinion. Not too many people, it's true, criticize Jackson's decision. It's one of the great opinions in American legal history. Only a fool would say otherwise. But I can think of one addition that would have made it better. A National Court should be mindful of its advantage in deciding cases after the State High Courts and the lower federal courts have considered them. Many of the stirring themes in the Jackson opinion had forerunners in the state court decisions, and he would have done well to mention them— not just for the sake of sharing credit but also for the sake of providing support for the First Amendment norms his opinion recognizes, if not creates. By 1943, as shown, there were plenty of thoughtful, eloquent, and impressive state court decisions on these issues from which to choose. A National Court humble enough to acknowledge that it is not infallible, just final,[241] should be humble enough to acknowledge, and wise enough to encourage, the good work of the state court judges who had already dealt with the issue. Not one of the decisions is cited, much less quoted.

7

Looking Forward: What the State Courts Can Do

SEVERAL THEMES EMERGE FROM the prior chapters. State constitutions create independent limits on state and local power, limits that may do more or less than their counterpart guarantees in the Federal Constitution. Tempting though it may be for institutional litigants to prioritize national civil rights victories over state court ones, the best approach is often complicated—and sometimes unknowable at the outset. Were the lawyers in *Rodriguez* and *Mapp* correct to think that a national victory at the U.S. Supreme Court was the only way, or even the best way, to protect those liberties? It's not clear. Sometimes the most important thing the advocate can do is to brighten, not blur, the lines of accountability, which is why *Rodriguez*'s removal of the federal courts from the field may have done as much for the cause of equitable school funding over the long run as the U.S. Supreme Court ever could have done. The *Mapp* story shows that victories at the U.S. Supreme Court are not cost-free, including for the very group of citizens the decisions purport to help. Would a greater appreciation of the independent roles of the state courts have prompted some courts to push back on the sweeping assumptions in *Buck v. Bell* or prompted the state and federal courts to push back more promptly against the wave of hate crimes against Jehovah's Witnesses? Through it all, history shows that the state courts at times have been more reliable protectors of individual liberties than the federal courts. At other times, less.

At all times, a litigant who targets the validity of a state or local law at a minimum ought to consider the possibility that a state constitutional claim should be added to the mix. In this chapter, I shift the discussion from the reasons why claimants should raise state constitutional claims and the historical lessons from when they have done so, and when they have not, to consideration of what can be done to increase the salience of state constitutional law—and to further the interaction, in truth the dialogue, between federal and state constitutional law. If there is a critical conviction of this book, it's that a chronic underappreciation of state constitutional law has been hurtful to state *and* federal law and the proper balance between state *and* federal courts in protecting individual liberty. While the state courts at times have played a critical role in advancing *some* constitutional rights, the question is whether there is room for them to play a greater role in the future.

Lockstepping

A grave threat to independent state constitutions, and a key impediment to the role of state courts in contributing to the dialogue of American constitutional law, is lockstepping: the tendency of some state courts to diminish their constitutions by interpreting them in reflexive imitation of the federal courts' interpretation of the Federal Constitution.[1] The issue arises when the Federal Constitution and a state constitution contain an identical or similarly worded guarantee and a litigant invokes both of them, by arguing that an arrest, say, violates the federal and state prohibitions on "unreasonable searches and seizures."[2] There is no reason to think, as an interpretive matter, that constitutional guarantees of independent sovereigns, even guarantees with the same or similar words, must be construed in the same way. Still less is there reason to think that a highly generalized guarantee, such as a prohibition on "unreasonable" searches, would have just one meaning over a range of differently situated sovereigns. Yet state courts frequently handle such cases by considering the federal constitutional claim first, after which they summarily announce that the state provision means the same thing,[3] occasionally at the beck and call of the state constitution itself.[4] So too of many other generally phrased constitutional guarantees found in the federal and state constitutions: "due process," "equal protection of the laws," "cruel and unusual punishment," "free speech," "free exercise of religion," and "takings" of property, to mention just a few that the state courts have frequently interpreted in reflexive lockstep with the federal guarantee.

Why the meaning of a federal guarantee in these areas (or any other) proves the meaning of an independent state guarantee is rarely explained and often seems inexplicable. If the court decisions of another sovereign ought to bear on the inquiry, those of a sister state should have the most to say about the point. Two state constitutions are more likely to share historical and linguistic roots. They necessarily will cover smaller jurisdictions than the National High Court. In almost all instances they will be construing individual-liberty guarantees that originated in state constitutions, not the Federal Constitution.[5] And they will be exercising a power—judicial review—that originated in state constitutional law, not in federal constitutional law.[6]

Why borrow in particular from the larger, far larger, jurisdiction? Federalism considerations may lead the U.S. Supreme Court to underenforce (or at least not to overenforce) constitutional guarantees in view of the number of people affected and the range of jurisdictions implicated.[7] No state supreme court by contrast has any reason to apply a "federalism discount" to its decisions,[8] making it odd for state courts to lean so heavily on the meaning of the Federal Constitution in construing their own.

Paradoxically, the most important article written about state constitutional law—"State Constitutions and the Protection of Individual Rights," by Justice William Brennan[9]—may have had the unintended consequence of setting us on this course. Recall that the possibility of dual-claim constitutional cases first became a widespread option roughly a half century ago after the U.S. Supreme Court had incorporated most of the provisions of the Bill of Rights into the liberty guarantee of the Fourteenth Amendment's Due Process Clause. In 1977, Justice Brennan, once a justice on the New Jersey Supreme Court, did not like what he saw at the National Court: fewer civil rights victories from the Burger Court than he had seen from the Warren Court. He wrote the article to press the state courts to fortify the breach, to grant relief by another name: a state constitution.[10] "It may not be wide of the mark," he wrote, "to suppose that . . . state courts discern, and disagree with, a trend in recent opinions of the United States Supreme Court to pull back from, or at least suspend for the time being, the . . . application of the federal Bill of Rights and the restraints of the due process and equal protection clauses of the fourteenth amendment."[11] State courts, he thus urged, "cannot rest when they have afforded their citizens the full protections of the federal Constitution" but should grant relief under their own constitutions instead.[12]

Much of Justice Brennan's article was laudable in ways that ought to be familiar by now. Claimants, sure enough, should prefer two arrows in their quiver—two chances, not one, to invalidate a state or local law. But the messenger and the message may have helped to perpetuate, if not to create, two damaging myths that, so far anyway, may have done as much harm as good for independent state constitutionalism.

The *messenger* may have prompted some state court advocates and judges to misperceive this option as a liberal ratchet, designed to give just some rights but not others a second chance in the state courts. Through little fault of Justice Brennan, it's easy to imagine a conservative state court judge's unfavorable reaction to his article. Having watched the U.S. Supreme Court identify many new liberal rights during the 1960s, having watched Justice Brennan lead the effort, and having perhaps become skeptical of some of those decisions, such a judge might understandably hesitate at the suggestion that the state courts should do still more. In that environment, the temptation of lockstepping becomes clear. With all of the innovation at the federal level, why add *more* one-directional innovation at the state level? Enough was enough. Better to let the state constitutional guarantees sink into irrelevance, the conservative judge might think, than to use them as a lever for still more rights innovation.

But there is a time, place, and person for everything. If 1977 was not the right year and if Justice Brennan was not the right person for advancing state constitutionalism in a way that resonated with *all* state court judges, that need not be so today. There's nothing about the state constitutions that necessarily points toward liberal or conservative rights. Independent state courts (and for that matter legislatures) may protect a range of rights, whether involving liberty, equality, or property, and enforce a wide range of structural guarantees, whether before or after the federal courts enter the picture. That the state constitutions provide a second avenue for invalidating a local law *says nothing* about what kind of law should be, or will be, challenged.[13]

In the past, the state courts have protected a large cross-section of rights: school funding and property rights; establishment and free exercise rights; obscenity and commercial speech; criminal procedure and contract rights; the right to privacy; and the right to bear arms.[14] In the future, this experience may set the stage for other innovations in other areas. Substantive due process protections in one direction or another? Limitations on executive branch agencies whether through revitalization of the nondelegation doctrine or limitations on theories of administrative deference?[15] Higher or lower walls between church and state? Fewer or more protections for new minority groups? Greater or lesser limits on economic regulation?[16] Whatever the reader may think about innovations in these areas, we should all be able to agree that the bolder a new idea, the better it is for just one State (or a few States) to test it before the whole country takes on the risks associated with implementing it.

Justice Brennan's *message* also had a flaw. It pushed one feature of state constitutional law (the authority of the States to construe their constitutions differently) at the expense of another (the independent basis for doing so). The suggested inquiry was not whether state constitutional law demanded a different answer from federal constitutional law based on local language, context, and history. So long as there is a progressive will, he implored, there is a new way for granting relief.[17] Instead of insisting on first-principle inquiries into the meaning of the state provisions, the article urged state courts to side with the dissenters in debates already held at the U.S. Supreme Court—under federal law no less![18] While state court judges and advocates assuredly have the authority to invoke dissents rather than majority opinions of the U.S. Supreme Court in construing their own constitutions, exclusive (or even heavy) reliance on debates about the meaning of a federal guarantee is not apt to dignify the state constitutions as independent sources of law. Much to the contrary. There will never be a healthy "discourse" between state and federal judges about the meaning of core guarantees in our American constitutions if the state judges merely take sides on the federal debates and federal authorities,[19] as opposed to marshaling the distinct state texts and histories and drawing their own conclusions from them.

The Brennan article, it is no doubt true, advanced state constitutional law in an essential and everlasting sense: It reminded advocates, through a former state court judge and a well-known Supreme Court Justice, that neglected state constitutional protections remain on the books and provide an alternative theory for relief. But in a state constitutional law equivalent of Stockholm syndrome, the article may have advanced the unfortunate myth that federal constitutional law remains front and center—the first line of inquiry—leaving state constitutional law as a second thought, as an argument of last, perhaps even desperate, resort.

That is an unfortunate and peculiar twist on how law customarily is developed in this country. Why live in a "top-down constitutional world" when we have the option of allowing the states to be the "vanguard—the first ones to decide whether to embrace or reject innovative legal claims"—and allowing the U.S. Supreme Court, informed by these experiences, to decide whether to federalize the issue.[20] In a process that Professor Joseph Blocher calls "reverse incorporation," the U.S. Supreme Court remains free, whether on living-constitutionalist, pragmatic, or originalist grounds, to learn from and, if appropriate, borrow from the States' experiences.[21]

Prioritizing State Law Claims

If the domination of federal constitutional law and its predictable stepchild, lockstepping, are the scourge of independent state constitutions and if these dynamics are interfering with the full development of American constitutional law, what is the remedy? The rest of this chapter and the one that follows offer a few ideas.

Start with process, the way most state courts sequence the resolution of federal and state claims. State court decisions that imitate federal court decisions not only seem to be prioritizing the wrong decisions in determining the meaning of their own constitutions, but they also seem to be inverting the right sequence for considering state and federal arguments.

In response to this problem, Hans Linde had a good idea—in 1970.[22] When state courts face state and federal constitutional claims in the same case, he proposed that they resolve the state claim first and consider the federal claim only if necessary, only if the court denies relief to the claimant under the state constitution. Linde proposed the idea as a professor at the University of Oregon and later had the opportunity, to his good fortune and ours, to put the idea into practice as a justice on the Oregon Supreme Court for fourteen years. He wrote many decisions and authored several articles implementing the principle.[23] The key insight of Linde's approach is that litigants and courts will be less likely to duck independent assessments of the state claim if they consider it first. If state court judges and lawyers tie themselves to the mast of first-order inquiries into their state constitutions, they will be less likely to succumb to the temptation to treat federal law as state law.

Since 1970, Linde's approach has not been widely accepted. Nearly a half century later, just three States follow this approach on a regular basis: Oregon, Maine, and New Hampshire.[24] Two other States—Washington and Vermont—use a variation on this approach. They start with the state constitutional claim but, in contrast to the state-first approach, proceed to resolve the federal claim no matter what happens with the state claim.[25]

That is not a promising pace of reform, whether one looks at the three States that embrace state primacy or the two others that embrace it in part. It's time to revive Linde's idea—to make state constitutional arguments the first line of defense in individual rights disputes—by explaining some of his reasons for using it and by adding some of my own.[26]

A state-first approach to litigation over constitutional rights honors the original design of the state and federal constitutions. State primacy in guarding individual rights flows from the U.S. Constitution and from one of its key structural guarantees of liberty: federalism. The Founders thought of the States as the first bulwarks of freedom.[27] The Constitution needed no Bill of Rights, Alexander Hamilton maintained, because the States would stand guard as "sentinels" watching over the People's rights.[28] And in the event of federal overreach, state governments were a sufficient "instrument of redress" to remedy the breach.[29] Hamilton lost that argument to the People, who preferred to add a belt—the Bill of Rights—to those suspenders. But that reality did not demote the state guarantees from the first line of defense if a state or local government refused to leave people alone or opted to meddle needlessly in their lives. The Founders also had faith in the state courts as protectors of liberty. They created one Supreme Court but left it to Congress to decide whether to create "inferior" courts, which implies that they had little doubt that state courts would enforce federal and state constitutional rights. Prioritizing the resolution of state constitutional claims in cases involving federal and state claims restores the States to what should be their proud place as the first responders to governmental dilutions of liberty and property.

That place accounts for the essential role of the States in determining the legal and policy context in which *all* federal constitutional challenges to state and local laws arise. Under the National Constitution, the States' reserved powers are "numerous and indefinite."[30] State law accordingly "extend[s] to all the objects which, in the ordinary course of affairs, concern the lives, liberties, and properties of the people, and the internal order, improvement, and prosperity of the State."[31] Lacking a general police power, the federal government by contrast holds powers "few and defined."[32] While the Fourteenth Amendment, for example, prohibits the States from depriving individuals of "property" without due process and Article I prohibits States from "impairing the Obligation of Contracts,"[33] the States still define what counts as property and what makes a contract.[34] Yet if the States are the lead players on the stage of private law, why treat them as the understudies of public law?[35] State constitutions no less than state statutes and common law decisions started out as, and remain, the place to *begin* any search for individual rights, whether in the context of property, contract, or any other rights.

The nature of a federal constitutional right confirms that state courts should address the state claim first. Pause over the issue at hand: Does state action violate the Federal Constitution? If the state constitution prevents state law from being enforced or prohibits a state official from acting, what work is left for the Federal Constitution to do? Why not consider the state constitutional claim first, given the possibility that it might eliminate any ultra vires state action at all?[36]

Supporting the point is the language under which most challenges to state action arise. That's the language of the Fourteenth Amendment to the U.S. Constitution: "nor shall any state deprive any person of life, liberty, or property, without due process of law; nor deny to any person within its jurisdiction the equal protection of the laws." How curious for a state court to review the federal claim first when it turns on language about the adequacy of the State's "process" and the adequacy of the State's "equal protection of the laws."[37] Nothing prohibits a state constitution from forming "part of the total state action in a case,"[38] supplying part of the "process" that is due or being part of "the [state] laws" to which equal protection applies. When a state court arrests the relevant state action under its own constitution, any deprivation of life, liberty, or property or denial of equal protection evaporates. As a matter of federal constitutional law, application of the state constitution is "logically prior to review of the effect of the state's total action" under the Federal Constitution[39] and indeed "first in time and first in logic."[40] By adhering to this natural sequence, state courts claim the rightful independence of their state constitutions.

Federal constitutional avoidance principles point in the same direction. In a case in federal court, the courts will "not pass upon a [federal] constitutional question . . . if there is also present some other ground upon which" to decide the case.[41] Federal courts for this reason generally resolve potentially dispositive state law claims first.[42] Why should litigation in state court be different? If the state constitution protects the right asserted, leaping to the federal claim flouts the "passive virtues" of judicial restraint no matter which court has jurisdiction.[43] If the state supreme court grants relief to the claimant on the state ground and provides a clear statement that it is doing so, the case is over, and the need to construe the federal constitutional provision disappears with it.

No version of the constitutional avoidance doctrine to my knowledge says that courts should consider the claim arising from the larger sovereign before they consider the claim arising from the smaller one. By deciding the federal claim first, state courts do most what one would expect them to do least: aggrandize federal law at the expense of state law.

Abstention and comity principles put an exclamation on the point. *Pullman* abstention requires federal courts to refrain from deciding federal constitutional claims when a case might turn on unsettled questions of state law.[44] That includes the state constitution.[45] If federal courts accord States this dignity, surely the States' *own* courts should do so too.[46] The rationales behind abstention are constitutional avoidance and comity, all to the end of avoiding needless conflict with the States as fellow sovereigns. But there should be two sides to the comity coin. If it's a good idea for the federal courts to avoid unduly interfering with the States by announcing federal rules without input about the meaning of state law, it's a good idea for the state courts to avoid conflict with their fellow sovereign—the federal government. *Both* sets of courts should follow the same sequence: resolve the state claim before taking on the federal claim and, even then, only if necessary.

Explanations for Prioritizing Federal Claims Do Not Hold Up

Most state courts do not prioritize state claims in handling cases that allege violations of state and federal constitutional rights. The competing schools of thought go by many names, the most prominent of which only an academic could love—the "interstitial" approach. But we should call that approach and any one like it what it is: a "secondary" approach. All that's at issue as a practical matter is this: Does the state court start with the state law claim or the federal claim? And all that's at issue as a policy matter is this: Is the state constitutional claim the first or second line of defense in individual rights cases? Is it the bulwark? Or the backstop?

Here's how one court, the New Mexico Supreme Court, described its interstitial/secondary sequencing of decision-making in a dual-claim case:

> Under the interstitial approach, the court asks first whether the right being asserted is protected under the federal constitution. If it is, then the state constitutional claim is not reached. If it is not, then the state constitution is examined. A state court adopting this approach may diverge from federal precedent for three reasons: a flawed federal analysis, structural differences between state and federal government, or distinctive state characteristics.[47]

This approach flouts foundational principles of federalism, comity, and the logic of most federal constitutional claims. But that reality would be of only theoretical import if this sequencing of decisions had little impact on the state courts and the independent interpretations of their own constitutions. If state courts, in prioritizing the resolution of federal claims, still dignified the independent meaning of their state constitutions, the stakes would not be high, and I would have lost interest in this subject long ago. But that is not what has happened. "To this day, most state courts adopt federal constitutional law as their own. Bowing to the nationalization of constitutional discourse, they tend to follow whatever doctrinal vocabulary is used by the United States Supreme Court, discussed in law reviews, and taught in the law schools."[48] Worse than that, the state courts often commit to following federal law wherever it leads them in the future—to the "rising and falling tides of federal case law both in method and specifics."[49] Who takes a voyage without knowing its destination?

Let's examine some of the explanations for prioritizing the resolution of federal claims and what invariably comes with it—lockstepping—to see if they hold up.

Some say that federal claims should be resolved first in dual-claim cases because state courts cannot construe their constitutions to offer *less* protection than the federal guarantee.[50] Wrong. State courts remain free to construe their constitutional guarantees to offer as little protection as they think appropriate, and only a state constitutional amendment can alter that decision. A few state courts have said as much.[51] The only thing state courts may not do is ignore the independent federal claim. It may be true that a state constitutional ruling that asks less of the government than existing federal constitutional law requires will not impact the parties before the court. But that does not make the ruling inconsequential. Once a state court establishes the interrelation between the two guarantees, it has established that no state constitutional inquiry is needed, a not-unhelpful development for future litigants and courts and assuredly an efficient one.

That's also a not-insignificant development for the U.S. Supreme Court, as it manages and assesses decisions of its own. Some state court rulings may implicate the meaning of a federal guarantee, such as the Eighth Amendment's prohibition on "cruel and unusual punishment." And some state court rulings may help to inform the original meaning of language in the Federal Constitution that first appeared in the state constitutions or may provide pragmatic reasons for following or steering clear of an approach embraced by the States. State courts have much to offer when they explain why the original, or for that matter pragmatic or living-constitutionalist, understanding of a guarantee under their care does not go as far as its federal counterpart.

To date, most state supreme courts willing to express their disagreement with precedents of the U.S. Supreme Court in construing their own constitutions do so only in explaining why the state constitution covers *more* ground. That is difficult to justify. A healthy form of comparative law—and that's just what this is—should attend to all comparisons, not just some. The state courts thus should explain the interrelation between the two sets of charters in both directions, whether the state guarantee covers more ground or less. Anything less reinforces a ratchet approach to state constitutionalism, one destined to fail over the long term.

Some worry about the potential inefficiencies of resolving state claims first in a world in which federal constitutional law is so well developed—and has become so much more developed than state constitutional law in the last five decades or so. Any clear-eyed proponent of prioritizing state claims must come to terms with this objection. Keep in mind that, by one count, 95 percent of the disputes resolved by courts in this country are filed in the state courts, as opposed to the federal ones.[52] Just one of those courts, the California Supreme Court, resolved thirty-seven state constitutional law disputes in 2005, while the U.S. Supreme Court resolved thirty federal constitutional law disputes that same year.[53] All of this makes it understandable that state courts would keep up with their burgeoning dockets by sticking to the calf-path rather than diverging from it.[54] Even though twenty-first-century state courts are as apt to be constitutional innovators as federal courts, decades of state court precedents remain on the books paralleling the federal precedents or at least starting their analyses with them. In the context of this burgeoning volume of cases, many state courts may think it unrealistic to change the order in which they address all such claims and the order in which they expect lawyers to brief all such claims.

One area of law offers an insight into the gravitational pull of precedents from the U.S. Supreme Court. Consider the state and federal experiences with *unincorporated* rights. Through the process of selective incorporation, the National Court has incorporated all but the following provisions in the first eight Amendments of the Bill of Rights: the Third Amendment's prohibition on the quartering of soldiers; the Fifth Amendment's grand jury indictment requirement; the Sixth Amendment's unanimous jury requirement in criminal cases; the Seventh Amendment's right to a jury trial in civil cases; and the Eighth Amendment's Excessive Fines Clause.[55] In these areas, the federal guarantee does not bind the States, meaning that the state courts have exclusive responsibility for the protection of these types of rights under their state constitutions in state court and meaning there is no possibility of dual-claim cases. The experience with one of these rights, the jury trial guarantee, offers a sobering lesson about the pull of federal precedent. Forty-seven States have jury-trial guarantees in their constitutions, and those guarantees provide the exclusive protection to individuals in state court civil cases. And yet a significant percentage of the States have followed federal precedent in construing their civil-trial guarantee.[56] If it is difficult for state courts to resist the appeal of leaning on federal precedent in areas where they have exclusive power over the issue, any ambitions for change in this area warrant caution.

But this consideration, powerful though it may be, comes with its own qualification. It might well be unrealistic to take all of this on at once. Yet nothing prevents a state court from identifying an area or areas that are particularly amenable to independent state constitutionalism in this State or that one. Then start there. A ground-up assessment of that constitutional right might show that it does less than the federal guarantee, ending any need to consider the issue again. Or the assessment may show that it goes further, making it unnecessary to worry about less-protective federal rights. Or the assessment may show nuances that favor state claims in some instances and federal ones in others. Once the state court has figured out one area of state-federal interaction, it can move to another.

Some fear confusion in the bar if the state courts delink the two constitutional inquiries, if two lines of constitutional law emerge in certain areas as opposed to one uniform approach. After all, the U.S. Supreme Court's multidecade experiment with dual standards for Bill of Rights guarantees applicable to the state and federal governments did not end well, with the Court ultimately collapsing the two.[57] But is confusion really a problem for a single State? If the state courts treat the two guarantees as distinct, the bench, bar, law enforcement, and citizenry usually will have to pay attention to just one standard: the more protective of the two.

Some point out that the secondary approach—preferencing the resolution of federal claims over state ones—pays tribute to the on-the-ground reality that the vast majority of lawyers start with the federal claim and brief it most thoroughly. Rarely, they add, do advocates provide an assessment of the independent meaning of the state guarantee premised on its language, its history, or early understandings of its meaning. What state courts often see at most is the argument that they should construe the state guarantee differently because they can or because the dissent rather than the majority in a U.S. Supreme Court case has the better of the . . . federal arguments. But a state court always may ask for additional briefing on the textual, historical, or precedent-driven reasons for construing a state guarantee independently of its federal counterpart. After a few such requests, lawyers (most of them anyway) will get the hint.

As for the unwillingness of many lawyers to do the groundwork needed for this kind of briefing, perhaps inadequate resources are the explanation in some cases. But that should not be true for institutional litigants, whether private ones (e.g., the ACLU, the NAACP, the Chamber of Commerce) or public ones (e.g., state attorneys general, local prosecutors, public defenders).[58] In an appropriate case, one would think it highly useful to figure out the underlying meaning of a state guarantee and to do the groundwork for figuring it out. As for the lawyer intimidated by the lack of guidance from modern state court precedents, I have little sympathy. For most lawyers, the chance to shape arguments on a clean slate is a gift, a rare and much appreciated opportunity.

Some worry that a state-first approach will diminish established federal constitutional norms that took many years to develop. Five years after Justice Brennan's 1977 article, the editors of the *Harvard Law Review* published a collection of student notes on "The Interpretation of State Constitutional Rights," which tried to turn Justice Brennan's article into an academic model.[59] The editors agreed with Justice Brennan that state courts should develop their own constitutional jurisprudence without mindlessly adopting federal doctrine as state doctrine. But they remained concerned about the possibility that state courts might ignore federal protections, which were "extensive," "well articulated," and broadly enforceable against the States.[60] To avoid requiring each State "to construct a complete system of fundamental rights from the ground up," the editors reasoned that the best approach to developing state constitutional law was a model that "recognizes federal doctrine as a settled floor of rights and asks whether and how to criticize, amplify, or supplement this doctrine to yield more extensive constitutional protections."[61] They thus proposed that state courts should "acknowledge the dominance of federal law and focus directly on the gap-filling potential of state constitutions."[62] What they proposed became the interstitial model—the secondary approach to interpretation.

Several state court justices agreed with the *Law Review*'s editors. Massachusetts Justice Herbert P. Wilkins wrote at the time: "If the Supreme Court has expressed broad rights under the federal Constitution, it is often superfluous to determine state constitutional principles in the same area."[63] Washington Supreme Court Justice Robert F. Utter maintained that state courts had a responsibility to analyze federal law even when it was not dispositive.[64] Because federalism concerns and "the institutional position of the federal Supreme Court cause[] it to 'underenforce' constitutional norms," Utter argued, the Supreme Court could always benefit from state court commentary on its decisions in parallel to analyses of their own constitutions.[65] Several scholars have supported this view as well.[66]

One should not lightly cast these arguments aside, not least because they have largely carried the day so far. Most American lawyers (and judges) are considerably more familiar with the Federal Constitution than they are with their State's constitution. Few lawyers know anything about their State's founders, their purposes in creating the State's constitution, the events that may have shaped their thinking, or "how the various provisions of the document fit together into a coherent whole."[67] By contrast, many features of state constitutions have their sources in a shared national and cultural heritage that embraces documents from Magna Carta and the Declaration of Independence to U.S. Supreme Court opinions, past and present. All of this leads many commentators to claim that state courts should use the Federal Constitution as a baseline instead of constructing each State's constitutional jurisprudence from the "ground up."[68] To "condemn state judiciaries for referring to federal doctrine when interpreting their own charters," it was said, "would force an irrational chauvinism on the state courts."[69]

But what one could have guessed would happen with this approach over the last half century has happened. Chauvinism, yes, but in exactly the wrong direction. A federal-first approach to constitutional inter-pretation has led to entrenched and still-growing federal domination in the dialogue of American constitutional law. Presumptions become destiny. If lawyers and judges presume the meaning of a guarantee in the Federal Constitution is the same for a similar guarantee in the state constitution, that is often where they will end up. Just look at the last five decades of experience if you have any doubt.

Any argument in favor of prioritizing federal law confuses what is with what should be. Sure, most lawyers are more familiar with the Federal Constitution, its history, and its debates than they are with their own state constitutions. But we should let this status quo lie only if we are content with it and with what it produces. Once a State prioritizes its own claims (even if just by doing so one guarantee at a time), that forces lawyers to brief the histories, structures, and texts of their particular constitutional provisions, allowing a distinct state law jurisprudence to emerge in some areas and not in others.[70] It's worth remembering that the U.S. Supreme Court has not always been perceived as the primary guardian and interpreter of rights. Some of the country's greatest judges, including James Kent, Benjamin Cardozo, and Roger Traynor, wrote celebrated (and innovative) opinions as state judges, and Cardozo did his most impactful work as a state court judge. As the *Buck v. Bell* story illustrates, national decisions are not invariably the soundest or the most rights-sensitive decisions.

If proponents of a federal-first model worry about the potential dilu-tion of federal constitutional law, they should be willing to account for (and justify) the actual dilution of state constitutionalism norms caused by their model. From an accountability perspective, state supreme court justices have the final say over the meaning of the States' constitutions. And Federal Supreme Court justices have the final say over the meaning of the U.S. Constitution. State court jurisprudence that starts and (often) ends with the state claim keeps the lines of accountability clean and true. But state court jurisprudence that blurs the line between federal and state norms blurs the line between who is accountable for state court decisions and who is not. The secondary approach permits state court judges, particularly elected state court judges, to convey the impression that federal law prompted the decision—that the U.S. Supreme Court made them do it. Accountability considerations firmly support the state-first model because it ensures that state courts take transparent responsibility for independently construing their constitutional guarantees or transparent responsibility for mimicking the federal approach. Whichever approach a state court wants, it should be clear which one it is adopting.

Nor is there any material risk that state court judges will diminish American constitutional norms by suddenly deciding, say, that their state constitutions do not offer key free speech protections. In areas like this one, the protections reflect norms built up by state and federal courts over a long time, and indeed reflect traditions started in the state constitutions. If that means the state courts frequently will replow deeply plowed ground and end up adhering to today's federal standards and tests anyway, so be it. That entrenches what should be entrenched: that certain constitutional norms are beyond reproach. But even universal truths have local dialects. The U.S. Constitution and a state constitution may equally value free speech while having different understandings of commercial speech. So too of regional understandings of privacy, education, speech, and family structures that stem from sources different from the text of the Federal Constitution.

The irreducible minimum is that state courts decide for themselves the meaning of their own constitutions, each with its own independent traditions and words. If state courts turn to their constitutions only when the Federal Constitution does not decide the question—or worse, only when they disagree with the U.S. Supreme Court's interpretation of the National Constitution—the documents will collect more dust and become more diminished. All with the risk that a day will come when we need them even more. So long as state courts give a "presumption of correctness" to U.S. Supreme Court decisions when it comes to interpreting their own constitutions, they will continue to "shift the debate away from analyzing the state constitution to a preoccupation with the shadow cast by the United States Supreme Court decision."[71]

Some fear that state primacy will lead state courts to view their constitutions in isolation without any reference to the Federal Constitution and decisions interpreting it. But that's not what's meant by urging state court judges to look to their constitutions *first*. It may be necessary to consult federal documents and precedents to understand some state constitutional provisions or even to decide how some state provisions should be construed. And the reverse is true. In each event, constitutional law—state and federal—will be richer if state judges do not assume one way or the other that the Federal Constitution will decide all fundamental questions and the state constitutions will at best provide supplements.

If there is a risk of chauvinism in all of this, it's the risk of assuming that the States can't be trusted to take individual rights seriously. The point of telling these American constitutional law stories in full is to burst some of these bubbles and to deflate a few others—to illustrate the risks of relying too heavily on the U.S. Supreme Court as the guardian of our rights, to show that the state supreme courts at times have been committed defenders of our rights, and to confirm that the right balance between the state and federal courts when it comes to rights protection is deeply complicated and relentlessly worth bringing into account.

In the final analysis, there assuredly are historical and practical explanations for linking the meaning of federal and state guarantees and for prioritizing consideration of the federal ones. But continuing to do so today as a matter of course is increasingly difficult to justify and, worse, all the more likely to deepen the inertia-driven channel that already exists.[72]

8

Looking Forward: What the Rest of the Legal Community Can Do

STATE COURT JUDGES FACE a practical limit in addressing the imbalance between the role of the Federal Constitution and its state counterparts in the development of American constitutional law. State judges, like basketball referees, call games. They don't play them. There's not much a state court can do when it comes to vindicating the independence of its state constitution if lawyers don't raise the claims under their own charters.

Utah v. Strieff illustrates the point.[1] The case arrived at the U.S. Supreme Court in 2016 on review of a decision of the Utah Supreme Court. All that was at issue before the Utah Supreme Court was an illegal-seizure claim under the Fourth Amendment because Edward Strieff challenged his seizure only on federal grounds, not state grounds as well. The Utah Constitution contains its own counterpart protection, which says: "The right of the people to be secure in their persons, houses, papers, and effects against unreasonable searches and seizures shall not be violated; and no warrant shall issue but upon probable cause supported by oath or affirmation, particularly describing the place to be searched, and the person or thing to be seized."[2] It is materially identical to the Fourth Amendment. Yet Strieff never sought relief under it. In a thoughtful 5–0 decision by Justice Thomas Lee, the Utah Supreme Court granted relief on the Fourth Amendment claim but could not grant relief on a state law ground never raised.[3] The U.S. Supreme Court reversed in a 5–3 decision.

Is it possible that Strieff went to jail because his lawyer did not read the Utah Constitution? Or because the Utah Supreme Court for too long had been unwilling to consider such claims? Or because our legal culture for too long has been unwilling to take these claims seriously? Let the reader be the judge. Is it possible that a lawyer who does not raise a promising state constitutional claim on behalf of his or her client violates the Sixth Amendment to the U.S. Constitution (or its equivalent in a state constitution), which guarantees the effective assistance of counsel? Let a future court decide.

When state courts prioritize the resolution of state constitutional claims and when they identify the requirements for raising an independent state constitutional claim,[4] that helps. But these efforts will not suffice by themselves. What's needed is a bench-bar partnership, as Justice Souter emphasized while serving as a justice on the New Hampshire Supreme Court. "It is the need of every appellate court," he implored, "for the participation of the bar in the process of trying to think sensibly and comprehensively about the questions that the judicial power has been established to answer. Nowhere is the need greater than in the field of State constitutional law, where we are asked so often to confront questions that have already been decided under the National Constitution. . . . If we are going to steer between [the extremes of 'too much reliance' on federal precedent and 'too little'], we will have to insist on developed advocacy from those who bring the cases before us."[5] There are as many chickens as eggs behind the absence of independent briefing of state constitutional claims.

Local Rules

So what can the rest of the legal community do to ensure that, as a matter of process, lawyers make informed decisions about their cases? One place to start is the States' rules of civil and appellate procedure as well as the local rules of each state court—a body of practice requirements put together by state legislatures, state court judges, advocates, clerks' offices, and professors. In each place, the rule makers would do well to require litigants who raise constitutional challenges to state or local laws to separate their briefing between the state and federal constitutional claims, whether at the trial level or the appellate level. Better yet, they should require litigants to brief the state claims first. All of these measures would remind litigants of the existence of the two types of claims and at a minimum prompt separate briefing of them.

One State goes an admirable step further. Reflecting the influence of Justice Linde, the Oregon State Bar publishes a practice guide for its attorneys on Oregon constitutional law. Written by two state court judges and three practitioners, the 2013 edition is over 500 pages long and helpfully tells lawyers about the independent role that Oregon constitutional law may play in helping their clients.

Any such practice guides or local rules also would provide a benefit to the state courts. It would remind them of the importance of clarifying the explanation of a decision to invalidate a state or local law or to overrule the actions of a state or local official. After *Michigan v. Long*, the U.S. Supreme Court presumes the reviewability of a state court decision involving federal and state claims—presumes, in other words, that the state court exercised the power of judicial review based on the federal ground rather than the state ground when the claimant successfully challenges the validity of a law on both grounds.[6] The only corrective is a clear statement that the state court's decision turns on state law.[7]

Bar Exams

The legal community can do something else. Each State holds a bar exam, passage of which is required to obtain a license to practice law in each State. More States should put questions about state constitutional law on their bar exams. Only seven States did so in recent years,[8] even as all fifty States require newly minted lawyers to take an oath to uphold the federal *and* state constitutions before they may practice in the State. Perhaps Edward Strieff wishes that Utah had put the topic on its bar exam.

How can States expect lawyers to take state constitutional law seriously if they don't take it seriously enough to put a few questions about the topic on the bar exam? If accountability follows money in government, it's assuredly true that accountability for understanding state constitutional law follows placement of the topic on the bar exam. Even just as a matter of symbolism, the topic warrants at least *one* question on each bar exam. How about this one? True or false: May a claimant successfully challenge the validity of a state or local law under the State's constitution even after the U.S. Supreme Court holds that relief is not available under an identically worded guarantee in the U.S. Constitution?

Law Schools

Lawyers can't make arguments they don't know anything about. American law faces a woeful education deficit when it comes to knowledge about our state constitutions, one that predates entry to law school, perhaps even to college. One national poll in 1988 showed that 52 percent of the adult population did not know their State had a constitution.[9] I doubt matters have improved since.

Most law schools do not teach state constitutional law, and none, to my knowledge, offers it as a core part of its curriculum. There are nearly 200 accredited and unaccredited law schools in the country.[10] During the 2007–08 school year, just twenty-four of them offered a course called "State Constitutional Law." Eleven law schools offered a state-specific version of the subject, for example, "Florida Constitutional Law." Forty-six law schools offered "State and Local Government Law," which covers some constitutional law but does not focus on it. Thirty-seven law schools offered "Local Government Law," which covers little if any state constitutional law. All told, eighty law schools (or less than half of the total) taught state constitutional law or a related course—and only twenty-four of them or at most thirty-five taught the subject fully.[11]

Is there a common denominator among the schools that offered the class during the 2007–08 school year? Here they are: Albany, American, Arizona State, Cleveland State, DePaul, Florida State, Fordham, Gonzaga, Indiana (Indianapolis), McGeorge, Michigan State, Minnesota, Ohio State, Oklahoma City, Pepperdine, Quinnipiac, Roger Williams, Rutgers (Newark), Temple, Tennessee, Widener, Yeshiva, Liberty, and Texas Wesleyan. Not one of the top fifteen law schools, as measured by *U.S. News & World Report*,[12] offered this general course during the 2007–08 school year.

Matters have improved, ever so slightly, since the 2007–08 school year. For the 2016 school year, twenty-eight (as opposed to twenty-four) law schools now offer the course: American, California (Hastings), Campbell, DePaul, Florida State, Gonzaga, Harvard, Indiana (Bloomington and Indianapolis), Louisiana State, Loyola (Los Angeles), New England, Northern Kentucky, Notre Dame, Ohio State, Oklahoma City, Pepperdine, Roger Williams, Rutgers (Camden), Samford, Iowa, Kansas, Kentucky, Minnesota, Missouri-Columbia, Wayne State, Widener, and Willamette. Thirteen of the law schools that offered it in the 2007 school year did not offer it in the 2015 or 2016 school year. In addition, twenty-five (as opposed to eleven) law schools offered a state-specific version of "State Constitutional Law" (e.g., "Florida Constitutional Law") in the 2016 school year.[13] All things considered, we see two modest steps forward (with more schools and a greater variety of schools offering the course) and one step back (with a baker's dozen of law schools no longer offering the course, at least for the two years I checked). In America circa 2018, the role of the fifty States in American constitutional law remains a persistently undertaught and underappreciated subject.

It's difficult for a law school to offer courses on a topic, I realize, if few professors offer to teach it. My impression is that most law schools that offer the course do so because an adjunct professor, as opposed to a tenured professor, has offered to teach the class. This defies explanation. Isn't one of the career objectives of most law professors to create a new field, to develop an underdeveloped field, or to offer a new perspective on an old field? How hard would it be to compete in the field of state constitutional law? Most of the professors in the area, including me, have other jobs. There are exceptions—Robert Williams of Rutgers being the most obvious—but on balance, the new law professor who can't compete here can't compete anywhere.

So many rich possibilities await in this field, and yet most new constitutional law professors seem intent on refining federal constitutional law still further, if indeed they engage the doctrine at all. Which path, I ask, is more attractive? To be the professor who points the way to the *eighth* distinct tier of review under federal equal protection jurisprudence, as opposed to the already catalogued seven tiers of review?[14] Or to be this professor: The one who proposes a new theory of equal protection for a State's constitution that accounts for the live-and-learn flaws of the federal experience? The one who encourages several state supreme courts to adopt the approach? And the one who develops an equal-protection approach at the state court level that, if all goes well, becomes a model for a reconfigured national approach based on its success in the States?[15]

A law school dean might object that now is not the time to be hiring new tenure-track professors or adding courses to a school's curriculum. Enrollment is down, and most law schools are trying to avoid doing less with less, struggling to preserve the offerings they now have even as they have fewer students and fewer resources. Fair enough. For some schools, now may not be a propitious time to add a separate course on state constitutional law. But if that's the case, it's worth remembering what treatises on constitutional law looked like in the nineteenth and early twentieth centuries. They covered both dimensions of the topic: state and federal constitutional law. To use one example, Cooley's *Treatise on the Constitutional Limitations Which Rest upon The Legislative Power of the States of the American Union* has these initial five chapters: Definitions; The Constitution of the United States; The Formation and Amendment of State Constitutions; Constructions of State Constitutions; and The Powers Which the Legislative Department May Exercise.[16] When the book turns to many chapters about the circumstances in which laws may be declared unconstitutional, it covers federal and state cases decided under the federal and state constitutions.[17]

Why not offer a course on *American* constitutional law, one that covers all facets of the topic? Yes, federal constitutional law has been a growth industry over the last seventy-five years, and it's hard to pack all of it into even two semester-long courses. But there's still something odd, and a tad misleading, about a class on individual constitutional rights that does not address the federal *and* state counterparts. Odder still is the course that purports to cover structure and yet fails to talk about the States' role in that structure. If law schools do not have the resources to offer separate courses on state constitutional law, they should at a minimum teach American constitutional law and tell students both sides of the story. How can one possibly understand the topic of constitutional law without understanding and appreciating its federal and state components? That's a little like offering a course on civil procedure without telling the students that there are federal court procedures and state ones.

There is one other oddity about the status quo. I have never met a law professor who is satisfied with the state of federal constitutional law, as interpreted by the U.S. Supreme Court. Nor have I ever read a law review article that offers unreserved praise for the state of federal constitutional law or the federal judges who interpret it. (I would have noticed the last point.) In the face of a complete absence of support by the legal academy for the status quo with respect to federal constitutional law—in the face, indeed, of frequent derision of it and scorn for it—why aren't law professors urging the state courts to avoid some of these problems by trying different approaches under their own constitutions? Think about it. No one seems to be happy with federal constitutional law, but very few people complain when the state courts incorporate every jot and tittle of federal constitutional law into their own constitutions. Go figure.

Federal Courts

Strange as it may be for a federal judge to write a book dedicated to increasing the salience of state constitutional law, it would be stranger still if he did not offer some ideas about how the federal courts could advance that goal. Federal law, as it happens, encourages respect for state law in several ways already—and other possibilities are in the offing. Begin with what is already in place. Several judge-created doctrines turn on the federalism imperative of dignifying state law, whether that law happens to be the State's constitution or not. Take abstention. Packaged in many forms, the basic idea is to discourage federal courts from intruding on sensitive and complicated issues of state law without giving the state courts a chance to review, and perhaps resolve, the matter first. A federal case embedded with a critical question of state constitutional law offers an opportunity for the federal courts to stay their hand until the state courts consider the matter.

Certification offers another avenue. All federal courts may certify questions of state law, including state constitutional law, to the pertinent state supreme court either because the answer may eliminate a federal question or because the state court has the final say in the matter anyway. In my experience, this option is not used as often as it could be for two reasons: It adds time, often a lot of time, to the lifespan of a case, and state courts often do not accept the certification request. A state supreme court worthy of its name can, and should, solve both problems. The state courts should make it clear that they take their final authority over the meaning of the state charter seriously by signaling to their sister federal courts that they are open to certification requests and, above all, that they will prioritize them—both by promptly answering the initial certification request and, if they accept the issue, by promptly resolving it. In a well-functioning federal system, state courts should welcome such requests and show it. By answering the initial request within weeks, not months. And, if they take the issue, by resolving it within months, not years. If state courts demonstrate that they welcome the dialogue by answering such questions promptly, federal courts, including the U.S. Supreme Court, should invoke the option, more often than they currently do.

Those are some of the ways in which the federal courts already strive to respect state law, including state constitutional law. But is there anything more they could do? And is there anything they could do with respect to the sequencing question in dual-claim cases? I have already given many good reasons to answer the state constitutional question before the federal one in a dual-claim case. Nothing prevents federal courts from doing just that in their own cases—by resolving the state claim first—and if necessary requiring the advocates to brief the state claim carefully and thoroughly. Influence by example is a path open to all federal and state courts in this area. The federal courts also are free to point out the relevance of state constitutional guarantees to certain disputes, as the Supreme Court has done from time to time,[18] or even to mention the benefits of sequencing the resolution of a state claim before a counterpart federal claim. In one of his year-end reports, Chief Justice Burger urged the state courts to take this path. "State Courts," he said "are responsible first for resolving issues arising under their constitutions and statutes and then for passing on matters concerning federal law."[19]

Beyond that, the U.S. Supreme Court might *require* the state courts to sequence their decisions by resolving the state constitutional claims first. But that possibility is a difficult sell. Such a heavy-handed mandate would hardly convey the kind of respect for the independent sovereign status of the state courts that federalism aims to encourage. How paradoxical for the U.S. Supreme Court to dictate to a state court how to sequence *its* decision-making in order to facilitate the development of *its* constitutional law. At any rate, precedent long ago rejected the idea, what would amount to a state-court exhaustion requirement for all federal claims under § 1983. The Supreme Court has already held that a § 1983 claimant, generally speaking, need not exhaust state remedies (including state constitutional remedies) before bringing a federal constitutional claim.[20]

That leaves one other possibility for increasing engagement between the state and federal courts and state and federal constitutional law. Even though the state courts handle (by some estimates) 95 percent of the litigation in this country and even though they handle a large number of cases that present federal issues, the Federal High Court devotes relatively little of its docket to reviewing state court decisions involving federal law.[21] And that's even though the U.S. Supreme Court has been just as likely over the last several years to reverse decisions by the state high courts as by the federal appellate courts.[22]

One possible explanation for this pattern is that the National Court has come to see infrequent review of state court decisions as a way to convey respect for the state courts. Little review of state court decisions, the thinking goes, is one way to dignify the independent sovereign status of the state courts. By leaving the state courts alone (or at least more alone than the federal courts), the U.S. Supreme Court may see itself as respecting their status in the system, perhaps even heightening it.

Let me push back in two modest ways on that perspective, one focused on fairness, the other on respect. Decreased review of state court decisions that turn on the Federal Constitution tilts the playing field against a frequent set of litigants in the state and federal system: state criminal defendants. Ever since 1996, AEDPA (the Anti-Terrorism and Effective Death Penalty Act, to be exact) has placed serious restrictions on the availability of federal habeas relief for individuals convicted of state crimes. Once direct review of the conviction ends, defendants must show that the state court's rejection of any federal constitutional claim is "unreasonable" as measured by U.S. Supreme Court precedent.[23] That's a high bar, as a state court's rejection of a claim on direct review will not be eligible for habeas relief so long as "fairminded jurists" could agree with the state court.[24] The question thus is not whether the state court erred but whether it erred unreasonably.

The upshot is that diminished direct review of federal claims by state criminal defendants insulates, or nearly insulates, those claims from federal review. Why do that? The point of AEDPA was to prevent *federal habeas courts* from interfering with the state criminal justice, not to prevent the U.S. Supreme Court from directly reviewing the state courts' handling of federal constitutional claims.

That's not just unfair to state criminal defendants in an absolute sense. It's unfair to them in a relative sense. Criminal defendants in the federal court system have better prospects of success in the U.S. Supreme Court as a result of this disparity. As the review patterns show over the last two decades, those convicted of federal crimes are more likely to obtain direct review of their constitutional claims by the U.S. Supreme Court. Instead of having just as many of their claims shunted to the significant hurdles of collateral review, those defendants face more promising odds of obtaining direct U.S. Supreme Court review. More frequent direct review of state court criminal cases would level this playing field.

Increased review of state court cases, whether criminal or civil, also might *increase* respect for state courts. Counterintuitive though that may sound, the question remains: What counts as respect? The current model seems premised on the idea that the best way for the U.S. Supreme Court to signal respect for state supreme courts is to let them be. But does ignoring the state courts, or at least infrequently reviewing their work, treat them as meaningful partners in the interpretation of the U.S. Constitution? One of the satisfying features of being a federal judge is participating in, and contributing to, the development of federal constitutional law. And that's so even when it means being reversed from time to time. Most state court judges, I suspect, would feel the same way.

Resolution of vexing constitutional law problems turns on ideas, mining for insights that fit within existing precedents but cope with new circumstances. It's difficult to understand why one wouldn't want all hands on deck for that enterprise. Increased review of state court decisions is another way of prompting increased engagement with them. More frequent review of state court *federal* constitutional rulings also would prompt more state court litigants and state court judges to pay attention to *state* constitutional rulings, which the U.S. Supreme Court has no power to review.

Now may be an opportune time to engage state courts. Even as most lawyers and most academics continue to assume that the election of most state court judges diminishes the quality of the pool of candidates for those jobs, a growing number of excellent practitioners and professors are joining the state courts. In truth, today's state *and* federal selection processes both have flaws—presumably because state and federal judges have come to exercise such considerable power over so many high-stakes debates in American society today. But it's dangerous to assume that the warts in these selection processes dissuade good lawyers from serving. I for one am increasingly skeptical that there is a meaningful difference between the quality of the work produced by the state high courts and federal courts of appeals.[25]

Federal *and* state courts perform better when the advocacy is better. State attorneys general offices are among the most prominent, if not the most prominent, litigants in state court—and frequent litigators in federal court. For many decades, American appellate courts faced a disparity between the trial and appellate advocacy of the federal versus the state attorneys general offices. That has changed and continues to change. In 1987, there were just eight state solicitors general.[26] By 2001, there were twenty-four state solicitors general.[27] Today, there are thirty-nine state solicitors general (occasionally called state solicitors or appellate chiefs), who preside over offices that are modeled after the (correctly) lauded federal Office of the Solicitor General.[28] More state solicitors general does not necessarily mean better state advocacy. It's just a title after all. But it appears to be an enticing title with enticing advocacy responsibilities in view of the number of excellent lawyers who have joined these offices. In my circuit, some of the best advocates today are assistant U.S. attorneys *and* state solicitors general (and their deputies and assistants). Just as we may be entering a golden age of state court judges, the same may be true for state advocates.

Better state advocacy promises better state constitutional law. Good state lawyers, I realize, generally will oppose the creation or recognition of new state constitutional rights. But even when that is the case, improved advocacy sharpens the debate, prompting more vigorous advocacy from public defenders and private counsel, all to the boon of the state court judges. Even when a state lawyer wins by showing that the state constitution does not go as far as its federal counterpart, that creates its own benefit: the proper independent resolution of a state constitutional claim, immediately useful for that State and eventually of potential use to the U.S. Supreme Court in interpreting the federal guarantee.

If change is to come in this area, it's likely to come from the state courts, not the federal courts. And it's likely to require considerable leadership from the local bench and bar. But it can happen. Professor Richard Price recently undertook an exhaustive study of Oregon appellate practices to determine how often lawyers raised state constitutional claims and how often they independently briefed them.[29] He examined three periods: 1970–78, 1980–84, and 1986–2000. After reading the briefs filed by the parties in the appeals filed during these periods (an impressive, if dreary, accomplishment), he noticed the gradual normalization of state constitutional law as the first, and primary, arguments raised, briefed, and addressed by the Oregon Supreme Court. But as suggested by the length of time he examined, this did not happen overnight. "[I]t is a difficult road," one that required "an unusual leadership commitment from the Oregon Supreme Court as a whole" and cooperation with the law schools and the bar over three decades.[30] That's about right. But the reward is a state legal system that takes its own constitution seriously, that is unlikely to revert any time soon, that is there when you need it—and that will *always* be in a position to contribute to the development of American constitutional law.

9

Epilogue

LET ME TIE TOGETHER some loose ends and untangle a few others. Why would a federal judge write a book that features state court judges and state constitutional law? Because there is room for improving state *and* federal constitutional law, and because the improvement of each will generate collateral benefits for both—for American constitutional law and for all of its component parts.

Renewing trust in state courts. By telling the stories of landmark rights disputes from the perspective of the federal and state constitutions as well as the federal and state courts, this book illustrates the role the States can play, and have played, in protecting individual rights. Convention suggests that only life-tenured federal judges, not elected state court judges, only the national government, not the States, can be trusted to enforce constitutional rights. The post-*Rodriguez* school-funding story and the post-*Mapp/Leon* exclusionary rule prove otherwise. They arise in settings that say a lot about a country—what kind of opportunity it gives children to have an equal start in life and how it treats those suspected of crime. In both settings, large numbers of States insisted on change even after the U.S. Supreme Court permitted continuity. The pre-*Buck* and pre-*Barnette* stories likewise arise in settings that say something about a country—how it treats individuals with disabilities, how and when it restricts an individual's right to procreate, and how it treats the free speech and free exercise rights of religious minorities and other dissenters.

When told in full, these stories provide a healthy counterweight to received wisdom. They show the risk of relying too heavily on the U.S. Supreme Court as the sole guardian of our liberties as well as the farsighted role the state courts have played before in dealing with threats to liberty. Even the most acclaimed individual rights decision in American history, *Brown v. Board of Education,* is more complicated than it might at first appear when it comes to the role of the States and national government in rights protection. It's worth remembering the other half of that story. The companion case to *Brown* was *Bolling v. Sharpe,* in which the Court demanded the end of segregation in the public schools of the District of Columbia, an enclave controlled by the federal government, not a State. Those who place complete faith in just *one* branch of American government to protect their rights will eventually be disappointed.

Nor are these stories restricted to the twentieth and twenty-first centuries. To use one example mentioned in a recent state supreme court case, the nineteenth century saw a marked contrast between the treatment of African Americans in the U.S. Supreme Court and in the Iowa High Court, with the Hawkeye State coming out on top.[1]

But do these stories stand alone? How do they fit into the history of litigation over other individual rights? That is no small topic, one that cannot be covered in full (or even in meaningful part) in an epilogue. But it's worth offering a few other examples and a few other data points, at a minimum to provoke continued thought about the States' role as guardians of liberty, with the possibility to convince that this role can grow.

The States' responses to the Supreme Court's 2005 decision in *Kelo v. City of New London*[2] offer a contemporary illustration of the capacity and willingness of state courts and legislatures to protect—or at least thoughtfully to consider protecting—other individual rights when the Supreme Court declines to do so. *Kelo* upheld a city's development plan for property acquired through eminent domain because it amounted to a "public use" within the meaning of the Takings Clause. The decision displaced Susette Kelo from her multigenerational family home (by permitting the city to replace it with a planned, though never built, corporate headquarters) and dispirited property-rights advocates (by seeming to allow all manner of future takings). The U.S. Supreme Court's opinion was not the last word on the issue, however.

Through state court decisions, state legislation, and state constitutional amendments, property-rights advocates since then have made considerable gains, in some instances perhaps obtaining more than a favorable *Kelo* decision could have offered them. State court rulings prompted some of the gains. Within roughly a year of *Kelo*, the Ohio and Oklahoma Supreme Courts extended their state constitutional protections against eminent domain beyond the federal baseline by holding that the potential economic benefit from a new private development alone does not justify the exercise of eminent domain under the State's constitution.[3] Both decisions directly repudiated the reasoning of *Kelo*.

Most state legislatures, however, refused to wait for similar court decisions. As of today, most states have enacted legislation that tightens restrictions on public use and the ways in which local governments may exercise eminent domain.[4] Seven States have limited the public purposes for which eminent domain is acceptable.[5] Roughly ten States have enacted laws limiting the States' power to exercise eminent domain.[6] Five others have adopted variations on these ideas.[7] Some States have sought to reduce the potential abuse of eminent domain by developing procedural changes, requiring state agencies to make stronger showings of public use, requiring agencies to create redevelopment plans, and setting notice and offer requirements to prevent "stealth" condemnation.[8] Only a handful of States have not enacted legislation in the wake of *Kelo*.[9]

All of this does not justify *Kelo* or for that matter prove that the States have compensated for its failings. The question throughout is what happens when the U.S. Supreme Court stays its hand, not whether it was right in doing so. Many critics of *Kelo* remain. As Professor Ilya Somin helpfully points out, some of the state and local responses are more cosmetic than real.[10] But it's difficult to deny—and I don't think anyone denies—that *Kelo* unleashed a wave of state responses that filled many, even if not all, of the gaps left by the U.S. Supreme Court's decision.

A variation on this story arose in response to the U.S. Supreme Court's decision in *Employment Division v. Smith*.[11] Oregon denied unemployment benefits to a man dismissed from his job for using peyote as a sacrament in a religious service of his Native American Church.

Because the relevant state laws—banning peyote use and denying employment benefits to those convicted of using it—were generally applicable and did not target this Native American faith or any other, the Court upheld the law in the face of a free exercise challenge to it premised on the First (and Fourteenth) Amendment. In doing so, the Court applied deferential review, not skeptical review, to the law.

What happened next is a remarkable story of federalism and of the unpredictable path it can take. The first meaningful response came from the national government, not the States, and it was one that was highly critical of *Smith*. In 1993, three years after *Smith*, Congress passed the Religious Freedom Restoration Act (RFRA) with near unanimity. Purporting to exercise its power to enforce the guarantees of the Fourteenth Amendment, RFRA effectively overruled *Smith* by requiring courts to apply strict scrutiny, not rational basis, to any local, state, or federal law that imposed a substantial burden on the exercise of any religious faith without regard to the neutrality or general applicability of the law. The U.S. Supreme Court did not take kindly to this assault on *Smith*. *City of Boerne v. Flores*[12] rejected this broad use of Congress's enforcement powers under the Fourteenth Amendment, reasoning that the national legislature had power to enforce free exercise rights only in response to state violations of the guarantee, not to redefine them in response to a decision of the U.S. Supreme Court it did not like.

Since 1997, when *City of Boerne* was decided, the federal and state legislatures have continued to respond to *Smith*. So too have the state courts. *City of Boerne* did not invalidate RFRA as applied to the federal government. That reality has kept the U.S. Supreme Court busy. Witness *O Centro Espirita*[13] and *Hobby Lobby*[14] and *Zubik*[15] and others sure to follow. In response to *City of Boerne*, Congress enacted the Religious Land Use and Institutionalized Persons Act in 2000, which applied strict scrutiny to land-use laws and prison regulations that burdened the religious practices of inmates. It has withstood constitutional challenge.[16]

Of equal significance, many state legislatures have enacted their own RFRAs, which likewise require courts to use rigorous scrutiny to assess the validity of a state or local law that interferes with the free exercise of religion.[17] The state courts have not hesitated to do what these laws require: apply strict scrutiny.[18] And many state courts have refused to follow *Smith* in construing the free exercise clauses that appear in all state constitutions, insisting that strict scrutiny or at a minimum something more than rational basis governs the claims.[19]

Think about all of these developments, all of this give in some directions and take in others, in the quarter century since *Smith*. Now *that* is a story of American constitutional law and American legislation, one that shows what can transpire when there is a rich judicial and legislative dialogue between and among the States and national government.

Same-sex marriage offers one last example. In 1972, in *Baker v. Nelson*, the U.S. Supreme Court determined in a summary affirmance that the Fourteenth Amendment does not require the States to authorize same-sex marriage.[20] It affirmed a decision of the Minnesota Supreme Court, which had held that the Fourteenth Amendment did not invalidate the State's definition of marriage as between a man and a woman. Not until thirty years later did that definition of marriage begin to change in a lasting way. Change began in the States, and the first change agents were the state courts. In 2003, in *Goodridge v. Department of Public Health*,[21] the Massachusetts Supreme Judicial Court relied on the Massachusetts Constitution to grant same-sex couples the right to marry. It's hard to imagine the U.S. Supreme Court's decision twelve years later in *Obergefell v. Hodges*[22] without *Goodridge* and without the additional state-level activity it prompted. Whether in state supreme courts or state houses, the states led this innovation in American law.

Obergefell recognized as much. In establishing a right to same-sex marriage under the Fourteenth Amendment and in overruling *Baker v. Nelson*, the Court observed that "the highest courts of many States have contributed to this ongoing dialogue in decisions interpreting their own State Constitutions."[23] Ongoing dialogue indeed. This was not just a conversation to which the States contributed; it was one in which they announced the first words. There is no *Obergefell* without *Goodridge*.

Long before *Obergefell*, the role of the state courts as a promising venue for civil rights prompted a fascinating debate between two prominent lawyers—law professors and civil rights advocates both—who shared world views but had different assessments of the state courts.

In 1977, Burt Neuborne wrote *The Myth of Parity*,[24] which maintained that the state courts would never rival the federal courts as a venue for innovative civil rights litigation.[25] In 1999, William Rubenstein responded with *The Myth of Superiority*.[26] Based on his experience as a gay-rights litigator, Rubenstein wrote that "gay litigants seeking to establish and vindicate civil rights have generally fared better in state courts than they have in federal courts."[27] He concluded the piece by "urg[ing] civil rights litigators generally to abandon a rebuttable presumption in favor of federal courts and to consider the possibility of a rebuttable presumption in favor of state courts."[28] For present purposes, it doesn't matter who is right. If these two highly regarded civil rights advocates cannot agree about the point based on their own court experiences, there must be more nuance to the issue than most people appreciate.

All of this prompts an essential question, one of the most crucial underlying this book. What is it about the issues in *Rodriguez, Mapp/ Leon, Buck*, or *Gobitis* (or for that matter, *Kelo* or *Smith* or *Baker*) that prevented Supreme Court defeats from becoming the death knell of the claimants' objectives and instead spurred equally promising, if not more promising, state and local initiatives? Why in these areas? Why not others?

A common thread in many of these examples—and others in which the States have been leaders rather than followers—is the complexity of the problem at hand. While national interest groups will invariably favor winner-take-all approaches, complexity often stands in the way. The more difficult it is to find a single answer to a problem, the more likely state-by-state variation is an appropriate way to handle the issue and the more likely a state court will pay attention to an advocate's argument that a single State ought to try a different approach from the one adopted by the National Court. Just as the intricacy of a problem might prompt different, even competing, answers, it might prompt state courts (and legislatures) to pace change at different speeds. In many areas of law affected by changing social norms, the most important question is not whether but when, not whether but by whom.

A second consideration prompted by these stories is accountability. When the U.S. Supreme Court shifts the spotlight from the national to the local stage, it clarifies the lines of authority. Once the Court makes it clear that any relief will come from the States or not at all, that has a powerful way of sharpening debate, raising the stakes in the States, sometimes accelerating change. *Rodriguez* and *Leon* and their aftermaths illustrate that possibility.

A third consideration relates to the selection method for most state court judges: elections. Dissonant though it may sound, judicial elections sometimes are the friend of innovative individual rights litigation, not its enemy. Some supposedly countermajoritarian constitutional issues are not countermajoritarian at all when presented effectively to elected state court judges. Just as there may be politically functional and politically dysfunctional issues in legislation, the same may be true in litigation. And the two do not always overlap. That reality may explain why these education, criminal procedure, property-rights, free exercise, and eventually marriage issues resonated with some state-elected judges but not life-tenured federal judges. In the Ohio school-funding litigation, in which I represented the State, I thought it helped the plaintiffs—the advocates of change—that the justices of the Ohio Supreme Court were elected. I say this not to plug one method of appointment over another but to show that traditional assumptions about judicial elections and constitutional guarantees may not always hold true.

Even the crudest electoral practicalities do not invariably warrant distrust in the capacity of state court judges to construe their constitutions independently. Truth be told, there are many settings in which judicial elections should lead to *more* state court independence from the U.S. Supreme Court, not less. Aren't there many federal constitutional rulings that *increase* the scope of a protected right and with which elected judges in some States disagree? And with which a majority of the electorate in those States disagree? Aren't there many federal constitutional rulings that *decrease* the scope of a protected right and with which elected judges in some States disagree? And with which a majority of the electorate in those States disagree? The answer of course will depend on the issue and the State. Think about it another way. Surely there are originalist justices on the state courts who disagree with living constitutionalist U.S. Supreme Court decisions. And surely the opposite is true. Electoral practicalities often should liberate, not confine, state court judges in following their own interpretive approaches.

That's just as it should be. Federalism offers a multihued palette from which to work, even after accounting for state judicial elections. It might horrify some state court judges, for example, to revive *Lochner* or reject *Blaisdell*[29] in deciding the meaning of their state liberty-of-contract and due process guarantees. But for others, this would be a welcome opportunity as a matter of legal reasoning—and in many States, electoral considerations would not get in the way. Exactly to the contrary: They would be a net plus. Some state court judges might be inclined to follow *Glucksberg*[30] (and its refusal to recognize a federal constitutional right to physician-assisted suicide) in construing the due process guarantee in their own constitution. But for others, this might present a welcome opportunity for asserting a state court's independence as a matter of legal reasoning or (for judges so inclined) local policy preferences. If there are going to be experiments of this sort, it makes eminent sense in a country of our size and diversity to conduct them in the States. Let one State (or a few) experiment with reviving *Lochner* or burying *Blaisdell* or *Glucksberg*. Then see what happens. The same goes for other cutting-edge issues. In view of the many questions that have arisen recently about administrative deference under *Chevron* and the related nondelegation doctrine,[31] one wonders why some state courts—and presumably state court advocates—assume the federal doctrines should be embraced in full in their States. I could go on and on with other examples—some that liberals would favor and some that conservatives would favor. In either direction, state judicial selection procedures do not prohibit the States from returning to the front lines of rights innovation. Elections sometimes make it easier.

Before leaving the topic of state judicial elections, one last point deserves mention. Some assume that state judicial elections diminish the quality of the judges who sit on the state courts. I am skeptical. But anyone wishing to figure this out, or better yet trying to measure the point, ought to consider this perspective. Ask which set of courts, the state or federal courts, has honored the language of their respective constitutions more faithfully? I do not know the answer, and the number of state courts suggests a range of answers. But I have a guess. On balance, I suspect that the federal judicial interpretations of the U.S. Constitution have migrated further from its terms than have most state court interpretations of their constitutions. If lack of trust in state courts turns on their fidelity to the language of their constitutions, that may be a game many state court justices are willing to lose.

Renewing the States' role in rights innovation offers benefits to all schools of constitutional interpretation. Up to this point, I have said little about the role of different schools of interpretation in thinking about these American constitutional law stories. That's because, for present purposes, it makes no difference to me whether the state and federal court decisions turn on originalism, living constitutionalism, or pragmatism, or for that matter whether the courts decided these cases correctly. Let me pause for a page or two to look at these stories through the lens of different interpretive methodologies.

For an originalist judge, much of this does not matter. If a constitution does not mention a right, there is little to quarrel about, whether in construing the Federal Constitution or a State Constitution. All that matters is whether the state or federal court's decision correctly identifies the publicly understood meaning of the guarantee at the time it was ratified—and stands by it. There is one meaningful exception. A federal judge faced with a question about the meaning of a federal guarantee modeled after a state guarantee will be quite grateful for, and should embrace, a renewed emphasis on state constitutionalism. In that context, originalist state court decisions offer powerful evidence about the initial public meaning of the federal guarantee—guidance that federal judges should be grateful to receive. Just look at the Court's right-to-bear-arms decision in *Heller* for a recent illustration.[32] State court decisions focused on the original meaning of state guarantees also will prompt more scholars and advocates to do the work of uncovering the relevant histories of the state constitutions.

What of living constitutionalists? In their eyes, the meaning of a constitution changes over time not because a given judge wants it to change or because he wishes to insert his personal belief into the constitution. It changes because objectively provable norms in the area have changed. For the adherent of this approach, state constitutional decisions offer a rich source of guidance—for other state courts and for the federal courts and especially for the U.S. Supreme Court. As to the National Court, what better source of evidence of the fluidity of social norms and mores than new interpretations of state constitutions by state court judges? If a theory does not have the support of the

American people of 1791, then its legitimacy at a minimum must have the support of the American people today.[33] Taking a cue from Justice Jackson, a living constitutionalist on the U.S. Supreme Court might do well to distinguish three settings in evaluating whether to adopt a constitutional right on a national scale: efforts to bring outlier States into line with a new national consensus, efforts to resolve a debate still brewing in the States, and efforts to overrule the States' long-held and uniform practices.[34] The first setting offers the best, and least controversial, reason for altering the meaning of federal constitutional guarantees over time.

State court decisions offer a different insight for the pragmatist. They show what works and what doesn't. What pragmatic jurist wants to nationalize a right when the end result may be self-defeating or worse? As the *Rodriguez* story shows, as some of the *Mapp* story suggests, and as the *Kelo* and *Smith* and *Baker* stories confirm, the answer to the pragmatist judge's question—"What happens if we do nothing?"—is not invariably that the States will do nothing. And it occasionally may be that the States will do more for a given cause than the federal courts ever could have done on their own.

By allowing the state courts to be the first responders in addressing innovative rights claims, the U.S. Supreme Court can gain valuable insights critical to all three schools of thought. The risks of error associated with a state-first approach are fewer. And the possibility of exporting ideas that work to other States and sometimes to the federal government is as promising when it comes to American constitutional law as it has been when it comes to other areas of law—criminal law, contracts, torts—in which the state and federal governments have overlapping responsibilities. Time has a way of showing which individual rights have centrifugal tendencies and which have centripetal ones. Yet all roads lead to the same place. A core feature of American government—federalism—works best if we encourage both halves of the equation to take seriously their responsibilities under it.

Recovering some of the structural virtues of the U.S. Constitution. Federalism also respects the initial design of the U.S. Constitution, and its carefully drawn, but difficult to preserve, balance of power. One way to measure the health of a legal system would be to print the country's legal texts on the left pages of a law book and the judiciary's interpretations of those texts on the corresponding right pages. The greater the gap between the meaning of the text and the courts' interpretations of them, the less healthy the legal system. And the more one can wonder: Who is the lawmaker? How is lawmaking done?

That's a particularly acute issue for a state or national charter. And it's a particularly acute risk for the U.S. Constitution, which is nearly impervious to change through amendment, a reality that simultaneously has placed pressure on the U.S. Supreme Court to alter it through interpretation *and* made each of those changes nearly unalterable. The problem with modifying the U.S. Constitution by interpretation rather than amendment is that each change increases the gap between our foundational charter and its meaning. And each change makes it more plausible to make still further changes. Over time, updating a constitution by interpretation runs the risk of skewing democratic government, cheapening law, and imperiling the body responsible for making the changes: the federal courts. It's not good for each new generation of lawyers either. How unfortunate to imprint each set of first-year law students with a lesson that no class on federal constitutional law can avoid—that some constitutional texts have come to look like hurdles to clear, not words to interpret, telling us more about the people who interpreted the document than about the people who ratified it.

An objective of this book is to urge a few modest steps toward closing the gap between *one* feature of the original design of American government and current practice by returning the States to the front lines of rights protection and rights innovation. As written, the U.S. Constitution was *not* designed to facilitate rights innovation, whether through Congress or the courts. The document contains one blocking mechanism after another, all quite appropriate given the potential breadth of power exercised by the federal branches. As written, the state constitutions were change incubators, governing smaller, often more congenial populations with shared world views. And the state constitutions were, and remain, easy to amend. Unlike the Federal Constitution, the state constitutions are readily amenable to adaptation, as most of them can be amended through popular majoritarian votes, and all of them can be amended more easily than the federal charter. The design of each charter signals that the States were meant to be the breakwater in rights protection and the national government the shoreline defense.

Increasing the salience of the state courts and state constitutional law honors some worthy traits of the original federal constitutional framework, most notably its conspicuous horizontal *and* vertical separations of powers. If there's one feature of American government worth preserving over every other, it's that differentiated lines of constitutional structure—honored and undiluted—preserve liberty. Only by retaining a balance of authority among the branches do we keep the most malignant risks to liberty at bay.

Retaining trust in the federal courts. One last reason to tell these American constitutional law stories relates to the federal courts. There are long-term risks with the national judicialization of so many American policies, a process started between 75 and 110 years or so ago (depending on whom you ask) and one that does not seem to have run its course. One explanation for that development, a fair one at that, is that the state courts (and state legislators and governors) failed to perform their independent roles in enforcing the structural protections and individual rights guarantees found in their own constitutions. A revival of independent state constitutionalism not only might return us to something approximating the original design, but it also might ease the pressure on the U.S. Supreme Court to be the key rights innovator in modern America. Why not put the state constitutions, state courts, and state legislatures on the front lines (or more precisely return them to the front lines) when it comes to rights innovation? Even if one accepts that many of the Warren Court decisions were for the good as a matter of policy, and even if one assumes that the States brought this diminishment of authority upon themselves, that does not tell us what to do next. All essential constitutional questions ultimately come down to structure. And structure concerns who, not what—who should be the leading change agents in society going forward, not looking backward. One point of telling these stories is to make the case that it's time to shift the balance back to the state courts.

A political reality confirms that this will not be easy. It's the same reason why it's so difficult to preserve distinct spheres of power between the state and national governments. Federalism has no constituency, and it never will. Since the death of the Federalist and the Anti-Federalist

Parties two centuries ago, no national political party to my knowledge has taken a consistent stand on the proper scope of power of Congress and the National Supreme Court. Most interest groups are the same. They care foremost about what the decision is, not who is making it, and indeed care about who is making the decision only to the extent that it might extend the reach of a preferred policy—aptly named fairweather federalists. Most interest groups (and most Americans) are plenty happy to see Congress nationalize an issue in their favor or, still better, to see the National Court sideline a policy opponent through a constitutional ruling. The constant for political parties, interest groups, and most Americans is opportunism, pursuing a near-term interest in a favored policy at the distant expense of empowering national legislative and judicial decision makers to make still more policy decisions.

While nearly all interest groups and most Americans seem to remain comfortable with using the U.S. Supreme Court (as opposed to the state courts) as their preferred change agent, it's easy to wonder how long this can last and to worry how it will end. So long as we insist on casting the Court in this role, two things are inevitable: The people will care deeply about who is on the Court, and the people will criticize the Court, as opposed to the elected branches, when five justices do not do their bidding. The confirmation process—picking justices to resolve structural and individual rights debates known and unknown for the next twenty-five to thirty years—is not well-equipped to handle the first development, and the Court as an institution is not well-equipped to respond to the second.

One way out of this problem is to lean more heavily on legislatures, whether state or federal, as the key source of rights protection. We could, in other words, wean ourselves from what Professor Sandy Levinson calls our "national obsession" with countermajoritarian, which is to say judicially enforceable, rights.[35] There is something to be said for his point, as there is ample room for constitutional *and* statutory rights. Statutory guarantees may be the proletariat of rights, but they often are the superior of the two. Wouldn't most people prefer to live in a society in which a majority of citizens look after and respect the rights of minority groups, discrete, insular, or otherwise, through majoritarian legislation rather than through a majority of nine justices? The 1964 Civil Rights Act and *Brown v. Board of Education* both offered critical protections, but a compelling case can be made that the Act is the more instrumental of the two when it comes to creating a culture in which respect defeats prejudice. All else being equal, the earned success of a victory in the halls of a legislature is more likely to hold and facilitate lasting change than a judicial decision.

But this seems like a partial answer, and a hopeful one at that. I, for one, see no end in sight to the country's appetite for judicial resolution of many of the essential policy issues of the day. And the more courts do, to repeat, the more plausible it is for the courts to do more. A culture of judicially enforceable rights may be here to stay. Americans seem to like judicially created rights, making us one of the most rights-conscious countries in history. Instead of swimming against this current, I wonder if it is worth swimming with it, by accepting judicially innovated rights—just with more emphasis at the local rather than at the national level and more debate about judicial versus legislative changes.

Whatever the prospects for change through state constitutions and state courts may have been in the 1950s and 1960s, I have a hard time understanding why they remain inappropriate vehicles for rights innovation in the twenty-first century—and why they should not be the lead change agents going forward. When Justice Brandeis launched the laboratory metaphor for policy innovation, he used the plural, not the singular, signaling an interest in hearing how the States in the first instance would respond to new challenges. A single laboratory of experimentation for fifty-one jurisdictions and 320 million people poses serious risks. A ground-up approach to developing constitutional doctrine allows the Court to learn from the States—useful to pragmatic justices interested in how ideas work on the ground, useful to originalist justices interested in what words first found in state constitutions mean. It gives both sides to a debate time to make their case. And it places less pressure on the U.S. Supreme Court. The Court may wait for, and nationalize, a dominant majority position, lowering the stakes of its decision in the process. Or it may treat occasionally indeterminate language in the way it should be treated, as allowing for fifty-one imperfect solutions rather than one imperfect solution.

NOTES

<hr/>

Chapter 2

1. *See* Randy J. Holland, *State Constitutions: Purpose and Function*, 69 Temp. L. Rev. 989, 989 (1996); William J. Brennan, Jr., *State Constitutions and the Protection of Individual Rights*, 90 Harv. L. Rev. 489, 501 (1977) ("each of the rights eventually recognized in the federal Bill of Rights had previously been protected in one or more state constitutions").

2. *See* Jeffrey S. Sutton, *Introduction: State Constitutions in the United States Federal System*, 77 Ohio St. L.J. 195, 196 (2016); Steven G. Calabresi et al., *State Bills of Rights in 1787 and 1791: What Individual Rights Are Really Deeply Rooted in American History and Tradition?*, 85 S. Cal. L. Rev. 1451, 1452 (2012); Robert F. Williams, *The State Constitutions of the Founding Decade: Pennsylvania's Radical 1776 Constitution and Its Influences on American Constitutionalism*, 62 Temp. L. Rev. 541, 541 (1989).

3. Am. Atheists, Inc. v. City of Detroit, 567 F.3d 278 (6th Cir. 2009).

4. Not all States face this problem. Lawyers and judges from Oregon, a State that prioritizes state constitutional law claims, tell me that they face a different problem: Litigants sometimes neglect to raise the *federal* claims. For more on the Oregon approach, see Chapter 7.

5. *See* Jeremy M. Christiansen, *State Search and Seizure: The Original Meaning*, 38 U. Haw. L. Rev. 63, 106 (2016) (observing that "[s]tate constitutional law is generally considered second-tier to federal constitutional law"); James A. Gardner, *The Failed Discourse of State Constitutionalism*, 90 Mich. L. Rev. 761, 780 (1992) (opining that "[o]ne of the most striking aspects of state constitutional decisions is

their relative infrequency" and observing that, in the sample of State high courts, only 21 percent of the docket decided state constitutional issues); James A. Gardner, *What Is a State Constitution?*, 24 Rutgers L.J. 1025, 1026 (1993) (observing that State high courts "turned only infrequently and grudgingly to their state constitutions"); Daniel Gordon, *Superconstitutions Saving the Shunned: The State Constitutions Masquerading as Weaklings*, 67 Temp. L. Rev. 965, 965 (1994) ("Litigators have so infrequently tapped state constitutions as a source of protection for individual rights that more than once during the last dozen or so years legal commentators and courts have published basic 'how to' instructions on the use of state constitutions."); Michael D. Blanchard, *The New Judicial Federalism: Deference Masquerading as Discourse and the Tyranny of the Locality in State Judicial Review of Education Finance*, 60 U. Pitt. L. Rev. 231, 288 (1998) ("In addition to the relative infrequency of state constitutional decisions, state supreme court opinions reflect a general avoidance of analysis of the state constitution altogether."); Erwin Chemerinsky, *Two Cheers for State Constitutional Law*, 62 Stan. L. Rev. 1695, 1700 (2010) (observing that, as a result of the infrequent use of state constitutional provisions, "many states do not have a tradition of using their state constitutions to provide rights greater than that in the United States Constitution").

6. Conn. Const. of 1776, *reprinted in* 1 The Federal and State Constitutions, Colonial Charters, and Other Organic Laws of the United States 257–58 (Ben Perley Poore ed., 2d ed. 1878) [hereinafter Constitutions]; Del. Const. of 1776, *reprinted in* Constitutions, *supra*, at 273–78; Ga. Const. of 1777, *reprinted in* Constitutions, *supra*, at 377–83; Md. Const. of 1776, *reprinted in* Constitutions, *supra*, at 817–28; Mass. Const. of 1780, *reprinted in* Constitutions, *supra*, at 956–73; N.H. Const. of 1776, *reprinted in* Constitutions, *supra*, at 1279–80; N.J. Const. of 1776, *reprinted in* Constitutions, *supra*, at 1310–14; N.Y. Const. of 1777, *reprinted in* Constitutions, *supra*, at 1328–39; N.C. Const. of 1776, *reprinted in* Constitutions, *supra*, at 1409–14; Pa. Const. of 1776, *reprinted in* Constitutions, *supra*, at 1540–48; S.C. Const. of 1776, *reprinted in* Constitutions, *supra*, at 1615–20; Va. Const. of 1776, *reprinted in* Constitutions, *supra*, at 1910–12. Rhode Island, the one state not on the list, operated under a charter from 1663 until it created its constitution in 1842. *See* R.I. Charter of 1663, *reprinted in* Constitutions, *supra*, at 1595–1603; R.I. Const. of 1842, *reprinted in* Constitutions, *supra*, at 1603–13. When Rhode Island finally came around to writing its own constitution, that did not happen without some controversy, one that made its way to the U.S. Supreme Court. *See* Luther v. Borden, 48 U.S. (7 How.) 1, 1–2 (1849). Vermont, though not recognized as a State at the time, held a convention and adopted its own

constitution in 1777. *See* VT. CONST. of 1777, *reprinted in* CONSTITUTIONS, *supra*, at 1857–65.

7. Gordon S. Wood, Foreword, *State Constitution-Making in the American Revolution*, 24 RUTGERS L.J. 911, 917 (1993) ("The American revolutionaries virtually established the modern idea of a written constitution.").

8. *Id.* at 911. *See generally* GORDON S. WOOD, THE CREATION OF THE AMERICAN REPUBLIC, 1776–1787 (1969).

9. U.S. Term Limits, Inc. v. Thornton, 514 U.S. 779, 838 (Kennedy, J., concurring).

10. *See, e.g.*, PA. CONST. art. I, § 7 (freedom of press and speech); VT. CONST. art. I (abolishing slavery); N.Y. CONST. art. I, § 2 (due process); WYO. CONST. art. VI, § 1 (women's right to vote).

11. *See, e.g.*, Brennan, *supra* note 1, at 501 ("Prior to the adoption of the federal Constitution, each of the rights eventually recognized in the federal Bill of Rights had previously been protected in one or more state constitutions."); Holland, *supra* note 1, at 997 ("[S]tate Declarations of Rights were the primary origin and model for the provisions set forth in the Federal Bill of Rights.").

12. District of Columbia v. Heller, 554 U.S. 570, 601 (2008).

13. City of Boerne v. Flores, 521 U.S. 507, 552–53 (1997) (O'Connor, J., dissenting).

14. *See, e.g.*, Borough of Duryea v. Guarnieri, 131 S. Ct. 2488, 2503 (2011) (Scalia, J., concurring) (right to petition); Kelo v. City of New London, 545 U.S. 469, 512 (2005) (Thomas, J., dissenting) (takings for public use); Crawford v. Washington, 541 U.S. 36, 48 (2004) (confrontation); Atwater v. City of Lago Vista, 532 U.S. 318, 339 (2001) (searches and seizures); Neder v. United States, 527 U.S. 1, 31 (1999) (Scalia, J., concurring in part and dissenting in part) (criminal jury trial).

15. *E.g.*, ALA. CONST. art. I, § 22; ARK. CONST. art. II, § 17; COLO. CONST. art. II, § 11; FLA. CONST. art. I, § 10; ME. CONST. art. I, § 11; N.D. CONST. art. I, § 18; N.H. CONST. pt. I, art. 23; R.I. CONST. art. I, § 12; TEX. CONST. art. I, § 16.

16. 32 U.S. 243 (1833).

17. *Id.* at 247 ("[T]he fifth amendment must be understood as restraining the power of the general government, not as applicable to the states.").

18. U.S. CONST. art. VI, cl. 2.

19. 17 U.S. 316 (1819).

20. *Id.* at 436 ("The result is a conviction that the states have no power, by taxation or otherwise, to retard, impede, burden, or in any manner control, the operations of the constitutional laws enacted by congress to carry into execution the powers vested in the general government.").

21. Saikrishna B. Prakash & John C. Yoo, *The Origins of Judicial Review*, 70 U. CHI. L. REV. 887, 929–39 (2003). *See, e.g.*, Commonwealth v. Caton, 8 Va. (4 Call) 5, 20 (1782) (holding invalid a pardon passed by one house

of the state legislature and rejected by the other); Symsbury Case, 1 Kirby 444, 452 (Conn. Super. Ct. 1785) (holding that the legislature could not alter a land grant without the grantees' consent). For more examples, see Prakash & Yoo, *supra* at 933 n.169.

22. Prakash & Yoo, *supra* note 21, at 933.

23. 5 U.S. 137 (1803).

24. *See* William E. Nelson, *Changing Conceptions of Judicial Review: The Evolution of Constitutional Theory in the States, 1790–1860*, 120 U. PA. L. REV. 1166, 1169–70 (1972) (discussing the early history of judicial review and its shaping by state courts). For various state court cases exercising judicial review, see Merrill v. Sherburne, 1 N.H. 199 (1818); Ward v. Barnard, 1 Aikens 121, 121 (Vt. 1825); Bingham v. Miller, 17 Ohio 445 (1848); Guy v. Hermance, 5 Cal. 73 (1855).

25. Third edition, Little, Brown and Company (1898).

26. *E.g.*, FRANCIS NEWTON THORPE, THE ESSENTIALS OF AMERICAN CONSTITUTIONAL LAW (G.P. Putnam's Sons 1917); LAWRENCE B. EVANS, LEADING CASES ON AMERICAN CONSTITUTIONAL LAW (Callaghan and Co. 1916); JAMES PARKER HALL, CONSTITUTIONAL LAW (La Salle Univ. 1915).

27. *See* Steven G. Calabresi & Sarah E. Agudo, *Individual Rights Under State Constitutions When the Fourteenth Amendment Was Ratified in 1868: What Rights Are Deeply Rooted in American History and Tradition?*, 87 TEX. L. REV. 7, 21 (2008).

28. Something similar happened with the Supreme Court's interpretation of Congress's power under the Commerce Clause. Most areas of regulation at the founding and until the Depression were perceived as being exclusive under state or federal power. Not until the post-Depression decisions do we shift from a country with largely exclusive powers (federal or state) to one with largely overlapping powers (federal and state). *See* Am. Beverage Ass'n v. Snyder, 735 F.3d 362, 377–78 (6th Cir. 2013) (Sutton, J., concurring). *See also* Ernest A. Young, *"The Ordinary Diet of the Law": The Presumption Against Preemption in the Roberts Court*, 2011 SUP. CT. REV. 253, 257–58.

29. McDonald v. City of Chicago, 561 U.S. 742 (2010).

30. Brennan, *supra* note 1, at 502; *see also* Ohio v. Robinette, 519 U.S. 33, 44 (1996) (Ginsburg, J., concurring) (noting that state courts may grant relief under state constitutions when the Federal Constitution does not provide a right to relief).

31. Michigan v. Long, 463 U.S. 1032 (1983).

32. JEAN EDWARD SMITH, JOHN MARSHALL: DEFINER OF A NATION 403 n.* (1996) (quoting JOSEPH QUINCY, FIGURES OF THE PAST (1883)).

33. Jeffrey S. Sutton, San Antonio Independent School District v. Rodriguez *and Its Aftermath*, 94 VA. L. REV. 1963, 1979 (2008); Jamison E. Colburn, *Rethinking Constitutionalism*, 28 RUTGERS L.J. 873, 898 (1997) (book

review); *see* Lawrence Gene Sager, *Fair Measure: The Legal Status of Underenforced Constitutional Norms*, 91 HARV. L. REV. 1212, 1218 (1978).

34. *See, e.g., Robinette*, 519 U.S. at 40 (Ginsburg, J., concurring) (describing the "unique vantage point" of state supreme court justices regarding traffic-stop searches).

35. A qualification or two is in order. In some areas of federal constitutional law, take obscenity as one, the U.S. Supreme Court has permitted the law to account for local community standards. *See, e.g.*, Miller v. California, 413 U.S. 15, 32 (1973) ("It is neither realistic nor constitutionally sound to read the First Amendment as requiring that the people of Maine or Mississippi accept public depiction of conduct found tolerable in Las Vegas, or New York City."). And some scholars have argued for local tailoring in other areas. *See, e.g.*, Joseph Blocher, *Firearm Localism*, 123 YALE L.J. 82 (2013).

36. *See* Robert F. Williams, *Forward: Looking Back at the New Judicial Federalism's First Generation*, 30 VAL. U. L. REV. xiii, xxiv (1996).

37. New State Ice Co. v. Liebmann, 285 U.S. 262, 311 (1932) (Brandeis, J., dissenting) ("It is one of the happy incidents of the federal system that a single courageous state may, if its citizens choose, serve as a laboratory; and try novel social and economic experiments without risk to the rest of the country.").

38. *See, e.g.*, Sutton, *supra* note 33, at 1981.

39. *See, e.g.*, RICHARD A. POSNER, HOW JUDGES THINK (2008). *See* Jeffrey S. Sutton, *A Review of Richard A. Posner, How Judges Think*, 108 MICH. L. REV. 859 (2010) (responding to Judge Posner's criticism of the political nature of judging in some cases).

40. *See* Craig v. Boren, 429 U.S. 190, 211–13 (1976) (Stevens, J., concurring).

41. *See generally* Emp't Div. v. Smith, 494 U.S. 872 (1990), superseded in part by statute, Religious Freedom Restoration Act (RFRA) of 1993, Pub. L. No. 103–141, 107 Stat. 1488 (1993), invalidated in part by City of Boerne v. Flores, 521 U.S. 507 (1997).

42. *See* Humphrey v. Lane, 728 N.E.2d 1039, 1043 (Ohio 2000) (applying a more stringent standard of review to religious liberty claims premised on the Ohio Constitution).

43. U.S. CONST. amend. V.

44. *See* Kelo v. City of New London, 545 U.S. 469, 483 (2005).

45. *See* City of Norwood v. Horney, 853 N.E.2d 1115, 1123 (Ohio 2006) (adopting more restrictive limits on economic-development takings); Bd. of Cty. Comm'rs v. Lowery, 136 P.3d 639, 652 (Okla. 2006) (same).

46. San Antonio Indep. Sch. Dist. v. Rodriguez, 411 U.S. 1 (1973); U.S. CONST. amend. XIV, § 1; *see* Chapter 3.

47. Sutton, *supra* note 33, at 1978–79.

48. *See, e.g.*, OHIO CONST. art. II, § 15(D) ("No bill shall contain more than one subject, which shall be clearly expressed in its title."); *id.* art. I, § 16

("[E]very person, for an injury done him in his land, goods, person, or reputation, shall have remedy by due course of law, and shall have justice administered without denial or delay."); CAL. CONST. art. IV, § 16(a) ("All laws of a general nature have uniform operation.").

49. *See, e.g.*, OHIO CONST. art. XII, § 13 (barring the taxation of food sold for human consumption); ALASKA CONST. art. VIII, § 15 (forbidding the creation of any "exclusive right or special privilege of fishery" within Alaskan waters, subject to certain exceptions).

50. Ten States—Delaware, Maine, Montana, New Hampshire, North Dakota, Rhode Island, South Dakota, Vermont, West Virginia, and Wyoming—do not have intermediate appellate courts and permit appeals of right to the state supreme court. *See* DEL. CODE ANN. tit. 10, § 142; ME. STAT. tit. 4, § 57; MONT. CONST. art. VII, § 2; N.H. SUP. CT. R. 7; N.D. CENT. CODE § 28-27-01; R.I. CONST. art. X, § 2; S.D. CONST. art. V, §§ 1, 2; VT. CONST. § 30; W. VA. CONST. art. VIII, § 3; WYO. CONST. art. 5, § 2. Eleven more states—Colorado, Florida, Georgia, Illinois, Indiana, Kansas, Louisiana, Mississippi, Missouri, Nebraska, and New York—provide appeals of right to the state supreme court when a trial court declares a statute unconstitutional. *See* COLO. REV. STAT. § 13-4-102; FLA. CONST. art V, § 3; GA. CONST. art. VI, § VI, ¶ II; ILL. SUP. CT. R. 302; IND. APP. R. 4; KAN. STAT. ANN. § 60-2101; LA. CONST. art. V, § 5; MISS. CODE ANN. § 9-4-3; MO. CONST. art. V, § 3; NEB. REV. STAT. § 24-1106; N.Y. CONST. art VI, § 3.

51. *See* Michael Wells, *Congress's Paramount Role in Setting the Scope of Federal Jurisdiction*, 85 NW. U. L. REV. 465, 476 (1991) (noting that state courts can be fonts of "innovation," can create "multiple avenues of relief," and can offer "differing points of view" when adjudicating constitutional rights).

52. 554 U.S. 570 (2008).

53. 576 U.S. ___, 135 S. Ct. 2584 (2015).

54. Kennedy v. Louisiana, 128 S. Ct. 2641 (2008).

55. Mesa Cty. Bd. of Cty. Comm'rs v. State, 203 P.3d 519, 536 (Colo. 2009); Claremont Sch. Dist. v. Governor, 635 A.2d 1375, 1376 (N.H. 1993).

56. Hageland Aviation Servs., Inc. v. Harms, 210 P.3d 444, 453 (Alaska 2009).

57. Varnum v. Brien, 763 N.W.2d 862, 903–07 (Iowa 2009); *In re* Marriage Cases, 183 P.3d 384, 452 (Cal. 2008) superseded by constitutional amendment, CAL. CONST. art. I, § 7.5, as recognized in Strauss v. Horton, 207 P.3d 48, 93, 122 (Cal. 2009).

58. Skeen v. State, 505 N.W.2d 299, 313 (Minn. 1993) (establishing a fundamental right to education); Billings v. City of Point Pleasant, 460 S.E.2d 436, 440 (W. Va. 1995) (establishing a fundamental right to run for office).

Chapter 3

1. 347 U.S. 483, 493 (1954).

2. 411 U.S. 1 (1973).

3. The groundwork for the *Rodriguez* case began when parents in the Edgewood Independent School District contacted Arthur Gochman, a civil rights attorney. The son of Jewish immigrants, Gochman had been drawn to civil rights litigation after seeing the effects of segregation firsthand as a young boy. The lead plaintiff in the case was Demetrio Rodriguez, a Navy veteran and member of the Air Force Reserve, who worked for a time at Kelly Air Force Base as a sheet metal worker. His daughter, Patty Rodriguez, is now a teacher at Lyndon B. Johnson Elementary School in Edgewood ISD, where her father filed the lawsuit.

4. *Rodriguez,* 411 U.S. at 11–12.

5. *Id.* at 12–13.

6. *Id.*

7. *Id.* at 85 & n.44, 86 & n.47, 136 app. III (Marshall, J., dissenting).

8. *Id.* at 47–48 & n.102.

9. *See* Richard Schragger, San Antonio v. Rodriguez *and the Legal Geography of School Finance Reform, in* CIVIL RIGHTS STORIES 85, 93–102 (Myriam E. Gilles & Risa L. Goluboff eds., 2008).

10. *See* JOHN C. JEFFRIES, JR., JUSTICE LEWIS F. POWELL, JR. 139–60 (Fordham Univ. Press 2001) (1994).

11. *Rodriguez,* 411 U.S. at 35.

12. *Id.* at 37.

13. *Id.* at 38–39.

14. *Id.* at 63 (Brennan, J., dissenting).

15. *Id.* at 67–68 (White, J., dissenting).

16. *Id.* at 64–67.

17. *Id.* at 111, 115–16, 122 (Marshall, J., dissenting).

18. *Id.* at 109.

19. Natalie Gomez-Velez, *Public School Governance and Democracy: Does Public Participation Matter?,* 53 VILL. L. REV. 297, 301 (2008).

20. *See* Joseph P. Viteritti, *The Inadequacy of Adequacy Guarantees: A Historical Commentary on State Constitutional Provisions That Are the Basis for School Finance Litigation,* 7 U. MD. L.J. RACE, RELIGION, GENDER & CLASS 58, 73–77 (2007).

21. Horace Mann, *Report for 1848, in* ANNUAL REPORTS ON EDUCATION 640, 669 (Lee & Shepherd eds., 1872), *available at* https://babel.hathitrust.org/cgi/pt?id=njp.32101068983400;view=1up;seq=679.

22. *E.g.,* MD. CONST. art. VIII, § 1; OHIO CONST. art. VI, § 2; *cf.* TEX. CONST. art. VII, § 1 (mandating the creation of an "efficient" system of public schools).

23. *See* Annette B. Johnson, *State Court Intervention in School Finance Reform,* 28 CLEV. ST. L. REV. 325, 328 (1979).

24. *Id.*

25. *Id.*

26. *Id.*

27. *See id.* at 328–29.

28. *Id.* at 329 & n.14.

29. *See generally* Frederick Eby, *The First Century of Public Education in Texas,* in TEXAS PUBLIC SCHOOLS SESQUICENTENNIAL HANDBOOK 35, 35–59 (2004); Marilyn Kuehlem, *Education Reforms from Gilmer-Aikin to Today,* in TEXAS PUBLIC SCHOOLS SESQUICENTENNIAL HANDBOOK 60, 60–63 (2004); Mark G. Yudof & Daniel C. Morgan, Rodriquez v. San Antonio Independent School District: *Gathering the Ayes of Texas—The Politics of School Finance Reform,* 38 LAW & CONTEMP. PROBS. 383, 383–91 (1974).

30. *Rodriguez,* 411 U.S. at 9–11.

31. *Id.* at 9 n.21.

32. *See id.* at 10–11.

33. *Brown,* 347 U.S. at 493.

34. *Rodriguez,* 411 U.S. at 41 n.85.

35. *Id.*

36. *Id.* at 133 n.100 (Marshall, J., dissenting).

37. Johnson, *supra* note 23, at 331 n.20.

38. *See* Caroline M. Hoxby, *All School Finance Equalizations Are Not Created Equal,* 116 Q.J. ECON. 1189, 1189–90 (2001).

39. *See* John A. Thompson & Stacey E. Marlow, *Hawaii, in* U.S. DEP'T OF EDUC., NAT'L CTR. FOR EDUC. STAT., PUBLIC SCHOOL FINANCE PROGRAMS OF THE UNITED STATES AND CANADA: 1998–99, at 1 (Catherine C. Sielke et al. compilers, 2001).

40. In the words of Mark Yudof, co-counsel for the plaintiffs in *Rodriguez*: "In short, a politics of consensus must be substituted for the politics of federal intervention. Reform groups must recognize that the President, the Congress, and the federal courts are unlikely to come to their rescue if they fail. At the most basic level, this requires the raising of the collective consciousness of the state, making the public in general, and educators and legislators in particular, more aware of the deficiencies and irrationalities of the current financing scheme." Yudof & Morgan, *supra* note 29, at 408–09.

41. *See, e.g.,* Dupree v. Alma Sch. Dist. No. 30, 651 S.W.2d 90, 93 (Ark. 1983); Serrano v. Priest, 487 P.2d 1241, 1257–60 (Cal. 1971); Horton v. Meskill, 376 A.2d 359, 374 (Conn. 1977); Pauley v. Kelly, 255 S.E.2d 859, 878 (W. Va. 1979); Washakie Cty. Sch. Dist. No. One v. Herschler, 606 P.2d 310, 333–35 (Wyo. 1980); *see also* Michael A. Rebell, *Educational Adequacy, Democracy, and the Courts, in* NAT'L RESEARCH COUNCIL, ACHIEVING HIGH EDUCATIONAL STANDARDS FOR ALL: CONFERENCE SUMMARY 218, 226–27 (Timothy Ready et al. eds., 2002); Molly S. McUsic, *The Future of* Brown v. Board of Education: *Economic Integration of the Public Schools,* 117 HARV. L. REV. 1334, 1344 (2004) ("Prior to 1989, virtually every school finance case made its equity claim under a state constitution's equal protection clause.").

42. *See* Rebell, *supra* note 41, at 227 (noting that, by 1988, defendants had prevailed in fifteen of the twenty-two States in which equity suits were filed).

43. *Id.* at 226–27.

44. OHIO CONST. art. VI, § 2.

45. *See* Rebell, *supra* note 41, at 228; James E. Ryan, *Schools, Race, and Money*, 109 YALE L.J. 249, 268 (1999).

46. *See* Rebell, *supra* note 41, at 228.

47. NAT'L ACCESS NETWORK, LITIGATION CHALLENGING CONSTITUTIONALITY OF K–12 FUNDING IN THE 50 STATES (Mar. 2010), http://www. schoolfunding.info/litigation/equityandadequacytable.pdf.

48. NAT'L ACCESS NETWORK, "EQUITY" AND "ADEQUACY" SCHOOL FUNDING LIABILITY COURT DECISIONS (Mar. 2010), http://www.schoolfunding. info/litigation/equityandadequacytable.pdf.

49. *See* McUsic, *supra* note 41, at 1344 & n.63.

50. *See* Edgewood Indep. Sch. Dist. v. Kirby (*Edgewood I*), 777 S.W.2d 391, 392 (Tex. 1989); Edgewood Indep. Sch. Dist. v. Kirby (*Edgewood II*), 804 S.W.2d 491, 492–93 (Tex. 1991); Carrollton-Farmers Branch Indep. Sch. Dist. v. Edgewood Indep. Sch. Dist. (*Edgewood III*), 826 S.W.2d 489, 503 (Tex. 1992).

51. TEX. CONST. art. VII, § 1.

52. *Edgewood I*, 777 S.W.2d at 397. The constitutional guarantee of an "efficient" education had been contentious from the beginning. In *Neeley v. W. Orange-Cove Consol. Indep. Sch. Dist.*, 176 S.W.3d 746, 785 (Tex. 2005), the Texas Supreme Court explained, "[T]he delegates to the Constitutional Convention of 1875 were deeply divided over how best to provide for a general diffusion of knowledge. . . . No subject was more controversial or more extensively debated." One attendee, John Johnson, called public education "the most important yet the most difficult question that has or will come before us." SETH S. McKAY, DEBATES IN THE CONSTITUTIONAL CONVENTION OF 1875, at 341 (1930). Delegate Henry Cline was responsible for including the word "efficient" in Article VII on Education. JOURNAL OF THE CONSTITUTIONAL CONVENTION OF THE STATE OF TEXAS OF 1875, at 318 (1875); *see also Edgewood I*, 777 S.W.2d at 395 n.4. Cline had first proposed the more common phrase "thorough and efficient," but the convention rejected this wording. *See* JOURNAL, at 396. "Texas thus became the first state to require only *efficiency* but not *thoroughness* in its school system." Brief for David R. Upham as Amicus Curiae Supporting Appellants, Morath v. Sterling City Indep. Sch. Dist., 59 Tex. Sup. J. 1428 (Tex. 2016) (No. D-1-GN-11-003130).

53. *Edgewood I*, 777 S.W.2d at 397.

54. *See* Edgewood Indep. Sch. Dist. v. Meno (*Edgewood IV*), 917 S.W.2d 717, 731 (Tex. 1995); Neely v. W. Orange-Cove Consol. Indep. Sch. Dist., 176 S.W.3d 746, 792 (Tex. 2005).

55. *W. Orange-Cove*, 176 S.W.3d at 758.

56. *See Edgewood IV*, 917 S.W.2d at 730.

57. *Id.* at 731.

58. *W. Orange-Cove*, 176 S.W.3d at 789.

59. *See* Schragger, *supra* note 9, at 107 (observing that "over thirty years after *Rodriguez*, Edgewood's schools are now comparatively well-funded").

60. *Id.*

61. DeRolph v. State (*DeRolph I*), 677 N.E.2d 733, 747 (Ohio 1997); DeRolph v. State (*DeRolph II*), 728 N.E.2d 993, 1020 (Ohio 2000). For what it is worth, I represented the State in *DeRolph I* at the Ohio Supreme Court and at the trial level on remand, losing both times.

62. *DeRolph I*, 677 N.E.2d at 747; *DeRolph II*, 728 N.E.2d at 1021.

63. DeRolph v. State (*DeRolph IV*), 780 N.E.2d 529, 530 (Ohio 2002).

64. *Id.* at 537 (Moyer, C.J., dissenting).

65. *DeRolph II*, 728 N.E.2d at 1005.

66. *See* DeRolph v. State (*DeRolph III*), 754 N.E.2d 1184, 1191 (Ohio 2001).

67. *Id.* at 1192–93.

68. *Id.* at 1199.

69. *Id.* at 1194.

70. *DeRolph III*, 754 N.E.2d at 1194; Ohio Sch. Facilities Comm'n Ann. Rep. 27 (2007).

71. Ohio Sch. Facilities Comm'n Ann. Rep. 27 (2007).

72. *Id.*

73. *See* Ohio Sch. Facilities Comm'n Ann. Rep. 12 (1999).

74. *DeRolph III*, 754 N.E.2d at 1196 (quoting *DeRolph I*, 677 N.E.2d at 742).

75. *Id.*

76. *Id.* According to Chief Justice Moyer, the author of the initial *DeRolph* dissent, "There's just no question that *DeRolph* has had a positive impact on schools." *Justices Discuss DeRolph School Ruling*, Cincinnati Post (Mar. 19, 2007), *available at* https://www.highbeam.com/doc/1G1-160867525.html.

77. *DeRolph III*, 754 N.E.2d 1184 (Ohio 2001).

78. DeRolph v. Ohio, 758 N.E.2d 1113 (Ohio 2001).

79. *DeRolph IV*, 780 N.E.2d 529 (Ohio 2002).

80. Ohio v. Lewis, 789 N.E.2d 195 (Ohio 2003).

81. *See, e.g.*, Ohio v. Robinette, 519 U.S. 33, 42–45 (1996) (Ginsburg, J., concurring in the judgment); *Rodriguez*, 411 U.S. at 133 n.100 (1973) (Marshall, J., dissenting); William J. Brennan, Jr., *State Constitutions and the Protection of Individual Rights*, 90 Harv. L. Rev. 489, 491 (1977).

82. Kansas v. Carr, 136 S. Ct. 633, 641–42 (2016) (citing Jeffrey S. Sutton, San Antonio Independent School District v. Rodriguez *and Its Aftermath*, 94 Va. L. Rev. 1963, 1971–77 (2008)).

83. Workman v. Bredesen, 486 F.3d 896, 907 (6th Cir. 2007).

84. EMILY ZACKIN, LOOKING FOR RIGHTS IN ALL THE WRONG PLACES: WHY STATE CONSTITUTIONS CONTAIN AMERICA'S POSITIVE RIGHTS (Princeton Univ. Press 2013); *see also* Jeffrey S. Sutton, *Courts as Change Agents: Do We Want More—or Less?*, 127 HARV. L. REV. 1419 (2014) (reviewing Zackin's book).

85. OHIO CONST. art. VI, § 2 (emphasis added).

86. *See* McUsic, *supra* note 41, at 1344.

87. *See* ZACKIN, *supra* note 84.

88. *See* Monique Oosse, Evaluation of April 1, 2000 School District Population Estimates Based on the Synthetic Ratio Method 53 tbl. 10 (U.S. Census Bureau, Population Div., Educ. & Soc. Stratification Branch, Working Paper No. 74, 2004), http://www.census.gov/population/www/documentation/twps0074/twps0074.pdf; NAT'L CTR. FOR EDUC. STATISTICS, NUMBER AND ENROLLMENT OF REGULAR PUBLIC SCHOOL DISTRICTS, BY ENROLLMENT SIZE OF DISTRICT: SELECTED YEARS, 1979–80 THROUGH 2005–06, http://nces.ed.gov/programs/digest/d07/tables/dt07_084.asp; U.S. CENSUS BUREAU, USA QUICKFACTS, http://quickfacts.census.gov/qfd/states/00000.html; U.S. CENSUS BUREAU, HISTORICAL NATIONAL POPULATION ESTIMATES, http://www.census.gov/popest/data/historical/1990s/index.html.

89. *Rodriguez*, 411 U.S. at 41.

90. *Id.* at 42 (quoting *Jefferson v. Hackney*, 406 U.S. 535, 546–47 (1972)).

91. *Id.* at 43; *see also* Lawrence Gene Sager, *Fair Measure: The Legal Status of Underenforced Constitutional Norms*, 91 HARV. L. REV. 1212, 1218 (1978).

92. *See* Missouri v. Jenkins, 515 U.S. 70 (1995).

93. *See, e.g.*, DeRolph I, 677 N.E.2d at 747; *DeRolph II*, 728 N.E.2d at 1020–22; *DeRolph III*, 754 N.E.2d at 1200–01.

94. *See* John G. Augenblick et al., *Equity and Adequacy in School Funding*, 7 FUTURE CHILD. 63, 64–66 (Winter 1997).

95. Michael Heise, *Litigated Learning and the Limits of Law*, 57 VAND. L. REV. 2417, 2438 (2004).

96. HAW. REV. STAT. § 27-1 (2008).

97. *See* Rebell, *supra* note 41, at 226–27; William H. Clune, *New Answers to Hard Questions Posed by* Rodriguez: *Ending the Separation of School Finance and Educational Policy by Bridging the Gap Between Wrong and Remedy*, 24 CONN. L. REV. 721, 732 (1992); McUsic, *supra* note 41, at 1347–54; Laurie Reynolds, *Skybox Schools: Public Education as Private Luxury*, 82 WASH. U. L.Q. 755, 782 (2004) (noting that "[i]n spite of [Colorado's experiment with spending] caps . . . district property wealth remains extremely relevant"); *id.* at 786–87 (noting that despite Washington's experiment with revenue redistribution from richer to poorer districts, "funding disparities . . . are returning to their pre-1978 inequality" due to political pressures); *id.* at 793–94 (describing the

"vehement opposition" by residents of wealthy districts to Vermont's redistributive plan, leading to an amendment that removed caps for all but the highest spending districts); Hanif S.P. Hirji, Note and Comment, *Inequalities in California's Public School System: The Undermining of* Serrano v. Priest *and the Need for a Minimum Standards System of Education*, 32 LOY. L.A. L. REV. 583, 600 (1999) (noting that California voters responded to a court-imposed system of spending caps by passing Proposition 13, which severely limited the State's ability to use local property tax revenues to equalize educational spending).

98. *See W. Orange-Cove*, 176 S.W.3d at 752–53, 787–88.

99. *See DeRolph I*, 677 N.E.2d at 792–93.

100. *See* Julian R. Betts, *Is There a Link Between School Inputs and Earnings? Fresh Scrutiny of an Old Literature, in* DOES MONEY MATTER? THE EFFECT OF SCHOOL RESOURCES ON STUDENT ACHIEVEMENT AND ADULT SUCCESS 141 (Gary Burtless ed., 1996); JAMES S. COLEMAN ET AL., EQUALITY OF EDUCATIONAL OPPORTUNITY (1966); Eric A. Hanushek, *Assessing the Effects of School Resources on Student Performance: An Update*, 19 EDUC. EVALUATION & POL'Y ANALYSIS 141 (1997); Molly McUsic, *The Use of Education Clauses in School Finance Reform*, 28 HARV. J. ON LEGIS. 307, 316 (1991); McUsic, *supra* note 41, at 1355.

101. *See generally* Goodwin Liu, *Interstate Inequality in Educational Opportunity*, 81 N.Y.U. L. REV. 2044 (2006).

Chapter 4

1. THOMAS N. MCINNIS, THE EVOLUTION OF THE FOURTH AMENDMENT 16 (2009).

2. Huckle v. Money, 95 Eng. Rep. 768, 769 (C.P. 1763).

3. *See* WILLIAM J. CUDDIHY, THE FOURTH AMENDMENT: ORIGINS AND ORIGINAL MEANING 602–1791, at 603, 609 (2009) (discussing the state constitutions of 1776–84); *see also* MCINNIS, *supra* note 1, at 47 n.15 (noting the dates of adoption).

4. *See* CUDDIHY, *supra* note 3, at 852–53.

5. Regina v. Leatham, 8 Cox C.C. 498, 501 (1861) (Crompton, J.); *see also* Jordan v. Lewis, 104 Eng. Rep. 618, 618 (K.B. 1740) (receiving in evidence a copy of an indictment wrongfully procured, concluding that the court could take no "notice in what manner it was obtained"); Legatt v. Tollervey, 104 Eng. Rep. 617, 619 (K.B. 1811) (admitting in evidence a copy of the record of a trial, even though it had been "surreptitiously taken," because the manner of its acquisition did not "affect the validity of the proof"). (Justice Wilde later would rely on both of these cases in *Commonwealth v. Dana*, 43 Mass. (2 Met.) 329, 337–38 (1841)).

6. United States v. Hughes, 26 F. Cas. 421, 425 (S.D.N.Y. 1875). The district court judge who handled *Hughes*, Samuel Blatchford, founded Blatchford, Seward & Griswold. The Seward in the firm was William

H. Seward, later the secretary of state in Lincoln's cabinet, and the firm
eventually became Cravath, Swaine and Moore. Blatchford was the first
judge to serve at all three levels of the federal judiciary, at least all three
levels of the federal judiciary that existed before the Evarts Act of 1891,
which created the modern circuit courts.

7. State v. Flynn, 36 N.H. 64, 70 (1858).

8. *See* Akhil Reed Amar, *What Belongs in a Criminal Trial: The Role of
    Exclusionary Rules: Against Exclusion (Except to Protect Truth or Prevent
    Privacy Violations)*, 20 Harv. J.L. & Pub. Pol'y 457, 459 (1997).

9. *See* Roger Roots, *The Originalist Case for the Fourth Amendment
    Exclusionary Rule*, 45 Gonz. L. Rev. 1, 11–12 (2010) (observing that, at
    the time of the American Revolution, "a justice or magistrate would
    deputize a private citizen to perform executive duties such as searches and
    arrests" when constables were not available); Orin Kerr, *Is the Exclusionary
    Rule Consistent with Originalism?*, Volokh Conspiracy (July 21, 2008,
    9:02 AM), http://www.volokh.com/posts/1216589577.shtml (noting
    that although professional police forces did not exist in common law
    England, agents of the king could obtain warrants to search citizens'
    homes) [hereinafter Kerr, *Consistent with Originalism*]; Orin S. Kerr,
    An Equilibrium-Adjustment Theory of the Fourth Amendment, 125 Harv.
    L. Rev. 476, 519 (2011) ("In eighteenth-century England, private citizens
    were empowered to investigate crimes in exchange for money; prisoners
    were offered pardons to become informers.").

10. *See, e.g.*, Akhil Reed Amar, The Constitution and Criminal
    Procedure: First Principles 21 (1997) ("In a series of landmark
    English cases—most famously, *Wilkes v. Wood*—oppressive general
    warrants were struck down in civil jury trespass actions brought against
    the officials who committed or authorized the unreasonable searches
    and seizures."); Comment, Laprease *and* Fuentes: *Replevin Reconsidered*,
    71 Colum. L. Rev. 886, 887–88 (1971) (citing 3 William Blackstone,
    Commentaries 147) (discussing the roots of the replevin action in the
    Statute of Marlbridge, which allowed a sheriff to take chattel immediately
    upon the filing of a complaint).

11. *See, e.g.*, Wilkes v. Wood, 98 Eng. Rep. 489, 498–99 (C.P. 1763)
    (upholding a damages award for a victim of a trespass by the king's
    officers); Huckle v. Money, 95 Eng. Rep. 768, 768–69 (C.P. 1763)
    (upholding a damages verdict won by a printer whose house had been
    searched under the authority of a general warrant).

12. *See* Grumon v. Raymond, 1 Conn. 40, 45 (1814) (recognizing cause
    of action in trespass for damages against officer who conducted
    unreasonable search); Sandford v. Nichols, 13 Mass. 286, 290 (1816)
    (noting probability that "very small damages will be recovered" for
    unreasonable search); Amar, *supra* note 10, at 21 ("In America, both
    before and after the Revolution, the civil trespass action tried to a jury

flourished as the obvious remedy against haughty customs officers, tax collectors, constables, marshals, and the like."); Roots, *supra* note 9, at 8–9 ("[G]overnment agents who engaged in illegal searches and seizures in the early republic were held liable for civil damages with great regularity. In general, these lawsuits were framed not as constitutional claims but as tort claims such as trespass").

13. *See* United States v. Casino, 286 F. 976, 978 (S.D.N.Y. 1923) ("[T]he owner of property unlawfully seized . . . may have trespass, or, if there be not statute to the contrary, replevin" (citation omitted)); Reed v. Legg, 2 Del. (2 Harr.) 173, 173–74 (1837) (indicating that allegedly stolen goods recovered during a search were immediately returned to their alleged rightful owner); Sanford v. Sornborger, 26 Neb. 295, 295 (1889) (replevin action to recover the possession of illegally seized books).

14. 1 S. GREENLEAF, A TREATISE ON THE LAW OF EVIDENCE, § 254a, at 325–26 (Croswell rev. 14th ed. 1883) (cited in BRADFORD P. WILSON, ENFORCING THE FOURTH AMENDMENT: A JURISPRUDENTIAL HISTORY 45–46 (Garland 1986)).

15. 4 J. WIGMORE, WIGMORE ON EVIDENCE, § 2183, at 626 (2d ed. 1923) (cited in WILSON, *supra* note 14, at 46 n.4).

16. United States v. La Jeune, 26 F. Cas. 832, 842 (C.C.D. Mass. 1822) (No. 15,551).

17. *Id.* at 843–44 (cited in WILSON, *supra* note 14, at 46–47).

18. *Dana*, 43 Mass. (2 Met.) at 337.

19. *See* WILSON, *supra* note 14, at 48 (citing state and federal cases).

20. Gindrat v. People, 138 Ill. 103, 105 (1891).

21. *Id.*

22. *Id.* at 105–06.

23. *Id.* at 106.

24. *Id.* at 110.

25. *Id.* at 110–11.

26. *Id.* at 105, 110.

27. *Id.* at 111.

28. *Flynn*, 36 N.H. at 72.

29. *Id.* at 71–72.

30. Williams v. State, 100 Ga. 511, 511–12 (1897).

31. *Id.* at 525.

32. *Id.* at 520.

33. *Id.*

34. *Id.* at 521.

35. Utah v. Strieff, 136 S. Ct. 2056, 2060–61 (2016); *see* Thomas Y. Davies, *Recovering the Original Fourth Amendment*, 98 MICH. L. REV. 547, 625 (1999).

36. *Strieff*, 136 S. Ct. at 2061; *see also* Jeremy M. Christiansen, *State Search and Seizure: The Original Meaning*, 38 U. HAW. L. REV. 63, 101 (2016).

37. 116 U.S. 616 (1886).

38. Boyd v. United States, 116 U.S. 616, 634 (1886).
39. U.S. CONST. amend. V.
40. *See* United States v. Hubbell, 530 U.S. 27, 55–56 (2000) (linking *Boyd* with the Court's Fifth Amendment interpretation and the common-law understanding of the self-incrimination privilege) (Thomas, J., concurring in the judgment).
41. *Boyd*, 116 U.S. at 622.
42. *Id.*
43. *Id.* at 633; *see* 1 WAYNE R. LaFAVE, SEARCH AND SEIZURE: A TREATISE ON THE FOURTH AMENDMENT § 1.1(b) (5th ed. 2012).
44. *Boyd*, 116 U.S. at 633.
45. *Id.*
46. *Id.*
47. *Id.*
48. *Id.* at 639 (Miller, J., concurring).
49. *Id.* at 640.
50. *See* Brief for Plaintiffs at 23, Boyd v. United States, 116 U.S. 616 (1886), *reprinted in* LANDMARK BRIEFS AND ARGUMENTS OF THE SUPREME COURT OF THE UNITED STATES: CONSTITUTIONAL LAW 502 (Philip B. Kurland & Gerhard Casper eds., 1975) ("The purpose was to compel Mr. Boyd to produce papers to establish his own criminal intent: to adduce for the benefit of the prosecution, evidence tending to convict him whenever the Government . . . should see fit to indict him for the very acts alleged here as a ground of forfeiture. It is also, in effect, a search for and seizure of Mr. Boyd's papers, etc.; 'unreasonable' *because* for the purpose and of the tendency, just indicated.").
51. WILSON, *supra* note 14, at 72–73 n.60.
52. State v. Slamon, 73 Vt. 212 (1901).
53. *Id.* at 213.
54. *Id.*
55. *Id.* at 213–15.
56. *Id.* at 214.
57. *Id.*
58. *Id.* at 214–15.
59. *Id.* at 215.
60. *Id.*
61. State v. Height, 117 Iowa 652, 660 (1902).
62. *Id.* at 653–55.
63. *Id.* at 665.
64. State v. Sheridan, 121 Iowa 164 (1903).
65. *Id.* at 166.
66. *Id.*
67. *Id.*
68. *Id.* at 167.

69. *Id.* at 168.
70. *See, e.g.*, Gindrat v. People, 138 Ill. 103, 108 (1891); Shields v. State, 104 Ala. 35, 38–39 (1894); Williams v. State, 100 Ga. 511, 513 (1897); State v. Pomeroy, 130 Mo. 489, 491 (1895).
71. WILSON, *supra* note 14, at 72–73 n.60.
72. *See* State v. Tonn, 195 Iowa 94 (1923).
73. *Id.* at 118 (Weaver, J., dissenting).
74. Adams v. New York, 192 U.S. 585, 597 (1904).
75. People v. Adams, 176 N.Y. 351, 356 (1903) ("Articles fourth and fifth of the amendments to the Constitution of the United States do not apply to actions in the state courts.").
76. *See* Barron v. Baltimore, 32 U.S. (7 Pet.) 243 (1833) (the Bill of Rights limits the federal government, not the States); Smith v. Maryland, 59 U.S. (18 How.) 71 (1855) (the Fourth Amendment does not apply to state officials).
77. *Adams*, 176 N.Y. at 353.
78. *Id.* at 358.
79. *Id.*
80. 192 U.S. at 598.
81. *Id.*
82. *Id.*
83. *Id.*
84. *Id.* at 596.
85. *Id.* at 594.
86. State v. Pence, 173 Ind. 99, 104 (1909).
87. *Id.*
88. Wolf v. Colorado, 338 U.S. 25, 28 (1949); *see* Mapp v. Ohio, 367 U.S. 643, 648 (1961); Hudson v. Michigan, 547 U.S. 586, 590 (2006) ("In *Weeks* . . . we adopted the federal exclusionary rule. . . ."); *id.* at 605 (Breyer, J., dissenting) (observing that the Court "first set forth the exclusionary principle" in *Weeks*); Herring v. United States, 555 U.S. 135, 143 (2009) (calling *Weeks* a "foundational exclusionary rule case"); Davis v. United States, 131 S. Ct. 2419, 2438 (2011) (citing *Weeks* as the source of "a rule that the Court adopted nearly a century ago for federal courts").
89. Weeks v. United States, 232 U.S. 383, 393 (1914).
90. *Id.* at 386.
91. *Id.* at 387.
92. *Id.* at 387–88.
93. A former secretary of state, Justice Day came from a long line of jurists. His father was Chief Justice of the Ohio Supreme Court, his maternal grandfather was an associate justice of the Ohio Supreme Court, and his maternal great-grandfather was Chief Justice of the Connecticut Supreme Court. His son, Luther Day, was a leading litigator at Day, Young, Veach & LeFever, which would become Jones Day. *William R. Day*, OYEZ, https://www.oyez.org/justices/william_r_day (last visited Jan. 10, 2017).

94. *Weeks*, 232 U.S. at 389.

95. *Id.* at 395–96 (quoting *Adams*, 176 N.Y. at 358).

96. *Id.* at 396.

97. *Id.*

98. *Id.* at 398.

99. WILSON, *supra* note 14, at 63 (citing *People v. Mayen*, 188 Cal. 237, 243 (1922)); *see* United States v. Mills, 185 F. 318, 320 (C.C.S.D.N.Y. 1911); Francis Barry McCarthy, *Counterfeit Interpretations of State Constitutions in Criminal Procedure*, 58 SYRACUSE L. REV. 79, 95 (2007).

100. WILSON, *supra* note 14, at 63; Kerr, *Consistent with Originalism, supra* note 9.

101. 338 U.S. at 28.

102. 367 U.S. at 648 (quoting *Weeks*, 323 U.S. at 398).

103. WILSON, *supra* note 14, at 64. *See* John Barker Waitz, Note and Comment, 22 MICH. L. REV. 210, 722 (1924); Thomas E. Atkinson, *Prohibition and the Doctrine of the Weeks Case*, 23 MICH. L. REV. 748 (1925); People v. Defore, 242 N.Y. 13, 15 (1926) (Cardozo, J.) (*Weeks* "held that articles wrongfully seized by agents of the federal government should have been returned to the defendant or excluded as evidence, if a timely motion to compel return has been made before the trial."); Orin Kerr, *Response to Paul on Originalism and the Exclusionary Rule*, VOLOKH CONSPIRACY (July 22, 2008, 6:45 PM), http://www.volokh.com/posts/1216689102.shtml (characterizing *Weeks* "as a return-of-property-case, not a suppress-evidence-because-the-law-was-broken case" and noting that there is "little Fourth Amendment case law from" 1789 to 1914: *Ex Parte Jackson; Boyd; Hale v. Henkel;* and *Adams*); Roots, *supra* note 9, at 12.

104. *See* WILSON, *supra* note 14, at 81 ("[I]t is not at all clear that there is something in the nature of a property right, strictly speaking, that would militate against using the knowledge gained by a trespass for the purpose of requesting, demanding, or seizing an individual's property under orderly and lawful process."); *see also* Atkinson, *supra* note 103, at 759–64; O'Connor v. Potter, 276 F. 32, 33 (D. Mass. 1921) ("It does not, however, follow that, simply because it happened to be taken from their premises, the petitioners are entitled to have this large amount of outlawed liquor returned to them."); Trupiano v. United States, 334 U.S. 699, 710 (1948) ("But since this property was contraband, they have no right to have it returned to them.").

105. Silverthorne Lumber v. United States, 251 U.S. 385, 392 (1920).

106. *Id.* at 391.

107. *Id.* at 392.

108. *See Wolf*, 338 U.S. at 29 & app.; *see also* State v. Chin Gim, 47 Nev. 431, 433 (1924); Flum v. State, 193 Ind. 585, 586 (1923); Billings v. State, 109 Neb. 596, 598 (1923).

109. 242 N.Y. at 13–14.

110. *Id.* at 14.

111. *Id.*
112. *Id.* at 15.
113. *Id.* at 20.
114. *Id.* at 19.
115. *Id.* at 14.
116. *Id.* at 23.
117. *Id.* at 21, 23.
118. *Id.* at 22.
119. *Id.* at 23.
120. *Silverthorne Lumber*, 251 U.S. at 392.
121. Ken I. Kersch, Constructing Civil Liberties: Discontinuities in the Development of American Constitutional Law 80–82 (Cambridge Univ. Press 2004).
122. *Wolf*, 338 U.S. at 27–28.
123. *See, e.g.*, McDonald v. City of Chicago, 561 U.S. 742, 765 (2010) (stating that it would be "incongruous" to apply different standards for the same claim between state and federal courts) (citing Malloy v. Hogan, 378 U.S. 1, 10–11 (1964)).
124. *Wolf*, 338 U.S. at 28–29.
125. *Id.* at 31.
126. *See* Elkins v. United States, 364 U.S. 206, app. (1960).
127. *Id.* at app. n.*.
128. *See id.* at app.
129. People v. Cahan, 44 Cal.2d 434, 442 (1955).
130. The Supreme Court's *Wolf* and *Elkins* decisions, for what it is worth, provide slightly different tallies. According to *Wolf*, twenty-seven States had ruled on the admissibility of evidence obtained by unlawful search and seizure before *Weeks. Wolf*, 338 U.S. at 29. *Elkins* says the number is twenty-eight. It also counts *People v. Le Doux*, 155 Cal. 535 (1909), as an example of a case where the State of California rejected the exclusionary rule before *Weeks. Elkins*, 364 U.S. at 225–26. No less important, *Wolf* said that only sixteen States had adopted the exclusionary rule pre-*Wolf*, whereas the court in *Elkins* claimed that eighteen states had already accepted it in some form. The court in *Elkins* also counted Oregon (State v. Laundy, 103 Ore. 443 (1922)) and Texas (Chapin v. State, 107 Tex. Crim. 477 (1927)) as having adopted the exclusionary rule before *Wolf*.
131. 367 U.S. 643 (1961).
132. Mapp v. Ohio, 367 U.S. 643, 644 (1961).
133. *Id.*
134. *Id.*
135. *Id.*
136. *Id.*
137. *Id.* at 645.
138. *Silverthorne Lumber*, 251 U.S. at 392.

139. *Mapp*, 367 U.S. at 645.
140. State v. Mapp, 170 Ohio St. 427, 430 (1960).
141. *Id.* at 431.
142. *Id.* at 438 (Herbert, J., dissenting).
143. LaFave, *supra* note 43, at § 1.1(e).
144. 342 U.S. 165, 172 (1952).
145. *See* Brief of Amici Curiae on Behalf of the American Civil Liberties
     Union and Ohio Civil Liberties Union, Mapp v. Ohio, 367 U.S. 643
     (No. 236); Oral Argument at 32:46, Mapp v. Ohio, 367 U.S. 643 (No.
     236). The brief's full analysis said: "It is our purpose by this paragraph to
     respectfully request that this Court re-examine this issue and conclude
     that the ordered liberty concept guaranteed to persons by the due process
     clause of the Fourteenth Amendment necessarily requires that evidence
     illegally obtained in violation thereof, not be admissible in state criminal
     proceedings."
146. *Mapp*, 367 U.S. at 651.
147. *Id.*
148. *Id.* (quoting *Cahan*, 44 Cal. 2d at 440).
149. *Id.* at 652.
150. *Id.* at 653, 659.
151. *Id.* at 653.
152. *Mapp*, 367 U.S. at 659 (quoting Olmstead v. United States, 277 U.S. 438,
     485 (1928) (Brandeis, J., dissenting)).
153. In *Olmstead*, the wiretapping case, Holmes (unlike Brandeis) was "not
     prepared to say that the penumbra of the Fourth and Fifth Amendments
     covers the defendant." *Olmstead*, 277 U.S. at 469 (Holmes, J., dissenting).
     Instead, he explained in dissent: "[I]f we are to confine ourselves to
     precedent and logic the reason for excluding evidence obtained by
     violating the Constitution seems to me logically to lead to excluding
     evidence obtained by a crime of the officers of the law." *Id.* at 471.
154. *Mapp*, 367 U.S. at 655.
155. *Id.* at 656 (quoting *Elkins*, 364 U.S. at 217).
156. *Id.* at 657–58.
157. *Id.* at 660.
158. United States v. Leon, 468 U.S. 897, 900 (1984).
159. *Id.* at 900–01 (quoting Alderman v. United States, 394 U.S. 165, 175
     (1969)).
160. *Id.* at 905–06.
161. *Id.* at 906.
162. *Id.*
163. *Id.* at 920–21.
164. *Id.* at 921.
165. *Id.* at 918.
166. *Id.* at 922.

167. 2 JENNIFER FRIESEN, STATE CONSTITUTIONAL LAW: LITIGATING
      INDIVIDUAL RIGHTS, CLAIMS AND DEFENSES § 11.05(2) (4th ed. 2006).
168. 122 Idaho 981 (1992).
169. State v. Guzman, 842 P.2d 660, 661–62 (1992).
170. *Id.* at 662.
171. *See* IDAHO CONST. art. I, § 17.
172. *Guzman*, 842 P.2d at 663 (Idaho 1992).
173. *Id.* (quoting State v. Arregui, 254 P. 788, 794–95 (Idaho 1927)).
174. *Id.* at 670.
175. *Id.* at 672.
176. *Id.* at 673.
177. *Id.* at 674.
178. *Id.* at 676.
179. *Id.* at 672.
180. *See id.* at 677–78 (Bakes, C.J., dissenting).
181. State v. Walker, 267 P.3d 210, 216 (Utah 2011).
182. *Id.* at 220.
183. *Id.* at 220–21.
184. *Id.* at 221.
185. *Id.*
186. *Id.* at 221–22; *see* Paul G. Cassell, *The Mysterious Creation of Search and
      Seizure Exclusionary Rules Under State Constitutions: The Utah Example*,
      1993 UTAH L. REV. 751 (1993).
187. *Walker*, 267 P.3d at 221 (emphasis in original).
188. *Id.* at 223.
189. *See* FRIESEN, *supra* note 167, at § 11.03[4].
190. *See* FLA. CONST. art. I, § 12 ("Articles or information obtained in violation
      of this right [to be secure against unreasonable searches and seizures]
      shall not be admissible in evidence if such articles or information would
      be inadmissible under decisions of the United States Supreme Court
      construing the 4th Amendment to the United States Constitution.");
      State v. Lavazzoli, 434 So.2d 321, 322 n.1 (Fla. 1983) ("Prior to the
      amendment, the right of a citizen of the State of Florida to be free
      from unreasonable searches and seizures was guaranteed independently
      of the similar protection provided by the fourth amendment to the
      United States Constitution. . . . The new amendment, however, links
      Florida's exclusionary rule to the federal exclusionary rule, making it also
      nothing more than a creature of judicial decisional policy and removing
      the 'independent protective force of state law.' "); CAL. CONST. art. I,
      § 28(f)(2) ("[R]elevant evidence shall not be excluded in any criminal
      proceeding, including pretrial and post conviction motions and hearings,
      or in any trial or hearing of a juvenile for a criminal offense, whether
      heard in juvenile or adult court."); *In re* Lance W., 37 Cal.3d 873, 886–87

(1985) (noting that the California amendment "eliminate[d] a judicially created remedy for violations of the search and seizure provisions of the . . . state Constitution . . . .").

191. *See* FRIESEN, *supra* note 167, at § 11.03[4]; LaFAVE, *supra* note 43, at § 1.5(b) (noting that "[w]hen . . . a state court finds that a certain arrest or search passes muster under the Fourth Amendment but that it violates the comparable provision of the state constitution, there does not appear to be any dissent from the conclusion that the fruits thereof must be suppressed from evidence" but citing Maryland as an exception); *see also* Fitzgerald v. State, 384 Md. 484, 500 (2004); Quinlan v. Sec'y of State, No. AP-12-030, 2012 WL 6650643, at *1 n.1 (Me. Super. Ct. Oct. 26, 2012) ("There is no independent exclusionary rule for unlawful searches and seizures under the Maine Constitution beyond the requirements of the federal constitution." (citing *State v. Giles*, 669 A.2d 192, 194 (Me. 1996))).

192. FRIESEN, *supra* note 167, at § 11.05[2]; Joseph Blocher, *Reverse Incorporation of State Constitutional Law*, 84 S. CAL. L. REV. 323, 373 (2011).

193. State v. Novembrino, 105 N.J. 95, 157 (1987).

194. State v. Oakes, 157 Vt. 171, 183 (1991).

195. *See, e.g.,* Dorsey v. State, 761 A.2d 807, 820 (Del. 2000) ("[T]here can be no good faith exception when the probable cause requirement in the Delaware Constitution is absent—as in this case."); State v. Marsala, 216 Conn. 150, 171 (1990) ("[W]e are simply unable to sanction a practice in which the validity of search warrants might be determined under a standard of 'close enough is good enough' instead of under the 'probable cause' standard mandated" by the state constitution).

196. *See* TEX. CODE CRIM. PROC. ANN. art. 38.23(a) ("No evidence obtained by an officer or other person in violation of any provisions of the Constitution or laws of the State of Texas, or of the Constitution or laws of the United States of America, shall be admitted in evidence against the accused on the trial of any criminal case."); Gonzales v. State, 148 Tex. Crim. 401 (1945); *see also* Wilson v. State, 311 S.W.3d 452, 458 n.23 (Tex. Crim. App. 2010) (observing that Texas's statutory exclusionary rule "imposes what is probably the broadest state exclusionary rule requirement of any American jurisdiction").

197. *See* TEX. CODE CRIM. PROC. ANN. art. 38.23(b) ("It is an exception to the provisions of Subsection (a) of this Article that the evidence was obtained by a law enforcement officer acting in objective good faith reliance upon a warrant issued by a neutral magistrate based on probable cause.").

198. *See* N.C. GEN. STAT. § 15A-974(a) (providing that upon a defendant's timely motion, evidence "must be suppressed" if either the federal or state constitution requires its exclusion, or if the evidence was obtained as a result of a "substantial violation" of state law); *id.* ("Evidence shall not be suppressed under this subdivision if the person committing the violation

of the provision or provisions under this Chapter acted under the objectively reasonable, good faith belief that the actions were lawful.").

199. *See* Gary v. State, 262 Ga. 573, 575–76 (1992) ("In light of the unequivocal language of [the statute], infusion of the *Leon* good faith exception into the statute would be tantamount to judicial legislation."); Commonwealth v. Upton, 394 Mass. 363, 366 (1985) ("G.L. c. 276 § 2B, provides a statutory prohibition against the admission of such evidence."); State v. McKnight, 291 S.C. 110 (1987) (similar).

200. WILLIAM J. STUNTZ, THE COLLAPSE OF AMERICAN CRIMINAL JUSTICE 99–100 (2011).

201. *Mapp*, 367 U.S. at 652 ("The experience of California that such other remedies have been worthless and futile is buttressed by the experience of other States.").

202. Elena Kagan, The Development and Erosion of the American Exclusionary Rule: A Study in Judicial Method (Apr. 20, 1983) (unpublished M.Phil. thesis, Worcester College, University of Oxford) (on file with the Collections in The Bodleian Library, University of Oxford). Thanks go to Professor Orin Kerr for pointing me to the thesis, which is worth a read and which offers what might be described as a progressive critique of *Mapp*.

203. *Id.* at 45 n.29, 54–55.

204. *Id.* at 54.

205. *See, e.g.,* Linkletter v. Walker, 381 U.S. 618 (1965).

206. *Leon*, 468 U.S. at 919; *see also* David Clark Esseks, *Errors in Good Faith: The* Leon *Exception Six Years Later*, 89 MICH. L. REV. 625, 652–58 (1990) (discussing the Court's dismantling of the exclusionary rule).

207. 28 U.S.C. § 2255(a) (2008) ("A prisoner in custody . . . claiming the right to be released upon the ground that the sentence was imposed in violation of the Constitution or laws of the United States . . . may move the court which imposed the sentence to vacate, set aside or correct the sentence.").

208. Kaufman v. United States, 394 U.S. 217 (1969).

209. United States v. Johnson, 457 U.S. 537, 562 n.20 (1982).

210. *See* Ray v. United States, 721 F.3d 758, 761–62 (6th Cir. 2013); Brock v. United States, 573 F.3d 497, 500 (7th Cir. 2009); United States v. Ishmael, 343 F.3d 741, 742–43 (5th Cir. 2003); United States v. Cook, 997 F.2d 1312, 1317 (10th Cir. 1993); United States v. Hearst, 638 F.2d 1190, 1196 (9th Cir. 1980).

211. Baranski v. United States, 515 F.3d 857, 859–60 (8th Cir. 2008).

212. 414 U.S. 338 (1974).

213. Kagan, *supra* note 202, at 79–80.

214. 428 U.S. 433 (1976).

215. Kagan, *supra* note 202, at 90 (citing cases mentioned in *Janis*, 428 U.S. at 455).

216. 392 U.S. 1.

217. Harold J. Spaeth et al., *2016 Supreme Court Database, Version 2016 Release 1*, WА. UNIV. LAW, http://supremecourtdatabase.org.

218. *See* State v. Baldon, 829 N.W.2d 785, 813 (2013) ("In the period following the incorporation revolution ending with *Mapp*, there is no doubt the strength and scope of the Fourth Amendment's protection has been dramatically reduced by the United States Supreme Court."); Ker v. California, 374 U.S. 23, 45 (1963) (Harlan, J., concurring in the judgment) (wondering if the Court would "relax Fourth Amendment standards in order to avoid unduly fettering the States"); California v. Acevedo, 500 U.S. 565, 582–83 (1991) (Scalia, J., concurring in the judgment) (noting the development of over twenty exceptions to the warrant requirement); Schneckloth v. Bustamonte, 412 U.S. 218, 234–46 (1973) (rejecting the higher standard to determine consent in *Johnson v. Zerbst*, 304 U.S. 458 (1938)). *See generally* Duncan v. Louisiana, 391 U.S. 145, 182 n.21 (1968) (Harlan, J., dissenting) (claiming that "a major danger" of incorporation is "that provisions of the Bill of Rights may be watered down in the needless pursuit of uniformity"); George C. Thomas III, *When Constitutional Worlds Collide: Resurrecting the Framers' Bill of Rights and Criminal Procedure*, 100 MICH. L. REV. 145, 150–51 (2001) (noting that in the aftermath of incorporation "the dilution of [the Bill of Rights] flowed backward[s]" and that "the process of incorporation took a sledgehammer to the federal criminal procedure guarantees"); State v. Short, 851 N.W.2d 474, 485–86 (Iowa 2014).

219. 381 U.S. 618 (1965).

220. *Id.* at 620.

221. *Id.* at 628–29.

222. *Id.* at 628.

223. *Id.* at 637.

224. *Id.* at 641.

225. *Id.* at 642.

226. *Id.* at 637.

227. *See* Johnson v. New Jersey, 384 U.S. 719, 732 (1966); Stovall v. Denno, 388 U.S. 293, 300 (1967).

228. Tehan v. Shott, 382 U.S. 406 (1966).

229. *Stovall*, 388 U.S. at 293.

230. *Johnson*, 384 U.S. 723 (1966).

231. 479 U.S. 314.

232. Jennifer E. Laurin, *Trawling for* Herring*: Lessons in Doctrinal Borrowing and Convergence*, 111 COLUM. L. REV. 670, 688–724 (2011) (demonstrating how *Leon*'s good faith standard was "borrowed" from the reasonable mistake standard of qualified immunity and explaining that the two standards have since "converged").

233. FLA. CONST. art. I, § 12 ("This right shall be construed in conformity with the 4th Amendment to the United States Constitution, as interpreted

by the United States Supreme Court."); CAL. CONST. art. I, § 28(f)(2)
("[R]elevant evidence shall not be excluded in any criminal proceeding,
including pretrial and post conviction motions and hearings, or in any
trial or hearing of a juvenile for a criminal offense, whether heard in
juvenile or adult court.").

234. MICHAEL W. FLAMM, LAW AND ORDER: STREET CRIME, CIVIL UNREST,
AND THE CRISIS OF LIBERALISM IN THE 1960S 134–35 (2005).
235. State v. Bradberry, 129 N.H. 68 (1986) (Souter, J., concurring).
236. 42 U.S.C. § 1983.
237. Bivens v. Six Unknown Named Agents, 403 U.S. 388 (1971).
238. *Id.*
239. Davis v. Passman, 442 U.S. 228 (1979).
240. Carlson v. Green, 446 U.S. 14 (1980).
241. Vance v. Rumfield, 701 F.3d 193, 198 (7th Cir. 2012) (en banc).
242. That is especially true for search-and-seizure questions that implicate new
technologies, as Professor Orin Kerr has forcefully pointed out. *See* Orin
Kerr, *The Fourth Amendment and New Technologies: Constitutional Myths
and the Case for Caution,* 102 MICH. L. REV. 801, 863 (2004).
243. 389 U.S. 347 (1967).
244. *Olmstead,* 277 U.S. at 474.
245. *Id.* at 476.
246. *Id.* at 478.
247. *Id.* at 485.
248. *Id.* at 472 (quoting McCulloch v. Maryland, 17 U.S. 316, 407 (1819)).
249. *Id.*
250. *Id.* (quoting Village of Euclid v. Ambler Realty Co., 272 U.S. 365, 387
(1926) (upholding a local zoning ordinance) and citing Buck v. Bell, 274
U.S. 200 (1927)).
251. *Id.*
252. *See* Thomas Y. Davies, *Foreword: Independent State Grounds: Should State
Courts Depart from the Fourth Amendment in Construing Their Own
Constitutions, and if so, on What Basis Beyond Simple Disagreement with
the United States Supreme Court's Result?,* 77 MISS. L.J. 1, 10 n.16 (2007)
(collecting cases); *compare* California v. Greenwood, 486 U.S. 35, 45 (1988)
(holding that warrantless trash searches do not violate an individual's
expectation of privacy), *with* State v. Crane, 149 N.M. 674, 676–77 (2011)
(recognizing a greater expectation of privacy in one's garbage under the
New Mexico Constitution); *compare* Mich. Dep't of State Police v. Sitz,
496 U.S. 444, 455 (1990) (holding that a traffic checkpoint program did
not violate the Fourth Amendment), *with* City of Seattle v. Mesiani,
110 Wash.2d 454, 457 (1988) (recognizing that the Washington State
Constitution offers broader protection against police DUI checkpoints);
compare Illinois v. Rodriguez, 497 U.S. 177, 186–87 (1990) (holding that
police may conduct a warrantless search when acting under the "apparent

consent" of a third party), *with* State v. Maristany, 133 N.J. 299, 305 (1993) (requiring that an officer's reliance on the apparent consent of a third party must be objectively reasonable under the New Jersey Constitution).

253. HOLLAND ET AL., STATE CONSTITUTIONAL LAW AND THE MODERN EXPERIENCE 409 (2d ed. 2015).

254. Stephen Henderson, *Learning from All Fifty States: How to Apply the Fourth Amendment and Its State Analogs to Protect Third Party Information from Unreasonable Search*, 55 CATH. UNIV. L. REV. 373 (2006).

255. For example, state courts have rejected the "one party consent" rule utilized by the federal courts and extended greater protection in cases of warrantless taping of conversations with informants; have invalidated the warrantless use of "pen registers," in direct opposition to Supreme Court precedent; and have rejected the "good faith" exception to the warrant requirement the Supreme Court laid down in *Leon. See* Paul Marcus, *State Constitutional Protection for Defendants in Criminal Prosecutions*, 20 ARIZ. ST. L.J. 151 (1988).

Chapter 5

1. *Eugenics*, OXFORD ENGLISH DICTIONARY (2016), *available at* http://www. oxforddictionaries.com/definition/english/eugenics.

2. Michael G. Silver, *Eugenics and Compulsory Sterilization Laws: Providing Redress for the Victims of a Shameful Era in United States History*, 72 GEO. WASH. L. REV. 862, 865 (2004).

3. Robert J. Cynkar, Buck v. Bell: *"Felt Necessities" v. Fundamental Values?*, 81 COLUM. L. REV. 1418, 1421 (1981).

4. *Id.*

5. *Id. see* BARBARA WEXLER, GENETICS AND GENETIC ENGINEERING 24 (2010).

6. PHILLIP R. REILLY, THE SURGICAL SOLUTION: A HISTORY OF INVOLUNTARY STERILIZATION IN THE UNITED STATES 2 (1991).

7. ADAM COHEN, IMBECILES: THE SUPREME COURT, AMERICAN EUGENICS, AND THE STERILIZATION OF CARRIE BUCK 46 (Penguin Press 2016).

8. *Id.* at 3.

9. *Id.*

10. FRANCIS GALTON, HEREDITARY GENIUS: AN INQUIRY INTO ITS LAWS AND CONSEQUENCES 14 (London: Macmillan 1869), *quoted in* REILLY, *supra* note 6, at 3.

11. Cynkar, *supra* note 3, at 1424 (quoting A. WIGGAM, THE NEW DECALOGUE OF SCIENCE 42–43 (1922)).

12. *Id.* at 1423.

13. *Id.* at 1422.

14. REILLY, *supra* note 6, at 42–43; Silver, *supra* note 2, at 865 n.27.

15. COHEN, *supra* note 7, at 57 (quoting Theodore Roosevelt, *Twisted Eugenics*, OUTLOOK, Jan. 3, 1914, 30–34).

16. *See* CHARLES DARWIN, ON THE ORIGIN OF SPECIES (1859).
17. *See* THOMAS ROBERT MALTHUS, AN ESSAY ON THE PRINCIPLE OF POPULATION (1798).
18. *See* HERBERT SPENCER, SOCIAL STATICS (1851).
19. REILLY, *supra* note 6, at 4 (quoting Spencer).
20. COHEN, *supra* note 7, at 322.
21. Cynkar, *supra* note 3, at 1429.
22. *Id.* at 1429–30.
23. REILLY, *supra* note 6, at 29.
24. Cynkar, *supra* note 3, at 1430.
25. *Id.*
26. REILLY, *supra* note 6, at 32.
27. Cynkar, *supra* note 3, at 1433.
28. REILLY, *supra* note 6, at 31.
29. Cynkar, *supra* note 3, at 1433.
30. REILLY, *supra* note 6, at 31–32 (quoting H.C. Sharp, *The Severing of the Vasa Deferentia and Its Relation to the Neuropsycopathic Constitution*, 75 N.Y. MED. J. 411 (1902)).
31. HARRY H. LAUGHLIN, EUGENICAL STERILIZATION IN THE UNITED STATES 15 (1922), *quoted in* REILLY, *supra* note 6, at 46–47.
32. REILLY, *supra* note 6, at 57–58.
33. Cynkar, *supra* note 3, at 1431 (quoting M. HALLER, EUGENICS: HEREDITARIAN ATTITUDES IN AMERICAN THOUGHT 124 (1963)).
34. REILLY, *supra* note 6, at 56.
35. *Id.* at 45–46.
36. *Id.* at 46.
37. *Id.* at 47.
38. *Id.*
39. *Id.* at 48.
40. Dr. Sharp apparently did not record all of his sterilizations, suggesting that the Indiana numbers understate that State's record. *Id.* at 40.
41. *Id.* at 49.
42. *Id.*
43. COHEN, *supra* note 7, at 84. Alabama and North Carolina enacted such laws that year.
44. REILLY, *supra* note 6, at 34, 48.
45. The governor of Nebraska at one point noted that eugenics legislation had more in common "with the pagan age than with the teachings of Christianity" and that "man is more than an animal." COHEN, *supra* note 7, at 101.
46. REILLY, *supra* note 6, at 48–49.
47. *Id.* at 51; *see also* COHEN, *supra* note 7, at 101.
48. *See* 1 JENNIFER FRIESEN, STATE CONSTITUTIONAL LAW §§ 2.02, 3.01[2] (4th ed. 2006).
49. Robinson v. California, 370 U.S. 660 (1962).

50. State v. Feilen, 126 P. 75, 76 (Wash. 1912).

51. LAUGHLIN, *supra* note 31, at 292.

52. *Feilen*, 126 P. at 76.

53. *Id.*

54. *See* WASH. CONST. art. I, § 14 ("excessive bail shall not be required, excessive fines imposed, nor cruel punishment inflicted").

55. *Feilen*, 126 P. at 76.

56. *See* Coker v. Georgia, 433 U.S. 584 (1977) (invalidating capital punishment for rape as imposing cruel and unusual punishment under the Federal Constitution).

57. *Feilen*, 126 P. at 76.

58. *Id.*

59. *Id.* at 77.

60. *Id.*

61. *Id.* at 77–78.

62. Lutz Kaelber, *Eugenics: Compulsory Sterilization in 50 American States, available at* http://www.uvm.edu/~lkaelber/eugenics/WA/WA.html/.

63. REILLY, *supra* note 6, at 51.

64. LAUGHLIN, *supra* note 31, at 91.

65. *Id.* at 292.

66. *Id.*

67. E.D. Twyman & C.S. Nelson, *Vas Deferens Anastomosis: Successful Repair Four Years Subsequent to Bilateral Vasectomy*, 42 UROL CUTANEOUS REV. 586 (1938) (reporting the first successful vasectomy reversal).

68. Mickle v. Herrichs, 262 F. 687 (D. Nev. 1918); *see* NEV. CONST. art. I, § 6 ("Excessive bail shall not be required, nor excessive fines imposed, nor shall cruel or unusual punishments inflicted.").

69. *See* Younger v. Harris, 401 U.S. 37, 54–55 (1971) (denying a federal court the power to enjoin, even on federal constitutional grounds, a pending state criminal proceeding).

70. *See* Estelle v. McGuire, 502 U.S. 62, 67–68 (1991); Pennhurst State Sch. v. Halderman, 465 U.S. 89, 105–06 (1984) (federal courts may not require state agents to follow state law).

71. *Mickle*, 262 F. at 687. *See* Steel Co. v. Citizens for a Better Env't, 523 U.S. 83, 93–94 (1998) (parties may not waive subject matter jurisdiction).

72. *Mickle*, 262 F. at 687.

73. *Id.*

74. LAUGHLIN, *supra* note 31, at 312–13.

75. *Mickle*, 262 F. at 688.

76. *Id.*

77. *Id.*

78. *Id.*

79. *Id.* at 689.

80. *Id.*

81. *Id.* at 690.

82. *Id.* at 691.
83. *Id.*
84. *Id.*
85. *Id.*
86. Biographical Directory of Federal Judges: Farrington, Edward Silsby, http://www.fjc.gov/servlet/nGetInfo?jid=736&cid=999&ctype=na&instat e=na (last visited June 20, 2016).
87. U.S. District Court for the District of Nevada: Judge Succession Chart, http://www.fjc.gov/history/home.nsf/page/courts_district_nv_sc.html (last visited June 28, 2016).
88. Biographical Directory of Federal Judges: Farrington, Edward Silsby, http://www.fjc.gov/servlet/nGetInfo?jid=736&cid=999&ctype=na&instat e=na (last visited June 20, 2016).
89. Skinner v. Oklahoma, 316 U.S. 535 (1942).
90. Smith v. Bd. of Exam'rs of Feeble-Minded, 85 N.J.L. 46 (N.J. 1913).
91. *Id.* at 49–50.
92. *Id.* at 51.
93. *Id.*
94. *Id.* at 51–52.
95. *Id.* at 52.
96. *Id.*
97. *Id.*
98. *Id.*
99. *Id.*
100. *Id.* at 52–53. *See also id.* at 53 ("[T]he large and underlying question is, how far is government constitutionally justified in the theoretical betterment of society by means of the surgical sterilization of certain of its unoffending, but undesirable, members?").
101. *Id.* at 53.
102. *Id.* at 54.
103. *Id.*
104. *Id.* at 55.
105. *Id.*
106. Cohen, *supra* note 7, at 273.
107. *Smith*, 85 N.J.L. at 51.
108. *See* Ohio v. Robinette, 519 U.S. 33, 42–43 (1996) (Ginsburg, J., concurring) ("When a State high court grounds a rule of criminal procedure in the Federal Constitution, the court thereby signals its view that the National Constitution would require the rule in all 50 States.").
109. State *ex rel.* State Bd. of Milk Control v. Newark Milk Co., 179 A. 116, 124 (N.J. 1935).
110. *See Smith*, 85 N.J.L. at 48 ("*Held*, that the statute in question was based upon a classification that bore no reasonable relation to the object of such police regulation," thereby denying "equal protection of the law.").

111. City of Cleburne v. Cleburne Living Ctr., 473 U.S. 432 (1985).
112. *The Rev. Joseph F. Garrison Dead*, N.Y. Times, Feb. 1, 1892, at 3.
113. William Edgar Sackett & John James Scannell, Scannell's New Jersey First Citizens: Biographies and Portraits of the Notable Living Men and Women of New Jersey 202 (1917).
114. *The Rev. Joseph F. Garrison Dead, supra* note 112, at 3.
115. Acts of the One Hundred and Thirty-Fifth Legislature of the State of New Jersey, Chapter 190 (Paterson, NJ: News Printing Co., State Printers, 1911).
116. *Cabinet Complete, Wilson Announces*, N.Y. Times, Mar. 4, 1913, at 1; *Surprise to Brother: Justice C.G. Garrison Asks Cause of Resignation*, Wash. Post, Feb. 11, 1916, at 5.
117. Jeffrey Alan Hodges, Dealing with Degeneracy: Michigan Eugenics in Context 138 (2002).
118. *Smith*, 85 N.J.L. at 51.
119. *Id.*
120. Laughlin, *supra* note 31, at 297–304.
121. *Id.* at 299.
122. *Id.* at 293.
123. *Id.* at 297.
124. *Id.* at 296, 300.
125. *Id.* at 295.
126. *Id.* at 296.
127. *Id.* at 370.
128. *See* Haynes v. Lapeer, 201 Mich. 138 (1918); *see also* E.S. Gosney & Paule Popenoe, Sterilization for Human Betterment 15 (1930) (In 1897, Michigan had been the first State to propose eugenics legislation, but it did not pass any such law until 1913.).
129. Laughlin, *supra* note 31, at 73.
130. *Id.*
131. Frances Oswald, *Eugenical Sterilization in the United States*, 36 Am. J. Psychol. 72 (July 1930).
132. *Haynes*, 201 Mich. at 141.
133. *Id.* at 142 (citing 6 R.C.L. 373 (William M. McKinny & Burdett A. Rich eds., 1914)).
134. *Id.* at 143.
135. Public Acts of Michigan, P.A. 285, 1923 (*reprinted in* Jeffrey Alan Hodges, Euthenics, Eugenics and Compulsory Sterilization 1897–1960, at 148 (1995)).
136. 231 Mich. 409 (1925).
137. Smith v. Wayne Cty. Probate Judge, 231 Mich. 409, 420–21 (1925) (noting that one section of the law unconstitutionally "carves a class out of a class" by applying only to feebleminded individuals who may be unable to support their children financially).

138. *Id.* at 427.

139. *Id.* at 428 (Wiest, J., dissenting).

140. Dean W. Kelley, In Memoriam Howard Wiest, Michigan Supreme Court Historical Society (Oct. 2, 1945), http://www.micourthistory.org/special-sessions/in-memoriam-howard-wiest/.

141. Charles P. Van Note, In Memoriam Howard Wiest, Michigan Supreme Court Historical Society (Oct. 2, 1945), http://www.micourthistory.org/special-sessions/in-memoriam-howard-wiest/.

142. *Smith*, 231 Mich. at 430 (Wiest, J., dissenting).

143. *Id.* at 432.

144. *Id.* at 433–34 (citing Weems v. United States, 217 U.S. 349 (1910), which mentioned castration as an impermissible form of punishment).

145. *Id.* at 447 ("If one breeds a fool, is the idea to sterilize the fool and also the breeders for fear they may repeat? If the feeble-minded breeds a normal, then is the idea to sterilize him because, under the theory of heredity, such progeny may throw back?").

146. 236 Mich. 478 (1926).

147. Haynes v. Lapeer Circuit Judge: *Eugenics in Michigan*, 88 Mich. B.J. S9, S12 (Jan. 2009).

148. *In re* Salloum, 236 Mich. 478 (1926).

149. Osborn v. Thomson, 169 N.Y.S. 638 (S. Ct. Albany Cty. 1918).

150. *Id.* at 639.

151. *Id.*

152. *Topics of the Times*, N.Y. Times, Nov. 25, 1900, at 18.

153. *Ex-Justice Rudd Dies in 79th Year*, N.Y. Times, Oct. 20, 1929, at 31.

154. *Osborn*, 169 N.Y.S. at 641.

155. *Id.*

156. *Id.* at 641–42.

157. *Id.* at 642.

158. *Id.* at 642–44.

159. U.S. Const. art. III, § 2.

160. *See* Opinion of the Justices of Supreme Judicial Court, 815 A.2d 791 (Me. 2002); *In re* Advisory Opinion to the Governor, 856 A.2d 320 (R.I. 2004).

161. *Osborn*, 169 N.Y.S. at 643.

162. *Id.*

163. *Id.* at 644.

164. *Id.*

165. *Id.* at 645.

166. *See* Osborn v. Thomas, 185 A.D. 902 (N.Y. App. Div. 1918).

167. Laughlin, *supra* note 31, at 26 (citing L. 1920, Chap. 619).

168. *Id.* at 82.

169. *Id.*

170. No. 15, 422 (Ore. Cir. Ct. Dec. 13, 1921), *reprinted in* LAUGHLIN, *supra* note 31, at 287–88.

171. LAUGHLIN, *supra* note 31, at 319.

172. *Id.* at 288.

173. *Id.* (quoting Munn v. Illinois, 94 U.S. 113, 142 (1877)).

174. *Id.* at 288–89.

175. Davis v. Berry, 216 F. 413 (S.D. Iowa 1914).

176. *Id.* at 414.

177. *Id.* at 415.

178. *See, e.g.*, Cummings v. Missouri, 71 U.S. 277, 325 (1866) (striking down an amendment to the Missouri Constitution requiring an oath of past and present loyalty as a bill of attainder); United States v. Brown, 381 U.S. 437, 449–50 (1965) (holding unconstitutional a federal law denying Communist Party members the right to serve as officers or employees in labor unions); United States v. Lovett, 328 U.S. 303, 315 (1946) (invalidating a federal law that denied salaries to named federal employees).

179. *Davis*, 216 F. at 416–17.

180. *Id.* at 416 (emphasis added).

181. *See, e.g., Cummings*, 71 U.S. 277 (1866) (limiting ex post facto laws and bills of attainder to the Due Process Clause of the Fifth Amendment and describing all three provisions as protections from retroactive deprivations); *cf. Brown*, 381 U.S. 437, 458–59 (1965) (noting some English bills of attainder were enacted for preventive purposes); Anthony Dick, Note, *The Substance of Punishment Under the Bill of Attainder Clause*, 63 STAN. L. REV. 1177, 1192 (2011).

182. *Davis*, 216 F. at 418–19 (Smith, J. concurring).

183. United States v. Munsingwear, Inc., 340 U.S. 36, 39–40 (1950).

184. Berry v. Davis, 242 U.S. 468, 470 (1917).

185. Williams v. Smith, 131 N.E. 2 (Ind. 1921).

186. *Id.*

187. *Id.*

188. REILLY, *supra* note 6, at 63, 66, 84.

189. *Id.* at 63.

190. *Id.* at 84.

191. As noted, Alabama and North Carolina enacted such laws in 1919. COHEN, *supra* note 7, at 84.

192. Paul A. Lombardo, *Three Generations, No Imbeciles: New Light on* Buck v. Bell, 60 N.Y.U. L. REV. 30, 35 (1985).

193. PAUL A. LOMBARDO, THREE GENERATIONS, NO IMBECILES: EUGENICS, THE SUPREME COURT AND *BUCK V. BELL* 19 (2008) (quoting *Virginia Acts of Assembly*, 1916, ch. 106).

194. *Id.* at 60–61.

195. *Id.* at 74.
196. *Id.*
197. *Id.* at 71; *see Ex Parte* Mallory, 122 Va. 298 (1918) (writ of habeas corpus for release of Mallory children); Mallory v. Va. Colony for the Feebleminded, 123 Va. 205 (1918) (writ of habeas corpus for Nannie Mallory).
198. LOMBARDO, *supra* note 193, at 91, 97–98.
199. *Id.* at 97.
200. *Id.* at 101 (quoting Minutes of August 6, 1924, Special Board of Directors of the Virginia State Colony for Epileptics and Feebleminded (1906–1937)).
201. *Id.* at 150.
202. COHEN, *supra* note 7, at 292.
203. LOMBARDO, *supra* note 193, at 106.
204. *Id.* at 107 (quoting Record at 36, Buck v. Bell, 274 U.S. 200 (1927) (order of Special Board to sterilize Carrie Buck)).
205. *Id.*
206. *Id.* at 148.
207. COHEN, *supra* note 7, at 51 (identifying the "fundamental problems with the eugenicists' science").
208. LOMBARDO, *supra* note 193, at 134 (quoting Record at 32, Buck v. Bell, 274 U.S. 200 (1927) (deposition of Harry Laughlin, quoting Albert Priddy)).
209. *Id.*
210. HODGES, *supra* note 117, at 138.
211. LOMBARDO, *supra* note 193, at 139; COHEN, *supra* note 7, at 19.
212. LOMBARDO, *supra* note 193, at 139; COHEN, *supra* note 7, at 290.
213. LOMBARDO, *supra* note 193, at 140.
214. *Id.* at 117 (quoting Record at 58, Buck v. Bell, 274 U.S. 200 (1927) (testimony of Caroline E. Wilhelm)).
215. *Id.* at 190.
216. *Id.* at 154 (emphasis added) (quoting December 7, 1925 Board minutes).
217. *Id.* at 216.
218. *Id.* at 56.
219. *Buck*, 274 U.S. at 207–08.
220. LOMBARDO, *supra* note 193, at 185.
221. *Id.* at 171.
222. Reply Br. for the Petitioner at 5, Buck v. Bell, 143 Va. 310 (1925).
223. 268 U.S. 510.
224. Lochner v. New York, 198 U.S. 45, 75 (1905) (Holmes, J., dissenting).
225. COHEN, *supra* note 7, at 277.
226. *Id.* at 273.
227. LOMBARDO, *supra* note 193, at 173 (quoting Letter from Oliver Wendell Holmes Jr. to Lewis Einstein, May 19, 1927, Papers of Oliver Wendell Holmes Jr., Library of Congress).

228. Cohen, *supra* note 7, at 299 (quoting Harry Laughlin, The Legal Status of Eugenical Sterilization: History and Analysis of Litigation Under the Virginia Sterilization Statute, Which Led to a Decision of the Supreme Court of the United States Upholding the Statute 53 (1930)).

229. Cohen, *supra* note 7, at 299.

230. Victoria F. Nourse, In Reckless Hands 31 (W.W. Norton & Co. 2008).

231. *Id.*

232. Cohen, *supra* note 7, at 300.

233. Jessica Baldanzi et al., *Eugenics in Indiana, available at* http://www. kobescent.com/eugenics.

234. *Id.*

235. Lombardo, *supra* note 193, at 294.

236. Julius Paul, "Three Generations of Imbeciles Are Enough": State Eugenic Sterilization in American Thought and Practice 557 (1965) (unpublished manuscript).

237. Cynkar, *supra* note 3, at 1454. Cohen, *supra* note 7, at 300 (noting that twenty-eight of the forty-eight States in 1931 had eugenic laws).

238. State *ex rel.* Smith v. Schaffer, 270 P. 604, 605 (Kan. 1928).

239. Lombardo, *supra* note 193, at 294. Cohen puts the number at 7,450 in Virginia. Cohen, *supra* note 7, at 319.

240. Lutz Kaelber, *Eugenics: Compulsory Sterilization in 50 American States, available at* http://www.uvm.edu/~lkaelber/eugenics/.

241. *Id.*

242. Lombardo, *supra* note 193, at 294.

243. Edward Larson, Sex, Race, and Science: Eugenics in the Deep South 8–9, 17 (Johns Hopkins Univ. Press 1995).

244. Cynkar, *supra* note 3, at 1454–55.

245. Lombardo, *supra* note 193, at 294.

246. Cohen, *supra* note 7, at 131.

247. *Id.* at 104.

248. *Id.* at 134–35.

249. *Id.* at 58.

250. *Id.* at 114.

251. Sandy O'Neill, First They Killed the "Crazies" and "Cripples": The Ablest Persecution and Murders of People with Disabilities by Nazi Germany, 1933–1945: An Anthropological Perspective 128 (2000) (citing Allan Chase, The Legacy of Malthus: The Social Costs of the New Scientific Racism (1977); Garland E. Allen, *Science Misapplied: The Eugenics Age Revisited*, 99.6 Tech. Rev. 22, 29 (1996); Dave Reynolds, *The Eugenics Apologies*, 24.6 Ragged Edge 13, 16 (2003)). Cynkar puts the number at 200,000, though he offers no citation for the point. *Supra* note 3, at 1456.

252. https://www.democracynow.org/2016/3/17/buck_v_bell_inside_the_scotus (interview with Adam Cohen).

253. For a powerful description of the *Skinner* story, see NOURSE, *supra* note 230.

254. *Skinner,* 316 U.S. at 536.

255. *Id.* at 537.

256. *Id.*

257. *Id.* at 536.

258. *Id.* at 538.

259. *Id.*

260. *Id.* at 542.

261. *Id.* at 539–40 (quoting *Buck,* 274 U.S. at 208).

262. *Id.* at 542.

263. *Id.* at 541.

264. *Id.*

265. *Id.* at 543–44 (Stone, J., concurring).

266. *Id.* at 544.

267. *Id.* at 545.

268. *Id.* at 546 (Jackson, J., concurring).

269. *Id.*

270. *Id.* at 541–42.

271. Philip R. Reilly, *Involuntary Sterilization in the United States: A Surgical Solution,* 62 Q. REV. BIOLOGY 153, 166 (June 1987).

272. LOMBARDO, *supra* note 193, at 242.

273. Silver, *supra* note 2, at 871.

274. Cook v. State, 9 Ore. App. 224 (1972).

275. *In re* Moore's Sterilization, 29 N.C. 95 (1976).

276. Silver, *supra* note 2, at 876.

277. Julie Sullivan, *State of Oregon Will Admit Sterilization Past,* PORTLAND OREGONIAN, Nov. 15, 2002.

278. Motes v. Hall Cty. Dep't of Family & Children Servs., 251 Ga. 373, 374 (1983).

279. *Id.*

280. *See In re* Hillstrom, 363 N.W.2d 871 (Minn. Ct. App. 1985); *In re* Romero, 790 P.2d 819, 820 (Colo. 1990).

281. McKinney v. McKinney, 305 Ark. 13 (1991).

282. *See Hearing Before the House Subcommittee on Surface Transportation,* 101st Cong. 293 (Sept. 1989).

283. 1941 Mo. Laws 344, § 1 (codified at Mo. REV. STAT. § 209.150).

284. *See* 1965 Wis. Sess. Laws 329, ch. 230.

285. Bd. of Trs. of the Univ. of Ala. v. Garrett, 531 U.S. 356, 368 n.5 (2001).

286. *Id.*

287. *See, e.g.,* CAL. CIV. CODE §§ 51, 54–55.2 (West 2016); FLA. STAT. §§ 760.08, 760.23–26 (2016); MASS GEN. LAWS ch. 272 §§ 92A, 98; MASS

GEN. LAWS ch. 93 § 103; N.J. STAT. ANN. § 10:5–12 (West 2016); TEX. LAB. CODE ANN. §§ 21.051–059, 128 (1995); Comm'n on Human Rights & Opportunities v. Sullivan Assocs., 250 Conn. 763, 804 (1999).

288. *See, e.g.*, Conservatorship of Valerie N. v. Valerie N., 40 Cal. 3d 143, 157–58 (1985); *see also Garrett*, 531 U.S. at 369 n. 6 ("there is no indication that any State had persisted in requiring such harsh measures as of 1990 when the ADA was adopted"); Tennessee v. Lane, 541 U.S. 509, 535 (2004) (Souter, J., concurring) (commenting that in upholding Title II of the ADA the Court "takes a welcome step" away from past discrimination like compelled sterilization); Lake v. Arnold, 112 F.3d 682, 687–88 (3d Cir. 1997) (holding that the language and intent of 42 U.S.C. § 1985 protect the mentally retarded).

289. LOMBARDO, *supra* note 193, at 31. Adam Cohen estimates the number at 60,000 to 70,000 between 1907 and 1983. COHEN, *supra* note 7, at 319.

290. Fulton Corp. v. Faulker, 516 U.S. 325, 345 (1996) (quoting H.L.A. Hart, *Positivism and the Separation of Law and Morals*, 71 HARV. L. REV. 593 (1958)).

291. *See* REILLY, *supra* note 6, at 44.

292. THE FEDERALIST No. 51 (James Madison).

293. COHEN, *supra* note 7, at 309.

294. *But see* Gonzales v. Raich, 455 U.S. 1 (2005); Wickard v. Filburn, 317 U.S. 111 (1942).

295. Friedemann Pfafflin & Jan Gross, *Involuntary Sterilization in Germany from 1933 to 1945 and Some Consequences for Today*, 5 INT'L J.L. & PSYCHIATRY 419 (1982).

296. COHEN, *supra* note 7, at 292 (quoting Stephen Jay Gould, *Carrie Buck's Daughter*, 2 CONST. COMMENT. 331, 338 (1985)).

297. COHEN, *supra* note 7, at 27, 290, 296, 272.

298. *Id.* at 19, 267.

299. *Id.* at 145.

300. *Id.* at 51.

301. For an historical account of judicial prohibitions on class legislation, see generally HOWARD GILLMAN, THE CONSTITUTION BESIEGED (Duke Univ. Press 1993).

302. Melissa L. Saunders, *Equal Protection, Class Legislation, and Colorblindness*, 96 MICH. L. REV. 245, 252 (1997).

303. *Id.* at 257–58.

304. City of Cleburne v. Cleburne Living Ctr., Inc., 473 U.S. 432 (1985).

Chapter 6

1. Gitlow v. New York, 268 U.S. 652 (1925).

2. Cantwell v. Connecticut, 310 U.S. 296 (1940).

3. PA. CONST. art. IX, § 7 (1790). For a compilation of state free speech provisions, see J. FRIESEN, STATE CONSTITUTIONAL LAW: LITIGATING INDIVIDUAL RIGHTS, CLAIMS, AND DEFENSES, app. 5 (4th ed. 2006).

4. N.Y. CONST. art. I, § 8.
5. IND. CONST. art. I, § 9.
6. S.C. CONST. art. 1, § 2.
7. MASS. CONST. art. 46, § 1; *see also* Va. Bill of Rights of 1776, § 16, reprinted in 2 FEDERAL AND STATE CONSTITUTIONS, COLONIAL CHARTERS, AND OTHER ORGANIC LAWS OF THE UNITED STATES 1908–1909 ("all men are equally entitled to the free exercise of religion"). For a full compilation of state free exercise guarantees, see FRIESEN, *supra* note 3, at app. 4B.
8. N.Y. CONST. art. I, § 3.
9. TEX. CONST. art. I, § 6.
10. 319 U.S. 624 (1943).
11. Minersville Sch. Dist. v. Gobitis, 310 U.S. 586, 600 (1940).
12. *Cf.* Peter D. Baird, *Legal Lore: Miranda Memories*, LITIGATION, Winter 1990, at 43, 46 (discussing Ernesto Miranda's difficulties after the landmark case bearing his name and his eventual death in obscurity).
13. *See* SHAWN FRANCIS PETERS, JUDGING JEHOVAH'S WITNESSES: RELIGIOUS PERSECUTION AND THE DAWN OF THE RIGHTS REVOLUTION 19 (2000); *see also* Richard Danzig, *Justice Frankfurter's Opinions in the Flag Salute Cases: Blending Logic and Psychologic in Constitutional Decisionmaking*, 36 STAN. L. REV. 675, 678–79 (1984) (reflecting on the spelling mistake).
14. *See* PETERS, *supra* note 13, at 19.
15. *Id.* at 19–20.
16. *Gobitis*, 310 U.S. at 591.
17. RICHARD J. ELLIS, TO THE FLAG: THE UNLIKELY HISTORY OF THE PLEDGE OF ALLEGIANCE 19 (2005).
18. Act of June 22, 1942, Pub. L. No. 77-623, § 7, 56 Stat. 377, 380.
19. Act of June 14, 1954, Pub. L. No. 83-396, 68 Stat. 249.
20. § 7, 56 Stat. at 380; *see also* PETERS, *supra* note 13, at 25 (discussing this "military-style salute" given during the pledge).
21. PETERS, *supra* note 13, at 28–29.
22. *Id.* at 25.
23. *Gobitis*, 310 U.S. at 591.
24. PETERS, *supra* note 13, at 25–26; *Exodus* 20:1–17.
25. PETERS, *supra* note 13, at 25–26.
26. *Gobitis*, 310 U.S. at 591.
27. PETERS, *supra* note 13, at 37–39.
28. Gobitis v. Minersville Sch. Dist., 24 F. Supp. 271, 272 (E.D. Pa. 1938).
29. Minersville Sch. Dist. v. Gobitis, 108 F.2d 683 (3d Cir. 1939).
30. PETERS, *supra* note 13, at 51–52.
31. *Id.* at 52, 65, 237.
32. *Id.* at 70–71.
33. *Id.* at 70.
34. *Id.* at 71.
35. *See id.* at 164–65.

36. *See* Selective Training and Service Act of 1940, Pub. L. No. 76-783, 54 Stat. 885.

37. *See* PETERS, *supra* note 13, at 260–61.

38. *See id.*

39. *Id.* at 262.

40. *Id.*

41. *See id.* at 72–95 (discussing a series of these attacks against the Witnesses).

42. *Id.* at 85 (and sources cited).

43. *Id.* at 108.

44. *Id.* at 77–82.

45. *Id.* at 85–87.

46. *Id.* at 89–92.

47. *Id.* at 213.

48. *Id.* at 210.

49. *Id.* at 84.

50. *Id.* at 67.

51. *Id.* at 69.

52. *Id.*

53. *Id.*

54. *Id.*

55. *Id.*

56. *See* Gregory L. Peterson et al., *Recollections of* West Virginia State Board of Education v. Barnette, 81 ST. JOHN'S L. REV. 755, 792 (2007).

57. *Barnette*, 319 U.S. at 626.

58. *Id.*

59. *Id.* at 629.

60. *Id.* at 629–30. The Barnett children would avoid truancy charges by presenting themselves at school each morning, only to have the principal send them home. Peterson et al., *supra* note 56, at 771.

61. *See Gobitis*, 24 F. Supp. at 273 (calculating the cost of tuition for 1935–38 for the two Gobitas children as totaling in excess of $1,400). The private school—Jones Kingdom School—that the Gobitas children began attending was an old farmhouse, renovated by a sympathetic individual and serving forty students in grades one through eight. PETERS, *supra* note 13, at 43. Walter Gobitas modified a delivery truck into a bus so that the children could all ride together for the daily one-hour commute. *Id.* at 44–45.

62. *See* Pub. L. 77–623.

63. *Barnette*, 319 U.S. at 638 n.17.

64. Act of June 22, 1942, Pub. L. 77–623, § 7, 56 Stat. 377; *see* 88 Cong. Rec. 3720–22 (1942) (describing the introduction of this language in the Senate version of the bill).

65. *See* Stephen A. Smith, *Patriotism, Pledging Allegiance, and Public Schools: Lessons from Washington County in the 1940s*, 64 ARK. HIST. Q. 55–56 (2005).

66. *Id.*

67. *Id.* at 66.

68. Act of Dec. 22, 1942, Pub. L. 77–829, §7, 56 Stat. 1074.

69. Smith, *supra* note 65, at 59–69.

70. Peterson et al., *supra* note 56, at 768.

71. *See* Dan Seligman, From *Gobitis* to *Barnette*: A Primer 2 (2006); Peterson et al., *supra* note 56, at 768.

72. Peterson et al., *supra* note 56, at 770.

73. Seligman, *supra* note 71, at 1.

74. Peterson et al., *supra* note 56, at 769.

75. Barnette v. W. Va. State Bd. of Educ., 47 F. Supp. 251, 255 (S.D. W. Va. 1942).

76. Peters, *supra* note 13, at 247.

77. *Id.* at 248.

78. *Barnette*, 319 U.S. at 642.

79. Noah Feldman, Scorpions: The Battles and Triumphs of FDR's Great Supreme Court Justices 46 (2010).

80. *Id.* at 42–43.

81. *See Barnette*, 319 U.S. at 642.

82. *Id.*

83. *Id.* at 646–47 (Frankfurter, J., dissenting).

84. In *Knox v. Lee*, 79 U.S. 457 (1871) (*Legal Tender Cases*), the Court overruled its decision from the prior term, *Hepburn v. Griswold*, 75 U.S. 603 (1870). The Court noted that *Hepburn* had been decided by an eight-member Court (and one of those members, Justice Grier, had stepped down before the decision was announced, though he had voted with the majority on the legal tender issue at conference). The first time the Supreme Court overruled one of its own opinions was in *Hudson v. Guestier*, 10 U.S. (6 Cranch) 281, 285 (1810), which overruled *Rose v. Himely*, 8 U.S. (4 Cranch) 241 (1808). *Graves v. People of the State of New York ex rel. O'Keefe*, 306 U.S. 466, 486 (1939), overruled *New York ex rel. Rogers v. Graves*, 299 U.S. 401 (1937), and *Brush v. Commissioner*, 300 U.S. 352 (1937), insofar as the earlier decisions had recognized implied constitutional immunity from income taxation for state and federal employees. *United States v. Rabinowitz*, 339 U.S. 56, 66 (1950), overruled *Trupiano v. United States*, 334 U.S. 699 (1948), which had made the requirement of a warrant for searches incident to arrest turn on the practicability of acquiring such a warrant. (*Rabinowitz*, for what it's worth, was later overruled in part by *Chimel v. California*, 395 U.S. 752 (1969)). *United States v. Scott*, 437 U.S. 82, 86–87 (1978), held that the Double Jeopardy Clause does not bar retrial of a defendant who successfully moves for termination on a ground unrelated to guilt or innocence, overruling the decision in *United States v. Jenkins*, 420 U.S. 358 (1975). *Payne v. Tennessee*, 501 U.S. 808 (1991), held that the

Eighth Amendment does not bar admission of victim impact evidence, overruling *South Carolina v. Gathers*, 490 U.S. 805 (1989). *United States v. Dixon*, 509 U.S. 688 (1993), rejected the "same conduct" double jeopardy test announced in *Grady v. Corbin*, 495 U.S. 508 (1990).

85. *See* Gitlow v. New York, 268 U.S. 652, 666 (1925); Cantwell v. Connecticut, 310 U.S. 296, 303 (1940).
86. PETERS, *supra* note 13, at 55–56.
87. *See id.* at 53–54. *See generally* Richard Danzig, *How Questions Begot Answers in Felix Frankfurter's First Flag Salute Opinion*, 1977 SUP. CT. REV. 257.
88. PETERS, *supra* note 13, at 65.
89. *Id.* at 54–55.
90. *Id.* at 55.
91. Schenck v. United States, 249 U.S. 47, 52 (1919).
92. *See Barnette*, 319 U.S. at 640–41.
93. PETERS, *supra* note 13, at 249.
94. Plessy v. Ferguson, 163 U.S. 537 (1896).
95. Korematsu v. United States, 323 U.S. 214 (1944).
96. Robert Harrison, *The Breakup of the Roosevelt Supreme Court: The Contribution of History and Biography*, 2 LAW & HIST. REV. 165, 166 (1984).
97. *See* Russell W. Galloway, Jr., *The Roosevelt Court: The Liberals Conquer (1937–1941) and Divide (1941–1946)*, 23 SANTA CLARA L. REV. 491, 508–15 (1983).
98. FELDMAN, *supra* note 79, at 203.
99. *See, e.g.*, W. Coast Hotel Co. v. Parrish, 300 U.S. 379 (1937) (upholding a Washington minimum wage law that fixed minimum wages for women and minors); *see also* BARRY CUSHMAN, RETHINKING THE NEW DEAL COURT: THE STRUCTURE OF A CONSTITUTIONAL REVOLUTION 84–97 (1998) (casting doubt on the conventional version of the "switch in time").
100. *See, e.g.*, Wickard v. Filburn, 317 U.S. 111 (1942) (holding that wheat grown by a farmer on private land for his own household's consumption was properly a subject for regulation by the Congress under the Commerce Clause).
101. *See* Galloway, *supra* note 97, at 528.
102. *The Supreme Court Database*, WASH. UNIV. Law (July 12, 2016), http://scdb.wustl.edu/data.php; EPSTEIN ET AL., THE SUPREME COURT COMPENDIUM: DATA, DECISIONS, AND DEVELOPMENTS 189–92, 199–209 (2015).
103. *See* Richard A. Posner, *The Rise and Fall of Judicial Self-Restraint*, 100 CALIF. L. REV. 519, 526–31, 542 (2012) (summarizing these individuals' approaches to judicial review).
104. United States v. Carolene Prods. Co., 304 U.S. 144 (1938).
105. *See id.* at 152–53 n.4. Footnote 4 says in part: "There may be narrower scope for operation of the presumption of constitutionality when

legislation appears on its face to be within a specific prohibition of the Constitution, such as those of the first ten amendments, which are deemed equally specific when held to be embraced within the Fourteenth. . . . It is unnecessary to consider now whether legislation which restricts those political processes which can ordinarily be expected to bring about repeal of undesirable legislation, is to be subjected to more exacting scrutiny under the general prohibitions of the Fourteenth Amendment than are most other types of legislation. . . . Nor need we enquire whether similar considerations enter into the review of statutes directed at particular religious, or national, or racial minorities: whether prejudice against discrete and insular minorities may be a special condition, which tends seriously to curtail the operation of those political processes ordinarily to be relied upon to protect minorities, and which may call for a correspondingly more searching judicial inquiry." (Citations omitted).

106.   FELDMAN, *supra* note 79, at 232.

107.   Frank H. Easterbrook, *Foreword* to ANTONIN SCALIA & BRYAN A. GARNER, READING LAW: THE INTERPRETATION OF LEGAL TEXTS, at xxi–xxvi (2012).

108.   *See* Galloway, *supra* note 97, at 535–36 tbls. 6–8 (showing the disagreement rates between and among the justices).

109.   *See, e.g., Gobitis*, 310 U.S. at 601 (Stone, J., dissenting).

110.   *See Barnette*, 319 U.S. at 634.

111.   *Id.*

112.   *See* Stephen M. Feldman, *The Theory and Politics of First Amendment Protections: Why Does the Supreme Court Favor Free Expression over Religious Freedom?*, 8 U. PA. J. CONST. L. 431, 476–77 (2006).

113.   Emp't Div. v. Smith, 494 U.S. 872, 878–79 (1990).

114.   PETERS, *supra* note 13, at 98, 113, 141.

115.   Act of June 22, 1942, Pub. L. No. 77–623, § 7, 56 Stat. 377, 380. Entitled a "Joint Resolution to codify and emphasize existing rules and customs pertaining to the display and use of the flag of the United States of America," it said "[t]hat the pledge of allegiance to the flag . . . [is] rendered by standing with the right hand over the heart; extending the right hand, palm upward, toward the flag at the words 'to the flag' and holding this position until the end, when the hand drops to the side. However, civilians will always show full respect to the flag when the pledge is given by merely standing at attention, men removing the headdress. Persons in uniform shall render the military salute."

116.   PETERS, *supra* note 13, at 246.

117.   319 U.S. at 638 n.17.

118.   Brown v. Bd. of Educ., 347 U.S. 483 (1954).

119.   Pub. L. No. 88-352, 78 Stat. 241; *see also* GERALD N. ROSENBERG, THE HOLLOW HOPE: CAN COURTS BRING ABOUT SOCIAL CHANGE? 39–159 (1991) (considering relative importance of *Brown* and the 1964 legislation

in accomplishing desegregation); Michael J. Klarman, Brown, *Racial Change, and the Civil Rights Movement*, 80 VA. L. REV. 7 (1994) (same).

120. *Cf.* FELDMAN, *supra* note 79, at 234 (elaborating on the view).

121. Felix Frankfurter, *Can the Supreme Court Guarantee Toleration?*, *in* FELIX FRANKFURTER ON THE SUPREME COURT: EXTRAJUDICIAL ESSAYS ON THE COURT AND THE CONSTITUTION 174 (Philip B. Kurland ed., Belknap Press 1970).

122. *Id.* at 175.

123. *Id.*

124. *Id.* at 176.

125. *Id.*

126. *Id.* at 175.

127. *Id.* at 178.

128. *Id.*

129. PETERS, *supra* note 13, at 56.

130. Kelo v. City of New London, 545 U.S. 469 (2005).

131. Posner, *supra* note 103, at 523, 526–27.

132. *See, e.g.*, James B. Thayer, *The Origin and Scope of the American Doctrine of Constitutional Law*, 7 HARV. L. REV. 129, 152 (1893).

133. 250 U.S. 616 (1919)

134. 347 U.S. 483 (1954).

135. Henslee v. Union Planters Nat'l Bank & Tr. Co., 335 U.S. 595, 600 (1949) (Frankfurter, J., dissenting).

136. For a State-by-State account of litigation in the States regarding flag salutes, see DAVID R. MANWARING, RENDER UNTO CAESAR: THE FLAG-SALUTE CONTROVERSY (1962), especially Chapters 4 and 9.

137. Hering v. State Bd. of Ed., 189 A. 629, 629 (N.J. Sup. Ct. 1937).

138. *Id.*

139. *Id.*

140. *Id.* at 629–30.

141. Nicholls v. Mayor of Lynn, 7 N.E.2d 577, 578 (Mass. 1937).

142. *Id.* at 579.

143. *Id.*

144. *Id.*

145. *Id.* at 579–80.

146. *Id.* at 580.

147. *Id.*

148. 98 U.S. 145, 166 (1878).

149. 293 U.S. 245, 265 (1934).

150. Leoles v. Landers, 192 S.E. 218, 222 (Ga. 1937); State *ex rel.* Bleich v. Bd. of Pub. Instruction, 190 So. 815, 816 (Fla. 1939); People *ex rel.* Fish v. Sandstrom, 18 N.E.2d 840 (N.Y. 1939) (affirming school's right to expel students who refuse to salute, but reversing conviction of parents for keeping children out of school). In *Reynolds v. Rayborn*, 116 S.W.2d 836

(Tex. Civ. App. 1938), a Texas court held that custody could not be denied
to a parent because he taught his daughter not to salute.

151. Leoles v. Landers, 184 Ga. 580, 585–86 (1937).
152. *Id.* at 586.
153. *Id.*
154. *Id.*
155. *Id.* at 587.
156. People v. Sandstrom, 279 N.Y. 523, 527–28 (1939).
157. *Id.* at 529.
158. *Id.* (quoting art. I, § 3).
159. *Id.* at 528.
160. *Id.*
161. *Id.* at 529–30.
162. *Id.* at 530.
163. *Id.* at 531.
164. *Id.* at 532.
165. *Id.*
166. *Id.*
167. *Id.* at 532–33.
168. *Id.* at 533.
169. *Id.*
170. *Id.*
171. *Id.* at 535 (internal quotations omitted).
172. *Id.* at 536–37.
173. *Id.* at 538.
174. *Id.* at 538–39.
175. *Id.* at 539 (internal quotation omitted).
176. *Id.*
177. Gabrielli v. Knickerbocker. The trial court's unreported decision is
      reprinted in "Refusing to Salute the Flag: An Important Court Decision,"
      32 *Liberty* no. 2 (1937).
178. Liberty, 23. *See also Bleich*, 190 So. 815, 817 (Fla. 1939) (Buford, J.,
      dissenting).
179. Liberty, 22.
180. Gabrielli v. Knickerbocker, 74 P.2d 290 (Cal. Dist. Ct. App. 1937).
181. Leoles v. Landers, 58 S. Ct. 364 (1937); Hering v. State Bd. of Ed., 303
      U.S. 624 (1938).
182. Gabrielli v. Knickerbocker, 82 P.2d 391, 394 (Cal. 1938).
183. *Id.* at 393.
184. 127 P.2d 518, 520–21 (Kan. 1942).
185. *Id.* at 519.
186. *Id.* at 521 (citing Jones v. City of Opelika, 316 U.S. 584 (1942)).
187. *Id.* at 523.
188. *Id.* at 521.

189. *Id.* at 522.
190. *Id.*
191. *Id.* (quoting Atchison St. Ry. Co. v. Mo. Pac. Ry. Co., 31 Kan. 660 (1884)).
192. *Id.*
193. This is not to say these courts were unanimous in affirming compulsory salutes. In his *Sandstrom* concurrence—effectively a dissent on the issue of compelled speech—Justice Lehman penned an eloquent defense of religious freedom and would have held salute requirements unconstitutional. 18 N.E.2d 840, 844–47. *See also* Justice Buford's dissent to the denial of a petition for rehearing in *Bleich*, 190 So. 815, 817–18.
194. *Smith*, 127 P.2d at 523.
195. *Id.*
196. *Id.*
197. *Id.*
198. 133 P.2d 803 (Wash. 1943).
199. *Id.* at 806.
200. *Id.* at 805–07.
201. *Id.* at 809.
202. *Id.* at 806.
203. *Id.*
204. *Id.* at 808.
205. *Id.* at 807.
206. *Id.*
207. *Id.* at 809.
208. *Id.*
209. *Id.*
210. *Id.*
211. *Id.*
212. *Id.*
213. *Id.*
214. *Id.*
215. State v. Mercante, mem. op. at 6 (W. Va. Cir. Ct. June 1, 1942).
216. *Id.*
217. *Id.* at 7.
218. *Id.*
219. *Id.*
220. *Id.* at 11–12.
221. *Id.* at 13.
222. Only one case from this period, best I can tell, involved a direct challenge to a flag-salute expulsion, the unpublished decision in *Brown v. Skustad*, Eleventh District Court, St. Louis County, Minnesota (1942). The Court rejected *Gobitis* and ruled the expulsion unconstitutional. Witnesses raised this issue as a defense in other cases, but judges tended to resolve

the claims on nonconstitutional grounds by rejecting the delinquency charge.

223. MANWARING, *supra* note 136, at 187.

224. *See* State v. Mercante, mem. op. at 10 (W. Va. Cir. Ct. Jun. 1, 1942) (West Virginia law requiring pupils to salute the flag and recite the pledge of allegiance was "in contravention of the Constitution of West Virginia"); *cf.* Kennedy v. City of Moscow, 39 F. Supp. 26, 29–30 (D. Idaho 1941) (holding that a statute requiring a person to salute the flag and recite the pledge of allegiance in the presence of a police officer before being issued a permit to distribute literature violated the Idaho Constitution).

225. *See also In re* Jones, 24 N.Y.S.2d 10 (N.Y. Child. Ct. 1940); *In re* Reed, 28 N.Y.S.2d 92 (App. Div. 1941); Commonwealth v. Johnson, 35 N.E.2d 801 (Mass. 1941); *In re* Latrecchia, 26 A.2d 881 (N.J. 1942); Commonwealth v. Nemchik, 36 Luzerne Leg. Reg. 247 (Pa. Q. Sess. 1942), cited in MANWARING, *supra* note 136, at 189. *But see* State v. Davis, 120 P.2d 808 (Ariz. 1942) (upholding conviction of parents because they required their child to refuse to salute the flag).

226. 20 A.2d 185, 186 (N.H. 1941).

227. *Id.* at 188.

228. *Id.*

229. 44 N.E.2d 888, 889 (Ill. 1942).

230. *Id.*

231. *Id.* at 893.

232. *See* MANWARING, *supra* note 136, at 240–43.

233. 147 P.2d 823 (Colo. 1944). Another notable case decided in the wake of *Barnette* is *Morgan v. Civil Serv. Comm'n*, 36 A.2d 898 (N.J. 1944) (prospective government employee's refusal to salute flag does not provide "good cause" to deny him the post).

234. *Zavilla*, 147 P.2d at 824–25.

235. *Id.* at 824.

236. *Id.* at 826.

237. *Id.* at 828.

238. *Id.* at 825.

239. Rodriguez de Quijas v. Shearson/Am. Express, Inc., 490 U.S. 477, 484 (1989) ("the Court of Appeals should follow the case which directly controls, leaving to this Court the prerogative of overruling its own decisions").

240. So long, that is, that the ruling did not violate another federal constitutional guarantee.

241. Brown v. Allen, 344 U.S. 443, 540 (1953) (Jackson, J., concurring in the result).

Chapter 7

1. *See* Joseph Blocher, *Reverse Incorporation of State Constitutional Law*, 84 S. CAL. L. REV. 323, 339 n.80 (2011) ("To this day, most state courts adopt

federal constitutional law as their own. Bowing to the nationalization of constitutional discourse, they 'tend to follow whatever doctrinal vocabulary is used by the United States Supreme Court, discussed in the law reviews, and taught in the law schools.'" (quoting Hans A. Linde, *E. Pluribus—Constitutional Theory and State Courts*, 18 GA. L. REV. 165, 186 (1984))).

2. U.S. CONST. amend. IV; *see also, e.g.*, MICH. CONST. art. 1, § 11; N.J. CONST. art. I, § 7.

3. *See, e.g.*, State v. Jenkins, 3 A.3d 806, 839 (Conn. 2010) (holding that "the Connecticut constitution does not provide criminal defendants with greater protections than does the federal constitution in the context of unrelated questioning, including requests for consent to search, made during routine traffic stops"); State v. Stevens, 367 N.W.2d 788, 796–97 (Wis. 1985) (holding that search of garbage did not violate Wisconsin or Federal Constitutions); *see also* People v. Collins, 475 N.W.2d 684, 691 (Mich. 1991) (stating that the Michigan constitutional provisions prohibiting "unreasonable searches and seizures" should "be construed to provide the same protection as that secured by the Fourth Amendment, absent 'compelling reason' to impose a different interpretation"); State *ex rel.* Rear Door Bookstore v. Tenth Dist. Court of Appeals, 588 N.E.2d 116, 123 (Ohio 1992) (declining to find greater free speech guarantees in the Ohio Constitution than in the Federal Constitution); *In re* F.C. III, 2 A.3d 1201, 1212 (Pa. 2010) ("[W]e find the due process rights implicated herein under our Constitution to be equal to those under the Fourteenth Amendment of the United States Constitution."); *cf.* Am. Atheists, Inc. v. City of Detroit Downtown Dev. Auth., 567 F.3d 278, 301 (6th Cir. 2009) (holding that, under Michigan law, the Establishment Clauses of the Michigan and Federal Constitutions are interpreted the same way).

4. *See, e.g.*, FLA. CONST. art. I, §§ 12, 17 (requiring that Florida courts construe the state constitutional right against unlawful searches, seizures, and excessive punishments "in conformity with" the Fourth and Eighth Amendments, respectively, as interpreted by the U.S. Supreme Court).

5. *See, e.g.*, William J. Brennan, Jr., *State Constitutions and the Protection of Individual Rights*, 90 HARV. L. REV. 489, 501 (1977) ("Prior to the adoption of the federal Constitution, each of the rights eventually recognized in the federal Bill of Rights had previously been protected in one or more state constitutions."); Randy J. Holland, *State Constitutions: Purpose and Function*, 69 TEMP. L. REV. 989, 997 (1996) ("[S]tate Declarations of Rights were the primary origin and model for the provisions set forth in the Federal Bill of Rights."); Gordon S. Wood, *Foreword: State Constitution-Making in the American Revolution*, 24 RUTGERS L.J. 911, 911 (1993) ("The office of our governors, the bicameral legislatures, tripartite separation of powers, bills of rights, and the unique use of constitutional conventions were all born during the state

constitution-making period between 1775 and the early 1780s, well before the federal constitution of 1787 was created.").

6. Blocher, *supra* note 1, at 334.

7. *See* Alexandra Natapoff, *Underenforcement*, 75 FORDHAM L. REV. 1715, 1747 (2006); Lawrence Gene Sager, *Fair Measure: The Legal Status of Underenforced Constitutional Norms*, 91 HARV. L. REV. 1212, 1218, 1248 (1978); *see also* Jeffrey S. Sutton, San Antonio Independent School District v. Rodriguez *and Its Aftermath*, 94 VA. L. REV. 1963, 1978–79 (2008).

8. Sutton, *supra* note 7, at 1979.

9. *See* Brennan, *supra* note 5.

10. *Id.* at 490.

11. *Id.* at 495.

12. *Id.* at 491.

13. *See* Blocher, *supra* note 1, at 338 (noting than an interest in independent state constitutional interpretation is not "confined to liberals" and need not be justified solely on "outcome oriented" grounds); *see also* Randall T. Shepard, *The Maturing Nature of State Constitution Jurisprudence*, 30 VAL. U. L. REV. 421, 421 (1996) ("[T]he continuing strength of this movement does not derive from a desire to continue, at the state level, the agenda of the Warren-Brennan Court. It derives from the aspiration of state court judges to be independent sources of law.").

14. *See, e.g.*, Edgewood Indep. Sch. Dist. v. Kirby, 777 S.W.2d 391 (Tex. 1989) (holding, in contrast to *Rodriguez*, that the State's school financing system violated the Texas Constitution); City of Norwood v. Horney, 853 N.E.2d 1115 (Ohio 2006) (holding, in contrast to *Kelo v. City of New London*, 545 U.S. 469 (2005), that an economic benefit alone does not satisfy the Ohio Constitution's public use requirement with respect to the exercise of eminent domain); Visser v. Nooksack Valley Sch. Dist. No. 506, 207 P.2d 198 (Wash. 1949) (holding, in contrast to *Everson v. Bd. of Educ.*, 330 U.S. 1 (1947), that state-funded bus transportation for parochial school students violated the Washington Constitution); Huffman v. State, 204 P.3d 339, 344 (Alaska 2009) (holding, in contrast to *Emp't Div. v. Smith*, 494 U.S. 872 (1990), that under the Alaska Constitution strict scrutiny applies to generally applicable laws that disproportionately impact faith-based practices); State v. Henry, 732 P.2d 9 (Or. 1987) (holding, in contrast to *Miller v. California*, 413 U.S. 15 (1973), that obscenity is protected speech under the Oregon Constitution); Gerawan Farming, Inc. v. Lyons, 12 P.3d 720 (Cal. 2000) (holding, in contrast to *Glickman v. Wileman Bros. & Elliott, Inc.*, 521 U.S. 457 (1997), that a marketing order requiring growers to finance generic advertising violated the California Constitution); State v. Marsala, 579 A.2d 58 (Conn. 1990) (holding, in contrast to *United States v. Leon*, 468 U.S. 897 (1984), that the Connecticut Constitution does not recognize a good faith exception to the exclusionary rule); Hageland

Aviation Servs., Inc. v. Harms, 210 P.3d 444 (Alaska 2009) (holding, in contrast to *Energy Reserves Grp., Inc. v. Kan. Power & Light Co.*, 459 U.S. 400 (1983), that the retroactive application of a statutory exemption to overtime laws that impaired private contracts violated the Alaska Constitution); Valley Hosp. Ass'n, Inc. v. Mat-Su Coal. for Choice, 948 P.2d 963 (Alaska 1997) (holding, in contrast to *Planned Parenthood of Se. Pa. v. Casey*, 505 U.S. 833 (1992), that Alaska's express right to privacy is more protective of abortion rights than is the Federal Constitution); Britt v. State, 681 S.E.2d 320 (N.C. 2009) (holding, in contrast to *District of Columbia v. Heller*, 554 U.S. 570 (2008), that a law prohibiting felons from possessing firearms violated the North Carolina Constitution).

15. Many state courts have not followed the U.S. Supreme Court's abandonment of the nondelegation doctrine. The "majority" of them "still apply a robust non-delegation doctrine under their state constitutions." Douglas H. Ginsburg & Steven Menashi, *Our Illiberal Administrative Law*, 10 N.Y.U. J. L. & LIBERTY 475, 492–93 (2016); *see, e.g.*, N.Y. Statewide Coal. of Hispanic Chambers of Commerce v. N.Y.C. Dep't of Health & Mental Hygiene, 23 N.Y.3d 681, 690–92 (2014) ("by choosing among competing policy goals, without any legislative delegation or guidance," the agency "engaged in law-making and thus infringed upon the legislative jurisdiction of the City Council"); *id.* at 696 (under the New York Constitution, an executive agency may not "assume[] for itself the open-ended discretion to choose ends that are the prerogative of a Legislature") (cited in Ginsburg & Menashi); Tex. Boll Weevil Eradication Found. v. Lewellen, 952 S.W.2d 454 (Tex. 1997); *see also* James Rossi, *Institutional Design and the Lingering Legacy of Antifederalist Separation of Powers Ideas in the States*, 52 VAND. L. REV. 1167, 1195–96 (1999) (identifying twenty States in which "statutes are periodically struck on nondelegation grounds" and twenty-three States in which "state courts are much more likely to strike down statutes [on nondelegation grounds] than their federal counterparts") (cited in Ginsburg & Menashi). These opinions could well serve as useful templates to justices who may be willing to revisit the federal nondelegation doctrine. *See, e.g.*, Dep't of Transp. v. Ass'n of Am. R.R., 135 S. Ct. 1225, 1240 (2015) (Thomas, J., concurring in the judgment).

16. Note, *Developments in the Law—The Interpretation of State Constitutional Rights*, 95 HARV. L. REV. 1324, 1463–93 (1982) (identifying many areas in which state constitutions impose greater limitations on economic regulation than the Federal Constitution); A.E. Dick Howard, *State Courts and Constitutional Rights in the Day of the Burger Court*, 62 VA. L. REV. 873, 879–891 (1976) (same).

17. *See* Brennan, *supra* note 5, at 491, 495–96.

18. *See id.* at 498–502; *see also* Blocher, *supra* note 1, at 337 ("Led by Justice Brennan . . . liberals urged state courts to 'step into the breach' left by the

Burger Court's 'contraction of federal rights and remedies on grounds
of federalism.'" (quoting William J. Brennan, Jr., *The Bill of Rights and
the States: The Revival of State Constitutions as Guardians of Individual
Rights*, 61 N.Y.U. L. REV. 535, 548 (1986))); Shepard, *supra* note 13, at 422
(suggesting that after "Justice Brennan began to find himself on the losing
end of [individual rights] cases," he "candidly announced that the war
should be waged on another front").

19. James A. Gardner, *The Failed Discourse of State Constitutionalism*, 90
MICH. L. REV. 761 (1992).

20. Jeffrey S. Sutton, Speech, *Why Teach—And Why Study—State
Constitutional Law*, 34 OKLA. CITY U. L. REV. 165, 176 (2009).

21. Blocher, *supra* note 1, at 347–49; *see also* Joseph Blocher, *What State
Constitutional Law Can Tell Us About the Federal Constitution*, 115 PENN.
ST. L. REV. 1035, 1036 (2011) (arguing that state doctrine may be used as
"persuasive authority in federal cases" but may also be used to "define
federal law"). Professor Blocher notes that in *Mapp v. Ohio*, the Supreme
Court "explicitly relied on the states' independent embrace of the
exclusionary rule" in deciding to incorporate it under the Fourteenth
Amendment. Blocher, *supra* note 1, at 372; *see also* Mapp v. Ohio, 367
U.S. 643, 651–52 (1961).

22. *See generally* Hans A. Linde, *Without "Due Process": Unconstitutional Law
in Oregon*, 49 OR. L. REV. 125, 133 (1970) [hereinafter Linde, *Without
"Due Process"*]; Hans A. Linde, *First Things First: Rediscovering the States'
Bills of Rights*, 9 U. BALT. L. REV. 379 (1980) [hereinafter Linde, *First
Things First*]; *see also* Delaware v. Van Arsdall, 475 U.S. 673, 701–04 (1986)
(Stevens, J., dissenting) (arguing that this sequence of analysis is "best
suited to facilitating the independent role of state constitutions and state
courts in our federal system").

23. Cole v. Dep't of Revenue, 655 P.2d 171, 173 (Or. 1982); Sterling v. Cupp,
625 P.2d 123, 125 (Or. 1981); State v. Flores, 570 P.2d 965, 971 (Or.
1977) (Linde, J., dissenting).

24. *See* Sterling v. Cupp, 625 P.2d 123, 126 (Or. 1981); State v. Ball, 471 A.2d
347, 350–52 (N.H. 1983); State v. Cadman, 476 A.2d 1148, 1150 (Me. 1984).

25. J. FRIESEN, STATE CONSTITUTIONAL LAW: LITIGATING INDIVIDUAL RIGHTS,
CLAIMS, AND DEFENSES, § 1.04 (4th ed. 2006); John W. Shaw, *Principled
Interpretations of State Constitutional Law—Why Don't the "Primacy" States
Practice What They Preach?*, 54 U. PITT. L. REV. 1019, 1028 (1993); Cornell
W. Clayton, *Toward a Theory of the Washington Constitution*, 37 GONZ.
L. REV. 41, 52 (2002) ("Accordingly, even if the court interprets the state
constitution to provide the rights sought by the litigants, [under the "dual
sovereignty" approach,] the Federal Constitution is also analyzed, thus
providing two independent bases for decision."); *see, e.g.*, State v. Coe,
679 P.2d 353 (Wash. 1984); City of Seattle v. Evans, 366 P.3d 906, 909–15
(Wash. 2015); State v. Badger, 450 A.2d 336, 346–47 (Vt. 1982); and State
v. Neil, 958 A.2d 1173, 1176–78 (Vt. 2008).

26. A soon-to-be published article explains how Justice Linde's approach influenced the Oregon Supreme Court and led to a rebirth of state constitutionalism in the State. Richard S. Price, *Linde's Legacy: The Triumph of Oregon State Constitutional Law, 1997–2000*, 80 Alb. L. Rev. (forthcoming).

27. *See* Stephen Kanter, *Sleeping Beauty Wide Awake: State Constitutions as Important Independent Sources of Individual Rights*, 15 Lewis & Clark L. Rev. 799, 801–02 (2011) ("One of the most pervasive arguments against a federal bill of rights was that it was unnecessary, and that the country would not have to worry about the federal government infringing individual rights, since that government was constructed as a limited, enumerated government, without authority to infringe anyone's rights. The obvious corollary was that the states would shoulder the primary responsibility for protecting citizens' individual rights.").

28. The Federalist No. 84 (Alexander Hamilton); *see also* Gregory v. Ashcroft, 501 U.S. 452, 458 (1991) ("Perhaps the principal benefit of the federalist system is a check on abuses of government power.").

29. The Federalist No. 28 (Alexander Hamilton).

30. The Federalist No. 45 (James Madison).

31. *Id.*

32. *Id.*; *see* United States v. Lopez, 514 U.S. 549, 566 (1995) ("The Constitution . . . withhold[s] from Congress a plenary police power that would authorize enactment of every type of legislation.").

33. U.S. Const. art. I, § 10, cl. 1.

34. *See* Bd. of Regents of State Colls. v. Roth, 408 U.S. 564, 577 (1972) ("Property interests, of course, are not created by the Constitution. Rather they are created and their dimensions are defined by existing rules or understandings that stem from an independent source such as state law."); Indiana *ex rel.* Anderson v. Brand, 303 U.S. 95, 100 (1938) (explaining that "the existence and nature of the contract" is "one primarily of state law").

35. Linde, *supra* note 1, at 380 (noting that "state courts routinely assume their charge to declare individual rights against other individuals or private entities" but hesitate to "assume the same responsibility for individual rights against public authority").

36. Sterling v. Cupp, 625 P.2d 123, 126 (Or. 1981) ("The proper sequence is to analyze the state's law, including its constitutional law, before reaching a federal constitutional claim. This is required, not for the sake either of parochialism or of style, but because the state does not deny any right claimed under the federal Constitution when the claim before the court in fact is fully met by state law.").

37. U.S. Const. amend. XIV, § 1, cl. 2.

38. Linde, *Without "Due Process"*, *supra* note 22, at 133.

39. *Id.* at 135.

40. Linde, *First Things First, supra* note 22, at 380.

41. *See* Ashwander v. TVA, 297 U.S. 288, 346–347 (1936) (Brandeis, J., concurring).

42. Siler v. Louisville & Nashville R.R. Co., 213 U.S. 175, 193 (1909); *see also* Hagans v. Lavine, 415 U.S. 528, 546 (1974) (collecting cases illustrating that "[t]he Court has characteristically dealt first with possibly dispositive state law claims pendent to federal constitutional claims").

43. *See* Alexander M. Bickel, *The Supreme Court 1960 Term Foreword: The Passive Virtues*, 75 Harv. L. Rev. 40 (1961).

44. *See* R.R. Comm'n of Tex. v. Pullman Co., 312 U.S. 496 (1941).

45. *See, e.g.*, Harris Cty. Comm'rs Court v. Moore, 420 U.S. 77, 84 (1975); Reetz v. Bozanich, 397 U.S. 82 (1970); City of Meridian v. S. Bell Tel. & Tel. Co., 358 U.S. 639, 641 (1959).

46. *Cf.* Alden v. Maine, 527 U.S. 706, 749 (1999) (holding that immunity from suit in federal court is not enough to preserve the States' sovereign dignity, for the indignity of subjecting a nonconsenting State to private suit exists "regardless of the forum").

47. State v. Sanchez, 350 P.3d 1169, 1174 (N.M. 2015) (internal quotations omitted).

48. Blocher, *supra* note 1, at 339.

49. State v. Kennedy, 666 P.2d 1316, 1323 (Or. 1983).

50. *See, e.g.*, Bell v. City of Boise, 834 F. Supp. 2d 1103, 1116 (D. Idaho 2011), *rev'd on other grounds*, 709 F.3d 890 (9th Cir. 2013) ("State constitutional provisions must provide at least as much protection as their federal counterparts but may also provide greater protections for the individual."); State v. Fields, 168 P.3d 955, 969 (Haw. 2007) ("[I]t is fundamental that, when interpreting our own constitution, our divergence from federal interpretations of the United States Constitution may not convey less protection than the federal standard.").

51. *See, e.g.*, State v. Tarantino, 587 A.2d 1095, 1098 (Me. 1991) (recognizing that Maine—as a matter of state law—does not have an exclusionary rule); State v. McKechnie, 690 A.2d 976, 978 n.1 (Me. 1997) (noting that Maine "ha[s] never required the *Miranda* warnings as a matter of state constitutional law"). *See generally* Barry Latzer, *Whose Federalism? Or, Why "Conservative" States Should Develop Their State Constitutional Law*, 61 Alb. L. Rev. 1399, 1405–06 (1998).

52. R. LaFountain et al., Nat'l Ctr. for State Courts, Examining the Work of State Courts: An Analysis of 2008 State Court Caseloads, at iv (2010), http://www.courtstatistics.org/~/media/Microsites/Files/CSP/EWSC-2008-Online.ashx.

53. Neal Devins, *How State Supreme Courts Take Consequences into Account: Toward a State-Centered Understanding of State Constitutionalism*, 62 Stan. L. Rev. 1629, 1635 n.27 (2010).

54. *See, e.g.*, Hon. John Christopher Anderson, *The Mysterious Lockstep Doctrine and the Future of Judicial Federalism in Illinois*, 44 Loy. U. Chi.

L.J. 965, 972–73 (2013) (citing two studies demonstrating that when state high courts reluctantly interpret their state constitutions, they "often use[] a lockstep approach," "routinely rely[ing] on United States Supreme Court analysis" rather than their own).

55. McDonald v. City of Chicago, 561 U.S. 742, 765 n.13 (2010).

56. Eric J. Hamilton, *Federalism and the State Civil Jury Rights*, 65 STAN. L. REV. 851, 852–54 (April 2013); *id.* at 890–900 (identifying each State's practice).

57. *See Mapp*, 367 U.S. at 655–57.

58. State public defenders' offices, it is true, face heavy case loads, and as a result may not have the resources to invest in serious legal research in every case. *See generally* Lawrence Herman, *Gideon and the Golden Thread*, 99 IOWA L. REV. 2015 (2014). But it surely is not too much to ask that, in areas where repeat claims arise, such as search and seizure or interrogation, that someone at some point do the historical research about the state guarantees.

59. *Developments in the Law—The Interpretation of State Constitutional Rights*, 95 HARV. L. REV. 1324 (1982) [hereinafter *Developments*].

60. *Id.* at 1357.

61. *Id.* at 1357–58; *see also* Stewart G. Pollock, *State Constitutions as Separate Sources of Fundamental Rights*, 35 RUTGERS L. REV. 707, 718–19 (1983).

62. *Developments, supra* note 59, at 1357.

63. Herbert P. Wilkins, *Judicial Treatment of the Massachusetts Declaration of Rights in Relation to Cognate Provisions of the United States Constitution*, 14 SUFFOLK U. L. REV. 887, 889 (1980).

64. Robert F. Utter, *Swimming in the Jaws of the Crocodile: State Court Comment on Federal Constitutional Issues When Disposing of Cases on State Constitutional Grounds*, 63 TEX. L. REV. 1025, 1049–50 (1985).

65. *Id.* at 1042.

66. James A. Gardner, *The Failed Discourse of State Constitutionalism*, 90 MICH. L. REV. 761 (1992) [hereinafter Gardner, *The Failed Discourse*]; James A. Gardner, *Whose Constitution Is It? Why Federalism and Constitutional Positivism Don't Mix*, 46 WM. & MARY L. REV. 1245, 1269–70 (2005).

67. Gardner, *The Failed Discourse, supra* note 66, at 765–66.

68. *Developments, supra* note 59, at 1358.

69. *Id.* at 1419.

70. Jack L. Landau, *Of Lessons Learned and Lessons Nearly Lost: The Linde Legacy and Oregon Constitutional Law*, 43 WILLAMETTE L. REV. 251, 256–59 (2007).

71. Robert F. Williams, *In the Glare of the Supreme Court: Continuing Methodology and Legitimacy Problems in Independent State Constitutional Rights Adjudication*, 72 NOTRE DAME L. REV. 1015, 1048–49 (1997).

72. *Cf.* LEARNED HAND, THE SPIRIT OF LIBERTY 241–42 (2d ed. 1954) ("[A]fter [administrative agencies] have proceeded a while they get their own sets of precedents . . . and they fall into grooves, just as the

judges do. When they get into grooves, then God save you to get them out of the grooves.").

Chapter 8

1. 136 S. Ct. 2056 (2016).
2. UTAH CONST. art. I, § 14.
3. Utah v. Strieff, 357 P.3d 532 (Utah 2015).
4. *See, e.g.,* State v. Dellorfano, 517 A.2d 1163, 1166 (N.H. 1986).
5. State v. Bradberry, 522 A.2d 1380, 1389 (N.H. 1986) (Souter, J., concurring).
6. Michigan v. Long, 463 U.S. 1032 (1983).
7. *Id.* at 1042.
8. Delaware, Florida, Indiana, Louisiana, Mississippi, Pennsylvania, and Tennessee each test state constitutional law (or at least state-specific criminal procedure guarantees) on the bar exam. *See* DEL. BD. B. EXAM'RS R. 12; FLA. BD. B. EXAM'RS R. 4–22; *Overview of the Indiana Bar Examination*, IND. BD. L. EXAM'RS, http://www.in.gov/judiciary/ble/2375. htm; LA. SUP. CT. R. XVII, § 7(A); MISS. B. R. IX.5; PA. B. ADMIS. R. 203, att. 1; TENN. SUP. CT. R. 7, art. IV, § 4.04. In 2009, that number was twelve. The decrease may stem from the growing number of States (now thirty-three) that use the Uniform Bar Examination (UBE) and the Multistate Essay Examination (MEE), a nationally administered, standardized bar exam. By its nature, the UBE cannot test state-specific subjects, such as state constitutional law. Six States that used to test state constitutional law on their bar exams a decade ago no longer do so. Two of these States—New York and Washington—have adapted by requiring applicants to take and pass a separate, state-specific examination, which does test state constitutional law. *See* N.Y. BD. L. EXAM'RS R. 6000.3(c); WASH. ADMIS. & PRAC. R. 5(b)(1). Another two—Arizona and Montana—require applicants to take a seminar on state law, including state constitutional law, prior to admittance. *See* ARIZ. SUP. CT. R. 34(j); MONT. B. ADMIS. R. VIII.
9. Robert F. Williams, *State Constitutional Law: Teaching and Scholarship*, 41 J. LEGAL EDUC. 243, 243 (1991).
10. LAW SCH. ADMISSION COUNCIL & AM. BAR ASS'N SECTION OF LEGAL EDUC. AND ADMISSIONS TO THE BAR, ABA-LSAC OFFICIAL GUIDE TO ABA-APPROVED LAW SCHOOLS, at i (2009 ed.).
11. The numbers are similar for the 2008–09 school year: Twenty-six schools offer "State Constitutional Law"; twenty-three offer a state-specific constitutional law class; thirty-two offer "State and Local Government Law"; and forty-one offer "Local Government Law."
12. *Schools of Law: The Top 100 Schools*, U.S. NEWS & WORLD REPORT, Apr. 9, 2007, at 92.

13. Spreadsheets on file with author.

14. R. Randall Kelso, *Standards of Review Under the Equal Protection Clause and Related Constitutional Doctrines Protecting Individual Rights: The "Base Plus Six" Model and Modern Supreme Court Practice*, 4 U. Pa. J. Const. L. 225, 226 (2002) ("Although traditional black-letter law continues to discuss three basic standards of review—minimum rationality review, intermediate or mid-level review, and strict scrutiny—actual Supreme Court cases continue to reflect the six standards of review discussed in my previous articles," as well as rational-basis review).

15. I do not want to overstate my case. Some examples indeed exist of worthy scholarship in this area, one of which (perhaps unsurprisingly) comes from Oregon. *See* Claudia Burton & Andrew Grade, *A Legislative History of the Oregon Constitution of 1857—Part I (Articles I & II)*, 37 Willamette L. Rev. 469, 519–20 (2001).

16. The treatise has eight editions from 1868 to 1927. They all are fairly similar in this respect.

17. *Id. See also* Henry Campbell Black, Handbook of American Constitutional Law, v–xi (2d ed. 1897) (devoting five chapters to the Federal Constitution and three to the state constitutions, with the remainder addressed equally to both).

18. *E.g.*, Ohio v. Robinette, 519 U.S. 33, 42 (1996) (Ginsburg, J., concurring); Oregon v. Hass, 420 U.S. 714, 719 (1975) ("a State is free *as a matter of its own law* to impose greater restrictions on police activity than those this Court holds to be necessary upon federal constitutional standards"); San Antonio Indep. Sch. Dist. v. Rodriguez, 411 U.S. 1, 133 n.100 (1973) (Marshall, J., dissenting) ("nothing in the Court's decision today should inhibit further review of state educational funding schemes under state constitutional provisions").

19. Year End Report on the Judiciary, 18 (1981).

20. Patsy v. Bd. of Regents, 457 U.S. 496 (1982). Someone interested in redesigning this system might borrow a page from the current approach to handling federal takings claims under the Fifth and Fourteenth Amendments. There, in contrast to the rule of *Patsy*, a federal takings claim is not ripe until the claimant has exhausted relief in the state courts, including by determining how much compensation is due for the taking. *See* Williamson Cty. Reg'l Planning Comm'n v. Hamilton Bank of Johnson City, 473 U.S. 172, 186–97 (1985). But the *Williamson* exhaustion rule does not apply to facial challenges, as opposed to as-applied challenges, to a state or local law. *See* Yee v. City of Escondido, 503 U.S. 519 (1992). The question is whether such an exhaustion rule, together with a significant exception to that rule for facial constitutional challenges, would work better or worse than the *Patsy* approach.

21. *The Supreme Court Database*, WASH. UNIV. LAW (last visited Feb. 13, 2017), http://scdb.wustl.edu/data.php (detailing the number of state court decisions reviewed each term beginning in 1946. The percentage of cases originating in state court from representative terms are: 1960, 27 percent; 1970, 26 percent; 1980, 27 percent; 1995, 12 percent; 2000, 18 percent; 2005, 18 percent; 2010, 12 percent).

22. *See Stat Pack October Term 2015*, SCOTUSBLOG (June 29, 2016), http://www.scotusblog.com/wp-content/uploads/2016/06/SB_scorecard_OT15.pdf (noting that, in the 2015 Term, the Court reversed state court decisions 85 percent of the time while it reversed the circuit courts of appeals 62 percent of the time).

23. 28 U.S.C. § 2254(d)(1).

24. Yarborough v. Alvarado, 541 U.S. 652, 664 (2004).

25. Anyone who doubts me should read the competing perspectives on independent state constitutionalism offered by Justices Appel and Mansfield of the Iowa Supreme Court in *State v. Short. Compare* 851 N.W.2d 474, 481–92, *with id.* at 519–27 (Mansfield, J., dissenting). The majority opinion by Justice Appel offers compelling arguments in favor of a vigorous state-specific model of interpretation, while the dissent by Justice Mansfield lays out the competing arguments in a fair and powerful manner.

26. James R. Layton, *The Evolving Role of the State Solicitor: Toward the Federal Model*, 3 J. APP. PRAC. & PROCESS 533, 534 (2001).

27. *Id.*

28. Current list supplied by Dan Schweitzer, Supreme Court Counsel to the National Association of Attorneys General, and on file with the author.

29. Richard S. Price, *Linde's Legacy: The Triumph of Oregon State Constitutional Law, 1970–2000*, 80 ALB. L. REV. (forthcoming).

30. *Id.* at 77.

Chapter 9

1. *Compare* Ableman v. Booth, 62 U.S. (21 How.) 506 (1858), *with In re* Ralph, 1 Morris 1 (Iowa 1839); *compare* Plessy v. Ferguson, 163 U.S. 537 (1896), *with* Coger v. Nw. Union Packet Co., 37 Iowa 145 (1873).

2. 545 U.S. 469 (2005).

3. *See* City of Norwood v. Horney, 853 N.E.2d 1115, 1123 (Ohio 2006); Bd. of Cty. Comm'rs v. Lowery, 136 P.3d 639, 652 (Okla. 2006).

4. *See* Steven J. Eagle & Lauren A. Perotti, *Coping with Kelo: A Potpourri of Legislative and Judicial Responses*, 42 REAL PROP. PROB. & TR. J. 799, 803 (2008).

5. *See id.* at 805–07 (Arizona, Georgia, Iowa, Minnesota, Montana, New Hampshire, and Virginia).

6. *See id.* at 807–08 (Alabama, Colorado, Connecticut, Michigan, Nebraska, North Dakota, Pennsylvania, South Dakota, Tennessee, and Texas).

7. *See id.* at 809 (Alaska, Georgia, Kentucky, Minnesota, and West Virginia).

8. *See id.* at 823.

9. *See id.* at 830, 832, 836–37, 839–41 (Arkansas, Hawaii, Massachusetts, Mississippi, New Jersey, New York, Oklahoma, and Rhode Island).

10. Ilya Somin, The Grasping Hand: *KELO v. CITY OF NEW LONDON* and the Limits of Eminent Domain (Univ. of Chi. Press 2015).

11. 494 U.S. 872 (1990).

12. 521 U.S. 507 (1997).

13. Gonzales v. O Centro Espirita Beneficente Uniao do Vegetal, 546 U.S. 418 (2006).

14. Burwell v. Hobby Lobby, 134 S. Ct. 2751 (2014).

15. Zubik v. Burwell, 136 S. Ct. 1557 (2016).

16. *See* Cutter v. Wilkinson, 544 U.S. 709 (2005) (holding that the Religious Land Use and Institutionalized Persons Act does not violate the Establishment Clause).

17. Ala. Const. art. I, § 3.01; Ariz. Rev. Stat. Ann. § 41-1493.01; Ark. Code Ann. tit. 16, § 123-401; Conn. Gen. Stat. § 52-571b; Fla. Stat. ch. 761.01–.061; Idaho Code § 73-402; 775 Ill. Comp. Stat. 35/1-99; Ind. Code Ann. § 34-13-9-1; Kan. Stat. Ann. § 60-5301 to 5305; Ky. Rev. Stat. Ann. § 446.350; La. Rev. Stat. Ann. § 13:5231-5242; Miss. Code Ann. § 11-61-1; Mo. Rev. Stat. § 1.302; N.M. Stat. Ann. § 28-22-1 to 22-5; Okla. Stat. tit. 51, § 251-58; 71 Pa. Cons. Stat. §2401-07; R.I. Gen. Laws 1956 § 42-80.1-1; S.C. Code Ann. § 1-32-30; Tenn. Code Ann. § 4-1-407; Tex. Civ. Prac. & Rem. Code Ann. § 110.001-.012; Va. Code Ann. § 57-2.02.

18. *E.g.*, Barr v. City of Sinton, 295 S.W.3d 287 (Tex. 2009) (invalidating a zoning ordinance used to prevent a man from providing free housing for recently released prisoners and free religious instruction as part of his ministry).

19. *See, e.g.*, Huffman v. State, 204 P.3d 339, 344 (Alaska 2009); State v. Adler, 118 P.3d 652, 661 (Haw. 2005); Rupert v. Portland, 605 A.2d 63, 65–66 (Me. 1992); Attorney General v. Desilets, 636 N.E.2d 233 (Mass. 1994); State v. Hershberger, 462 N.W.2d 393, 397 (Minn. 1990); Humphrey v. Lane, 728 N.E.2d 1039 (Ohio 2000); First Covenant Church of Seattle v. City of Seattle, 840 P.2d 174, 187–88 (Wash. 1992); Coulee Catholic Sch. v. Labor & Indus. Review Comm'n, 768 N.W.2d 868, 886 (Wis. 2009).

20. 409 U.S. 810 (1972).

21. 798 N.E.2d 941 (Mass. 2003).

22. 135 S. Ct. 2584 (2015).

23. *Id.* at 2597.

24. Burt Neuborne, *The Myth of Parity*, 90 Harv. L. Rev. 1105 (1977).

25. *See also* Burt Neuborne, *Parity Revisited: The Uses of a Judicial Forum of Excellence*, 44 DePaul L. Rev. 797 (1995).

26. William B. Rubenstein, *The Myth of Superiority*, 16 CONST. COMMENT. 599 (1999).

27. *Id.* at 599.

28. *Id.* at 625.

29. Home Bldg. & Loan Ass'n v. Blaisdell, 290 U.S. 398 (1934) (holding that Minnesota's suspension of banks' contractual rights did not violate the Contract Clause in the U.S. Constitution).

30. Washington v. Glucksberg, 521 U.S. 702 (1997) (holding that the Due Process Clause does not create a right to physician-assisted suicide).

31. *Compare* PHILIP HAMBURGER, IS ADMINISTRATIVE LAW UNLAWFUL? (2014) *with* Adrian Vermeule, *No*, 93 TEX. L. REV. 1547 (book review).

32. District of Columbia v. Heller, 554 U.S. 570 (2008) (holding that the Second Amendment protects an individual right to bear arms).

33. Jeffrey S. Sutton, *Courts as Change Agents: Do We Want More—Or Less?*, 127 HARV. L. REV. 1419, 1442 (2014) (book review).

34. *Id.* at 1442–43.

35. Sanford Levinson, *Courts as Participants in "Dialogue": A View from American States*, 59 U. KAN. L. REV. 791, 791 (2011).

INDEX